Hearing
Our Teacher's Voice

The pursuit of faithfulness at
Bethany Christian Schools

1954-2004

Hearing
Our Teacher's Voice

The pursuit of faithfulness at
Bethany Christian Schools

1954-2004

Devon Schrock, editor

Acknowledgments

This book, true to the institution it describes, is about a community and by a community. Of particular note are the persons on the steering committee, having met many times, carefully planning, then supervising, the effort. Special thanks go to former Bethany science teacher Roy Hartzler, chair, for his fine support, time, and energy; Allan Dueck, Bethany principal, for providing materials and ongoing support; Wilmer Hollinger, former history and government teacher; Maribeth Diener '72 Friesen; Rachel Lapp '91; and Sylvia Steiner '56 Miller. Very special thanks go to Dee Helmuth '66 Birkey for her extensive and superb work on the design and layout of our book.

A heartfelt thank you to our writers: former sociology teacher Leonard Gross, chapter one; Wilmer Hollinger, chapter two; Becky Bontrager '71 Horst, chapter three; Bethany parent Sally Weaver Glick, chapter four; Bryan '78 and Anita Yoder '78 Kehr, chapter five; and James Krabill '69, chapter six. Each of them spent much time researching and writing, then refining, the chapters.

Many others rendered significant service. An important contribution came from those who provided the vignettes for the book, giving it a more personal dimension. Others were very helpful in a variety of ways: former librarian and teacher Royal Bauer; Susan Gingerich and Karen Shenk of the development office; Helen Hostetler, Ruth Kaufmann, and Clarice Ens Warkentin, volunteers in the development office; and Denise Risser '89, administrative assistant.

We also are grateful to our proofreaders (all present or former faculty and staff) for their help in checking the chapters for factual accuracy: Royal Bauer, Beth Berry, Dan Bodiker, Irene Gross, Leonard Gross, Wilmer Hollinger, Galen Johns, Marvin Nafziger, Allen Peachey, and John Zook. For final editorial critique we thank historian James Hertzler; Rachel Lapp; and Mary Swartley, former teacher and administrator. Special thanks to Dan Shenk '68, who gave us professional editing help.

Ruthann Gardner '58 Miller led the search in gathering photographs, while J. Kevin Miller, communications coordinator, provided invaluable assistance in photo identification. Other volunteers helped to clarify factual data, identify photos, and generate and index the name and word lists.

Several spouses also lent much help and support. Thanks as well to the many others who, through their work and encouragement, made this book possible.

–Devon Schrock, Editor
English teacher, 1977-99

Published in the United States of America in 2004 by
Bethany Christian Schools
2904 South Main Street
Goshen, Indiana 46526-5499
T: (574) 534-2567
E: info@bethanycs.net
www.bethanycs.net

Library of Congress Control Number: 2004106077

The paper used in this publication meets the requirements of the American National Standard for
Permanence of Paper for Printed Library Materials.

Printed by Evangel Press, Nappanee, Indiana 46550

Cover and interior layout and design by Dee Birkey

Table of contents

Continued on next page ...

Table of contents ... *cont.*

Introduction

by Devon Schrock

It is a common perception that the 1950s ushered in a time to resume the pursuit of the American dream and plan for still grander things. The awful violence of World War II had ended; the disturbance of the 1960s was yet to disrupt the order and tranquility of the time. People were inclined to "like Ike" and wore buttons to say so. It was unmistakably an era of good feeling. And the Mennonites of the Indiana-Michigan Conference, now settled securely in their own quiet communities, were largely caught up in this optimism.

But all was not well within; among church leaders there was a growing uneasiness concerning that perennial problem: the church versus the world. These men (unfortunately, all of them *were* men) sensed a transition in the making and a new era coming. The decades ahead would call for new and more effective means to combat the corrupting influence of a culture becoming ever more sensual and secular. Such an era dare not just happen but must be planned, be shaped by people of conscience, by those who had centered their lives in the Mennonite Church and in its Lord. Mennonite distrust of the secular world had grown out of historical memory, albeit imprecise, of centuries past. These mid-twentieth century Conference ministers in their ponderings were neither prophets nor mystics; there remains no report of

The decades ahead would call for new and more effective means to combat the corrupting influence of a culture becoming ever more sensual and secular.

**They knew no way
to foretell the future,
but they did know the force
of their own convictions.
And they looked with
a careful concern at
the church's young people …**

their having heard voices, or having seen visions. They knew no way to foretell the future, but they did know the force of their own convictions. And they looked with a careful concern at the church's young people, wondering at the nature of the forces that would shape them in the time to come.

Certain questions must have been persistent: How could the church most effectively confront the powerful influence of the mass culture that threatened to envelop it? Might it indeed be best to focus on the church's young people, the group most vulnerable to societal influence? How could they as ministers be assured that the young people sheltered and nurtured in the church would be able to discern the gap between the two kingdoms: that of the world and that of Christ? And what were the spiritual and doctrinal teachings they should impart to these cherished persons that would be the future church?

Theirs was an era when doctrine was the thing; Daniel Kauffman's *Manual of Bible Doctrines* had exerted a powerful influence on church life (and in fact has an implicit impact on chapter one of our story). Could the teaching and enforcing of rules make secure the era to come? Should the church's purpose be to restrict or to make free?

Another influence was Fundamentalism, not in its explicit form, but in respect to its emphasis on the Bible's fundamental truths, its authenticity and inspiration, its concern with the cross and the resurrection as basic for salvation and for guidance in the Christian life. Evangelism had become almost a Mennonite institution. Preacher S. F. Coffman's extensive work as an evangelist in the late nineteenth century had borne witness to that; it was obvious in his success in persuading many to accept the new birth in Christ.

From the Coffman era through the mid-twentieth century, congregations in the Indiana-Michigan Conference came to expect one to three weeks of revival meetings as basic to church life. It is of interest here that Coffman was not only a highly gifted preacher but was also instrumental in establishing Elkhart Institute, which was ultimately to become Goshen College.

In his book *The Mennonites in Indiana and Michigan*, J. C. Wenger, speaking to mid-century Mennonites, makes clear the early link between the new birth and the nonconformed life:

> The New Testament writers recognize that the heart of Christianity lies
> not in externals but in the new birth, union with Christ, and Holy Spirit
> sanctification. But because Christians have been delivered from the world and
> its sin they cannot any longer follow the fashions and dictates of a sensuous
> and sensate culture. Christians are not to fashion themselves after this wicked
> world, but are to be transformed by the renewing of their minds.[1]

In matters of Christian education, the Conference ministry as well as laity recognized the Scriptural basis for Wenger's remarks. They knew well the text, "Train up a child in the way he should go: and when he is old, he will not depart from it" (Prov. 22:6, KJV). They were well acquainted with another text, the one alluded to here by Wenger, and one that spoke yet more gravely to them: "And be not conformed to this world: but be ye transformed by the renewing of your minds, that ye may prove what is that good, and acceptable, and perfect, will of God" (Rom. 12:2, KJV). They were also mindful of certain more explicit texts, ones they saw as corollaries of the Romans passage, such as the I Corinthians teaching of covered heads for women and their subordination to men. Furthermore, they were aware of recently established Mennonite high schools that were given the assignment, among other things, to reinforce the exterior disciplines symbolic of separation from the world. It was such awareness that underlay Bethany Christian High School's establishment in 1954.

Conservative influences were pervasive in the wider church at the time of Bethany's founding, a significant one being the widespread influence of the Kauffman book. By careful attention to that small volume, the newly ordained minister could acquire the guidance he needed to carry out his sacred calling. College and seminary

They knew well the text, 'Train up a child in the way he should go: and when he is old, he will not depart from it' (Prov. 22:6 KJV).

education were perceived to add little to its message; there were in fact very few Indiana-Mennonite ministers before mid-century who had acquired seminary training.

Yet among the earlier, unpaid "farmer preachers," it must be said, were individuals of high ability and character. They preached, counseled, baptized, and presided over weddings and funerals; they brought spiritual nurture to their congregations; they were a vital and integral part of the simple rural life that once helped stabilize the church. They were solid men of integrity, whose only training (beyond Kauffman's book) was a thoroughgoing Biblical knowledge, and universally from the King James Version. Even with the introduction of the Revised Standard Version in 1950, the text of choice for Mennonite ministers remained the KJV. Their solid Biblical knowledge was complemented by experience, and often by very good pastoral sensibilities. And to say that these men possessed little concern for the education of youth would be a mistake. Many such men of the forties and fifties must have supported the new Conference high school idea. These traditional preachers that were so prevalent and effective before the war era and after would also face the challenge of higher education. But they would still endure for a time, until seminary-trained ministers gradually found acceptance and preference.

Most Mennonites of the Indiana-Michigan area found little fault with the grade school education of the early twentieth century. The teachers in charge of the one-room schools were men and women of the community. They were well known persons that typically had only eight years of schooling themselves (and thus remained untroubled by higher learning). Such teachers became well integrated into the close rural communities, and at times were Mennonites teaching children of their own church people. Few if any influences were present to threaten and corrupt, whether social, academic, or doctrinal. Consequently, there was little incentive to change. Then with the coming of the public high school, only a few Mennonite parents of the twenties and thirties encouraged their children to attend.

The worldview of the early twentieth century Mennonite Church, from the present perspective, was limited and narrow. Although Goshen College had come

Their solid Biblical knowledge was complemented by experience, and often by very good pastoral sensibilities.

into existence in 1903, its influence in the Indiana-Michigan Conference region was limited—and its educational program was poorly understood. A grade school education and practical experience seemed to have complemented well the Mennonite tendency to noninvolvement and to the pursuit of a quiet, simple, even idyllic, life on the land.

Present-day Mennonites may look askance at church leadership, life, and worldview 50 to 75 years ago, may see it as a time far too narrow and provincial. But both leaders and followers, the shepherds and the sheep of that era, sought a life of separation and humility; they perceived the beliefs they held to be those of the New Testament church, assuming the believers of the first century to have been simple people like Mennonites, separated from the world and of limited education. It seems unlikely from its history, however, that the early church did not share the Mennonite suspicion of education. But they likely possessed some other qualities of good Mennonites, such as hard work and frugality, one may suppose!

There was also among Mennonites an assumption that their church doctrines and ways were constructed on sixteenth century Anabaptist foundations. Mennonite bishop and historian J. C. Wenger, through his preaching and writing, brought a much better sense of church history to many people of the Indiana-Michigan Conference.

But a more extensive study of early Anabaptism brought an even greater awakening to the church. As our first two chapters show, the impetus for this change came in the person of Harold S. Bender, who was surely one of the movers and shakers of the twentieth century Mennonite Church and who gave his extraordinary energy and ability to the founding of Bethany Christian High School. He had articulated a new Mennonite vision that looked both to past and future. His Mennonite classic, *The Anabaptist Vision,* introduced an ideal of church life and community that would profoundly affect the Indiana-Michigan Conference and the school it would mandate. Of course its founders could not have known to what degree their assumptions about church and world might eventually change—to be brought on in part through their establishing a Conference high school.

... The Anabaptist Vision, introduced an ideal of church life and community that would profoundly affect the Indiana-Michigan Mennonite Conference and the school it would mandate.

> ... their time of service
> also brought ...
> a new personal awareness,
> not only of the other world
> they had seen,
> but also of the realization
> that they could bear witness
> to their convictions
> in a new way
> and make a difference.

But another dynamic, dark and disturbing, confronted the church of the mid-twentieth century. The awful conflict that shook the world in the 1940s would affect the Mennonite Church as well. Many Mennonite young men, being part of a peace church, had to decide whether or not they would hold fast to its historical stance of nonresistance.

Most of them remained true to their Mennonite faith. Many served near home in mental hospitals, others farther away in conservation units. The story of the impact of Civilian Public Service men and their work during World War II, particularly of their dedication to the mentally ill, brought a new awareness of mental institutions and mental health care to American citizens. But their time of service also brought to these men a new personal awareness, not only of the other world they had seen, but also of the realization that they could bear witness to their convictions in a new way and make a difference.

However, there remained a shadow side. A survey taken by Mennonite Central Committee of the years before December 1944[2] showed that a high percentage of drafted young men from the various Mennonite groups had accepted a 1-A classification and had taken up arms as combatants. Mennonite historian Theron Schlabach has pointed to a passage in *Mennonites in American Society,* showing that Bender encountered these survey statistics with considerable dismay:

> A ... census in November of 1942 showed that a disconcerting pattern was continuing. MC data showed that eight hundred members were in CPS and 320 in the military. Harold Bender was shocked. 'A 30 percent failure is a bad record,' he exclaimed. 'Only 70 percent! Is this a passing grade...? Bender (and others) did not blame only youth. He said the dismal figures were a direct challenge to pastors, bishops, parents, and congregations.[3]

It should be noted that registered young men who had a high school education were the highest percentage of those accepting a 1-A classification. And it may also be, as Schlabach suspects, that this incident was the genesis of Bethany, that Bender in that very context decided on the necessity of a Conference high school.[4]

It may seem remarkable indeed that so many Mennonite young men were willing to take up arms, considering the horrendous nature of the war and their early years growing up in the Mennonite community. Bender evidently saw in this a serious deficiency in Mennonite education.

Those young people from the peace churches who enlisted in Mennonite Central Committee's European voluntary service or PAX program after the war also encountered something that their quiet Mennonite lives never could teach them: they saw the refugees and the rubble, the awful devastation of property and people. Here was the evil of war—and the ambiguity. Hitler's Reich was itself evil beyond doubt, but the allies had achieved victory partly through their use of atomic mega-weapons and by their utter devastation of many great German and Japanese cities. The many young Mennonite men (and women) who saw the effects of the war could not return home unchanged. Their experience brought a new dimension to education in the church. Any attempt at isolation now would mean a shunning of reality; the church would need to engage the world as never before.

Forward-looking Conference leaders, such as Amos Hostetler and Guy F. Hershberger, as well as many fathers and mothers, knew these things and in the early forties began to prepare the seedbed in which a Christian high school could germinate and grow. For them the health of the church did not lie in a retreat into the old nonconformity; they sensed that something new was afoot and that it must be met at the most basic level—the education of their young people through the establishment of a Conference high school. The Mennonite Church's long-held suspicion of education had been cast in doubt. In fact there was a new consciousness becoming widespread in the Mennonite Church, resulting in a general inclination to build high schools.

However, Indiana-Michigan concerns were unlike those that shaped the Lancaster Mennonite or Iowa Mennonite high schools, a primary motive for them having been

> The many ... who saw the effects of the war could not return home unchanged. Their experience brought a new dimension to education in the church.

to maintain nonconformity in their children. Indiana-Michigan leaders sought to protect their young people from worldly ways without exercising such close control, so that much of Bethany policy would arise from within.

Their concern was, as our first chapter records, to have a "Christian school," even though they were tardy in conceiving a carefully designed program of engaging the world, which involved considerable complexity. The pursuit of a liberal education required that the school glean from the culture of the Western world whatever truth, beauty, and reality it might offer, and bring to the task an alternative understanding. As an arm of the church, Bethany must measure the way of the world by the Rule of Christ. This constraint would demand some rejection, sorting, and sifting, but finally it must allow Christ to claim the domain that is truly his. This search for knowledge must go beyond the confines of the old walls of separation; of necessity it needed to assume a new paradigm: that of a loom weaving a web, not simply an entwining of religious material, but something partaking of two worlds, the sacred and secular, ultimately to create an interweaving and bring into being a tapestry greater and finer than any of its individual parts.

The realization of such an ideal came only with time, even though a new consciousness had put it in place. As our book attempts to show, the actual creation of a design came late, as is shown in the fifth chapter (1980s). This task has called for continuing discernment. And not all perceptions have been the same.

Education at Bethany has evolved; forward movement has been sometimes slow and halting. It has reflected the changes in understanding over these 50 years. There has needed to be a holding back at times, as well as a letting go, demanding on the material side much risk, but on the spiritual side much faith. Achievement is always partly dependent on influences beyond the teachers' domain.

An example of the spiritual came in an unusual manner, and may at first have seemed to lack significance: that is the use of first names for students and teachers, a practice of something that has become basic to the spirit of Bethany. This was first proposed in part as an attempt to draw the student body and faculty together

> As an arm of the church, Bethany must measure the way of the world by the Rule of Christ.

during Bethany's time of adolescent turmoil. The idea came from two thoughtful young teachers who believed the use of first names would be in harmony with the Mennonite conception of community. But the school was not then ready for such a policy. As time passed, however, first name communication became both acceptable and natural; contrary to what some had thought, the practice did not destroy order and respect, but lifted student-teacher relationships to a new and higher plane. In fact it ultimately became for the school one of the most basic models of community—and of Anabaptist faith.

In our first chapter Leonard Gross, as a church historian and former Bethany teacher, examines the gradual, sometimes hesitant, movement toward the founding of a school. From the evidence here presented, the founders' efforts did not lack purpose but were short on definition, although Harold S. Bender made an eloquent case for following a middle-of-the road path. Thus he did not assume the building of a fortress against the world; nor did Conference leaders of foresight, such as Amos Hostetler, who had been promoting the idea of a Conference high school for some years. But with the entrance of Harold Bender into the planning, means and matter merged into a new reality for the Indiana-Michigan Mennonite Conference—Bethany Christian High School. Gross sees in this the foreshadowing of a new conception of the church versus world problem; he thus introduces the warp and woof metaphor as a central theme of our book.

Wilmer Hollinger, a well-loved history teacher, shows how the school slowly and bravely achieved a solid beginning. The continuing influence of Bender and the hiring of the first administrators and faculty proved to be propitious; especially the hiring of John S. Steiner.[5] Here began the ideal of the school as an arm of the church. Hollinger describes a faculty willing to sacrifice for the sake of their students, young people that proved to be both gifted and highly motivated.

But the school like the wider church was significantly affected by the turmoil of the sixties. The mood of the time had entered the doors of Bethany. Bethany parent Rebecca Bontrager Horst is particularly able to tell the story of the time,

… first name communication became both acceptable and natural; …
it ultimately became …
one of the most basic models of community—and of Anabaptist faith.

> ... it is evident that human presence— here the presence of leadership fitted for the time and place— became paramount for the school's ability to accomplish its mission.

having participated in it as a Bethany student. She describes it, appropriately, as a time of Bethany's adolescence, when the effectiveness of the school seemed sometimes in doubt.

If Bethany Christian High School experienced a significant time of fruition, it was surely forming during the era described by Bethany parent Sally Weaver Glick. In fact one might well name this the beginning of a Bethany renaissance. Again, as in the two first chapters, it is evident that human presence—here the presence of leadership fitted for the time and place—became paramount for the school's ability to accomplish its mission.

And "mission" became the appropriate term, as Bryan and Anita Yoder Kehr, both former students and now Bethany parents (and Bryan a teacher), so well demonstrate. As the school came into the nineties, what was once only vaguely evident became clearly understood, described, and promulgated. And here even more powerfully the presence of people, both administration and staff, yes, and student body as well, came together in a most salutary manner.

It becomes alumnus James Krabill's task to determine and describe the nature of the transition that showed itself to be so very evident at the turn of the century. It could be said here that there was some parallel to the school's founding in the fifties: that with change came uncertainty. But now again the engagement of strong and effective leadership, though not without difficulty and disappointment, facilitated the transition from the "Bill Hooley" era with its informality, friendship and sense of community, along with clear and solid educational purpose, to a time of new effort. Again human presence became significant, for in this new era the leadership established, in a remarkable way, the Bethany Christian Middle School, and enabled a younger faculty to come into what may now be described even more appropriately as "the Bethany community."

Notes

1. John C. Wenger, *Studies in Anabaptist and Mennonite History: The Mennonites in Indiana and Michigan* (Scottdale, PA: Mennonite Publishing House, 1961) 448.

2. Melvin Gingerich, *Service for Peace: A History of Mennonite Civilian Public Service* (Akron, PA: The Mennonite Central Committee, 1949) 90-91.

3. Quoted by Paul Toews from a draft census by Howard Charles in *Mennonite Experience in America Vol. 4: Mennonites in American Society, 1930-1970: Modernity and the Persistence of Religious Community*. (Scottdale, PA: Mennonite Publishing House, 1996) 149.

4. In a recent conversation with writer.

5. Steiner's full name was "John Menno Simons Steiner." But hereafter he will be designated as simply "John S. Steiner" or "John Steiner."

Chapter 1

Bethany's Vigorous Birth
1945-54

by Leonard Gross

*Future construction site of Bethany Christian High School, State Road 15 South,
Goshen, Indiana.*

Fifty years ago, on September 7, 1954, Bethany Christian High School, later renamed Bethany Christian Schools, was born vigorous and healthy—after long years of gestation. What appears in the following chapters of this volume brings together Bethany's history: its beginnings and the intricate story of its evolving growth and change. What appears in this chapter, however, is the story of what led up to Bethany's birth five decades ago.

To capture the rationale behind the Bethany idea, we go back to 1948, a time of major transformation for the Indiana-Michigan Mennonite Conference, indeed, a quiet revolution. The constituency was now acquiring a new understanding of separation from the world, one quite different from before. During the first half of the twentieth century, most Mennonites understood nonconformity to be a set of restrictions and rules to be followed. It was a time when Conference worked at "problems" at every turn. The new vision, in contrast, was more positive and forward looking. It focused on the task of strengthening the primary community of those attempting to follow in the way of Jesus. Part of this task was to create reconciling

The new vision ... was more positive and forward looking.

Photo: 1948 Indiana-Michigan Conference Report, Mennonite Church USA Archives

Guy F. Hershberger
Photo: *Elkhart Truth*

This report signals a shift in the idea of the Mennonite way of life in general, and in particular in the idea of the education of young people.

relationships, one with another, as a spiritual body. Another part was consciously concerned with the cultural side of community—creating its own way of life within an imperfect world.[1]

The action in 1948 which led so directly to transformation came by way of a report of the Community Life Study Committee. The task of this new committee, appointed in 1947, was "to carefully review the entire structure of our community life, home, social, and economic, and bring Biblical and wholesome recommendations to our next annual conference." The influence of Goshen College Professor Guy F. Hershberger had pervaded Conference that year via his Conference address, "Strengthening our Christian Community: In Economic Life."[2] It proved of great importance in the birth of a Conference high school.

The report of the Community Life Study Committee takes up six full pages, in small print, of the published minutes for 1948. The committee, with Guy F. Hershberger at the helm, came up with a detailed and solid, all-encompassing report, in five parts: on the church and the community; the home and the community; the school and the community; social life and the community; and economic life and the community. The substance, spirit, copiousness, and vision of the report clearly show Hershberger's influence.

This report signals a shift in the idea of the Mennonite way of life in general, and in particular in the idea of the education of young people. Part Three is so significant that it merits full quotation, for here the education of young people is understood to be an important element in furthering the quest for a meaningful life together—within an imperfect world:

The School and the Community. One reply to our questionnaire has the following statement: "I believe Christian education is one of the needs in our communities today, especially in the high school. We Christians have lost the value of Christian education. We give our children over to the world to educate them in the things and ways of the world. Then when they are learned in all the wisdom of Egypt (world) we expect them to remain Christian. Our teaching program seems to be out of balance. Biblical teaching is 'Thou shalt teach thy children.' We need Christian day schools with consecrated Christian teachers."

Your committee believes that much good is being done by our public school system. Yet it must be recognized that schools vary a great deal from community to community; that they can do very little by way of effective religious instruction; that in the nature of the case their emphasis must be largely secular; that extracurricular activities frequently include undesirable features which help to break down Christian standards; and that the total impact of the life of the public high school makes it difficult for young people in our present militaristic world to maintain a firm stand for the principle of nonresistance. Christian parents should also keep in mind that the public school, its activities and programs, will take the central place in children's thinking unless a strong home interest is cultivated, enlisting the loyalty of the entire family.

The committee presented a recommendation for each of its five areas of concern, with the recommendation for adoption by Conference on Part Three reading:

The School. Resolved, that we urge diligence on the part of all parents that the influence of the school on their children be in harmony with our professed Christian standards; and that the Conference through the Church High School Study Committee continue its work looking forward toward the establishment of a Christian High School for the young people of our district.

It is evident here that Conference was ready to give direction to a new school; it should reflect the Christian standards of the church. It is also evident that the idea of community as part of the Anabaptist vision had yet to be spelled out.[3] The report was accepted, with the first three resolutions adopted, including the one on the

'Christian parents should also keep in mind that the public school, its activities and programs, will take the central place in children's thinking ...'

school and community. The following year the other two resolutions also passed, with minor changes.

We break into the developing story at this point, anticipating some of the deeper issues underlying the idea of a Mennonite high school in the late 1940s. Implicit within this new educational mandate was the assumption that the Mennonite Church needed to strengthen creatively its own "redeemed" social order, up to now seen as a somewhat closed community of believers ("neither in nor of the world"). However, another perspective, somewhat at odds with the old, was also subtly coming into play: that we as a believing community, although not of the world, were still in it ("in but not of the world"), in it and somehow dynamically related to it.

We wanted to remain a close-knit community. Yet we also began seeing the need to relate in a new manner to general society, our eyes having only recently been opened in part by the events of the Second World War. Worldwide relief needs were suggesting new approaches in our engagement with the world. Willy-nilly we were thrust into the world, and we began wondering to what degree we really did understand the nations that make up this world—their cultures and histories.

In this manner, Mennonites were beginning to realize that, to be aligned with the New Testament church and its mission, they most certainly needed to be "in the world," and that this meant relating in a new manner to general society. This new awareness led to concerted Mennonite efforts in developing deeper understandings of both societies—the "redeemed" and the "fallen," the sacred and the secular, the church and the state.

Such thoughts in turn raised the fundamental question of how the sacred ought to relate to the secular, including the question of Christianity's relationship to the arts, the sciences, and learning in general. Would the placing of the two spheres in juxtaposition necessarily imply separation, or could there be some accommodation between, and integration of, the two without compromise? Furthermore, could each sphere maintain its integrity if interrelating were to take place? Going even further, could the two spheres interact in specific ways with one another, producing a weave

Willy-nilly we
were thrust into
the world ...

... how the
sacred ought
to relate to the
secular ...

of the two (the warp of society and the woof of Christianity, as it were), creating in this manner a fully "Christian" tapestry?

Such questions and their attempted answers were integral to the quiet revolution in process and would define the central task and vision of the new Conference high school now being more earnestly pursued. That pursuit would be a striving for a stronger, more viable faith community and, in such a pursuit, the presence of a Conference high school was seen as vital.

Guy F. Hershberger's lending his support to the church high school idea in 1948 was significant for at least two reasons. It gave further impetus to the church high school idea, first suggested on the Conference floor by Ira S. Johns in 1940, by bringing it forward clearly in the constituency's awareness. Furthermore, as a part of the first comprehensive vision ever created for Indiana-Michigan Mennonites, it transformed the Conference rationale for such a school by showing it to be an essential part of a larger community design.

Both of these reasons ultimately came into play, although some older ways of thinking and believing did not soon die out, as may be seen the very next year, in 1949, when the Conference Rules and Discipline were updated and included the following rules: the regulation coat with no necktie for ministers, which all brethren were also encouraged to wear; no mustache or fashionable beard for the brethren; sisters to wear the bonnet or a form of plain headdress, and to have long uncut hair. The rules also forbade wearing of gold, pearls or costly array, including wedding rings; instead, modesty in apparel and appearance should prevail.[4]

In fact, during the first dozen years or so of its early life, the school also experienced this conservative bent—obvious, for example, in how players should be attired in interscholastic sports.

About this time the Church High School Study Committee,[5] by now in its third year of existence, had circulated a questionnaire among the constituency and found that interest for a Conference high school had waned. It thus decided to go to the congregations to promote the idea.[6] The results were generally positive. Parents of

Elizabeth and Ira S. Johns
Photo: Mennonite Church USA Archives

"The warp of society, the woof of Christianity: A fully 'Christian' tapestry?"

Cain/Christ: The old creation, the new creation

by Nancy Eash '62 (Myers)

Our course in Sociology this year followed two lines. One was the scientific study of the individual in society, which would be the usual sociology course.

We learned that man, although he has certain inborn drives, is mostly a product of his culture. Man's drives, his basic nature, are greatly modified because he lives in the society of others. The main problem of sociology, then, is to help man to adjust better to society, and to thus be more normal. The word "normal" implies there is a standard set, a norm. What is social science's norm? They have no set goal at present, sociologists say, sometime they will have one. Perhaps "average" would be a name for their present aim. Certainly, making men average cannot be an ultimate goal. Will science ever find an ultimate answer?

The second part of the course dealt with science's relation to Christianity. The limitations of science were pointed out by a look at the creation and fall of man.

It all starts with Adam. When God created Adam, he made him in his own image. He gave him a certain amount of authority. But most of all he made Adam free – free to have the right relationship with God; free to worship his Creator. When Adam made his first wrong choice, he broke this relationship.

He was no longer free, for his actions were now predetermined. Man was now to live in pain and pleasure, with neither one winning out. Man now was to begin searching for a definite answer. This searching is symbolized in Cain, the first man who knew nothing of what this right relationship was. Science is also a result of the fall. It also represents searching, but science cannot see past Cain and can therefore find no ultimate answer.

But Christianity has the answer. When God drove Adam and Eve from the Garden of Eden, he gave them a promise. He promised that someday he would send someone who would bind their broken relationships. This person was Jesus Christ. He was not only God who redeemed man, but he was also a man. In fact he was the only real man: he was man as man was meant to be. It is in Jesus that we find the answer science will always be searching for. He is our goal; he is our norm: to be "normal" we must measure up to him.

Who was Jesus? From the records we have of his life on earth, we can conclude that Jesus of Nazareth was a real person in the full sense of the word. It is difficult to characterize him, because he was so many different things at once. He was authoritative and humble, severe and gentle; he found meaning in his culture, yet was not afraid to rebel against the bad parts of it. He was everything to the greatest degree.

Jesus was a true person who was very much a part of his society, yet was not bound by it.

The Christian uses the life of Christ to work out his own view of society and attitude toward life in this world. Our attitude must be somewhere between conventionalism and rebellion. We must accept those things in our society which are good or neutral, but we must not be afraid to object to or try to change those which are bad.

There remains a tension between science, which is searching, and Christianity, which has the answer. Science resents Christianity because it claims to have the answer, and science is still searching. Yet Christians, because they are still human, need science because they have not found all the answers. Science's function is to control a world which will never be wholly redeemed to a right relationship with God.

—"Two sphere" living: a student summary of sociology, written in 1962, reproduced here in its entirety. From 1959 to 1964, sociology was taught by Leonard Gross.

Photo: 1962 *Witmarsum*

180 children responded affirmatively but with a diversity of expectations. Some Michigan people wanted a school somewhere in Michigan, and some parents were interested in boarding facilities. There was also "some impatience that a school has not been started already." With this new interest, the committee, headed by Amos O. Hostetler, recommended to Conference in 1950 that it

> authorize a high school committee to draft a constitution which should be presented to a special session of conference in December for approval or rejection. If approved, conference should appoint administrative committees such as building committees, board of trustees, and religious welfare committees to further the work of the school.

Amos O. Hostetler
Photo: Mennonite Church USA Archives

Conference adopted this recommendation and called a special session into being on December 6, 1950, which gave a green light for pushing ahead with plans for a Conference high school. The committee's name was changed to Church High School Committee, having as its new mandate:

- to present the need for a church-controlled high school to the churches in our conference;
- to start a church high school building fund for those who may wish to contribute to it;
- to work out a plan for a school or schools which will serve the largest number of young people in the conference;
- to present specific plans and recommendations for financing a church high school;
- to investigate further the possible effect of our starting a high school upon already existing … Mennonite high schools.

'There was … some impatience that a school had not been started already.'

Simon Gingerich:
Indiana-Michigan Conference considers a church high school

At an annual meeting of the Indiana-Michigan Conference, delegates discussed possibilities for the development of a church high school. The debate was lively. Persuasive reasons were offered both pro and con for considering such a venture. The idea was not new. It had been discussed informally for a number of years. Now it seemed such a school was a lively possibility and the public discussion was moving toward a favorable vote.

My memory and perception is that Harold S. Bender, aware of the ongoing discussion, skillfully waited until it appeared to be moving toward action. He then gave public leadership by entering the debate, saying in effect, "We have talked about this for years. Let's move ahead now by taking the necessary action." Bender, I believe, wrote the motion that was adopted by the Conference, initiating the development of the high school. I am sure that records and minutes document Bender's considerable involvement in the planning and development of the school.

One of the factors that somewhat clouded discussions for a new church high school was the nearby presence of Goshen College. Do

Continued on page 30 …

Gingerich ... *cont. from page 29*

we need another school? How will a proposed high school relate to our churches and our Conference? These were important questions that were not easily answered, particularly in the context of a history of somewhat uncomfortable relationships between the college and the Conference.

As the discussion on the Conference floor moved toward a vote, someone, perhaps Harold Bender, suggested that it would be appropriate for the Conference to hear from Goshen College. President Ernest E. Miller was present, likely expecting that he would be invited to speak. At the invitation of the moderator, President Miller went to the podium. He generously thanked the Conference for the invitation to speak on behalf of the college. He commented on his lifetime involvement in Christian education and indicated his personal support of a church high school. He further said that he thought the staff and teachers at the college would support the planning of such a school.

President Miller then told a story from his family's experience in India. He said that after the birth of their son, Donald, he took four-year-old Thelma to see her new brother and their mother. After their visit, Ernest and Thelma sat down for tea and talked about the new baby. Thelma had some reservations. With some apprehension, she said, "But Daddy, you won't forget about me now, will you?"

President Miller closed his brief comments with that appeal, saying, "You won't forget about Goshen College now, will you?"

With a change in name, came also a change in assignment, which had suddenly shifted from the talking stages to that of needed action on many levels. How careful would need to be the development of the many layers that it takes to bring a new school into being!

In 1951 the newly appointed Church High School Committee, no longer a "study" committee, was composed of Harold S. Bender, Erie E. Bontrager, Amos O. Hostetler, Ira S. Johns, and Wayne J. Wenger. The composition of the committee changed somewhat for 1952-53, and included Harold S. Bender (Sec.), Amos Hostetler, (Chairman), Ira S. Johns, C. Norman Kraus, and R. F. Yoder. The presence of Harold Bender on the committee almost immediately breathed new life into the church high school movement and gave it a renewed sense of purpose.

Indiana-Michigan High School Board chosen by the 1953 Annual Conference to build and operate an accredited Christian school (from left): Harold S. Bender (Sec.), Russell Krabill, H. Ernest Bennett (Tr.), Conference Moderator Paul M. Miller serving ex-officio, Amos O. Hostetler (Pres.), Ora M. Yoder, and Annas Miller (Vice-Pres.). Photo: United Building Campaign brochure, Mennonite Church USA Archives

Harold S. Bender, "Executive Officer"

By 1953 seminary dean and worldwide Mennonite leader Harold S. Bender had entered center stage in the Conference high school initiative. On Thursday, June 4 of that year, in the regular session of the Indiana-Michigan Mennonite Conference, "Amos O. Hostetler, chairman of the Church High School Committee, made suitable remarks and introduced Harold Bender, secretary of the committee, who gave the report of the committee. Report accepted." At this exact moment within the history of the Indiana-Michigan Conference, Amos Hostetler, long-time proponent of a Conference high school, in effect turned over the mantle to Bender. During that same Conference, the following individuals were elected/appointed to the new Bethany Christian High School Board: Amos Hostetler (Pres.), Annas Miller (Vice-Pres.), Harold S. Bender (Sec.), H. Ernest Bennett (Tr.), Russell Krabill, and Ora M. Yoder, with Conference Moderator Paul M. Miller serving ex-officio.

Annas Miller's recollections

In a 1971 interview, Board member and well-known Goshen businessman Annas Miller spoke about the year which predated the opening of Bethany. Not knowing of Amos Hostetler's quietly persistent attempts to found a Mennonite high school, going all the way back to 1945, Annas Miller pointed to Harold Bender as first putting forth the idea of a Christian high school. Miller's comments revisit the original concern of the proponents:

> Harold Bender was instrumental, I think, from the beginning, in the planning of Bethany. He was brought in, and was much interested in this, and was on the Board a number of years. There was talk of beginning a high school among a number of people in the Conference, for a number of years. But with Harold Bender's connection with education, and his interest in a Christian high school, he became one of the most active people in it because of his ability and experience. Bethany began, not out of a dissatisfaction with public schools, but

... Harold S. Bender had entered center stage ...

Harold S. Bender
Photo: Mennonite Church USA Archives

Annas Miller
Photo: 1955 *Witmarsum*

Christianity ... integrated into a secular education ...

Russell Krabill
Photo: 1955 *Witmarsum*

... Annas Miller, experienced in building and finance.

Amos Hostetler breaking ground, March 13, 1954.
Photo: Russell Krabill slide collection

rather, out of an interest in an emphasis on Christianity and the teaching of the Bible to be included in an education, integrated into a secular education, which is felt to be important—something of very great importance—to young people during their high school years. This is a time when many young people make pretty much their decisions in life, and are influenced a great deal by high school.

In the task of selling the school to the church constituency, I was involved right from the beginning, in 1953, when Conference acted ... We simply acted together, hiring another person, I think, to work on the fundraising program underway and this person went out to all the churches. It was quite successful.

Russell Krabill, in his own words

In an interview in 2001, Russell Krabill, active Conference leader and Bethany Board member from the start, reminisced about Bethany's beginning. Within the thirty-one Board meetings preceding September 7, 1954, when Bethany opened its doors, the Board had built and organized the school and hired faculty—all within one year's time!

Krabill reflected on the central significance of Harold Bender, the Bethany steam engine and mastermind, who conceptualized the high school idea and then transformed idea into reality. Krabill, however, also took note of the many others, without whose efforts Bethany would not have happened. He mentioned Mennonite missions leader H. Ernest Bennett by name, experienced in administration and building construction, and Mennonite businessman Annas Miller, experienced in building and finance. Krabill saw himself as the errand boy: "We had a lot of volunteer labor, and I would call people and try to get them to come help build the school—digging the foundation, and putting up the framework. I did a lot of phoning and trying to round up volunteers for the school."

Bringing in a principal with just the right touch was of utmost significance, and as Krabill notes, the Board entered this search very carefully, all the while keeping an eagle eye on one particular experienced administrator from Kansas:

The Board was anxious to get John Steiner as principal. John Steiner was conservative, yet not ultra-conservative. It was not his vision that we should build a school to maintain the strict doctrines of Indiana-Michigan Conference. Instead, he was concerned that the school not be a whole lot different, culturally, from the local congregations. In this regard, I have pictures of chapel services when coverings were worn for several years after Bethany started.

John S. Steiner
Photo: Royal Bauer collection

Krabill was in part responsible for bringing C. J. Holaway on board as teacher-administrator, a leader who would fill an important niche within the new school's administration as principal. He also proved to be a competent teacher of Latin and Spanish:

C. J. Holaway
Photo: Royal Bauer collection

I think I was partly instrumental in helping C. J. Holaway get on board. He was a teacher in the Nappanee area for many years. I heard he was retiring, and I thought he would be a good man. We approached him, and he consented, and he really threw himself into Bethany. He was in public education all those years, and then switched to be in a parochial situation, which wasn't a very popular thing to do in the eyes of public colleagues. Just from memory I do not recall, other than John Steiner and C. J. Holaway, about the people we engaged as faculty, although I was on the Board when we interviewed them.

Why Bethany at this time?

Russell Krabill also spoke to the question of the timing of Bethany's birth. When asked whether the push for a church high school was in response to the recent Second World War, Krabill's comments elaborate on Miller's:

"Warp and Woof"
The relationship of Christianity (the Church and the Christian) to the State
by Jeanette Slabach '64 (Campbell)

First we ask two questions: what is the current role of government, and what should the role of government be? The textbook only assumes problems and tells about control, not cure. For this reason we must step out of the world situation and see the world's predicament from God's view. The world has a great many problems such as crime, sickness, war, etc. The Christian's problem is not how to overcome these problems but how to live within this system. We see that man has made progress, but where he has stepped out of the boundaries, chaos results. Man's greatest problem is that he wants to be master. War and suffering do have a good side because men learn from mistakes and experience. Here is the paradox of life. We live and depend on something we don't understand. How we can live under this system lies in being. The answer is only partial. First we must see God as creator. He is lord of history and controls it. Adam wanted to be his own master and then came the fall. This is where secular history begins. *Heilsgeschichte,* or holy history, is history seen from God's viewpoint. Christ is where the secular and religious meet. The Christian's predicament is how to live on both levels. Christ of course is the answer. We follow Him by becoming Christ's and do what he would have done. We obey our government if it doesn't conflict with God's will and then take the consequences [where it does conflict]. God's will for the Christian and the church is definitely Christ; and for the world, the universal law and to some extent the Ten Commandments.

The world has come of age. For centuries, God was used as a stop-gap, as a fill-in for the unknown. With the coming of the scientific era God was pushed back farther and farther until today God isn't needed at all. Everything is answered by psychology, even the after-death. The church has always taken a negative view of the secularization of the world, but it is really for the good. We now see the world for what it really is and has always been. Now we can see the lines sharply, and witness to bring them to the real God and not back into superstition. The world cannot understand that there will always be a difference between the church and world. Because we can see history from God's view, *Heilsgeschichte,* we of course see it differently. Only individuals can believe and take the "leap of faith" necessary for becoming Christians. Therefore Christians will always be able to see history in a more complete form. Science has necessarily set limits for itself and Christians can see over and around them. In Revelation 5:1-10, the story of history is told. There is a scroll with seven seals, which is the history of the world. No one is worthy to open this book or fulfill history, except Christ.

Americans and Christians in America have the idea that only here in the Free World can Christianity grow. This is not true. Christianity can and does grow in Communist countries. Democracy is the best system of government, but it is no more, maybe even less, Christian than Communism. The difference between the church and state is the goals we have set. The Christians have set their goal to redo what Adam did wrong. How is this possible? Only through Christ. And who is Christ? We see Christ from the outside as the Christ who came to earth as God revealed. This is the love aspect of God, the service, the doing which Christ portrayed. We see Christ on the inside. This is the Holy Spirit. By faith we accept Christ and follow his guiding. We see Him from above. This is the hope of the second coming of Christ. Any of these three can be carried too far. The problem is to have a balanced Christ. Social religion has gone out on a tangent by overemphasizing the love of everyone for everyone else. Mysticism has decided it's only "God and I" and ignored the other two. Certain Christian sects have overemphasized God's coming back so that little attention is paid to the right now. The key to finding a balanced Christ is love.

Nonresistance is the negative approach to the Christian's policy of love and service. Nonresistance was implicit in all of Christ's life. The church has always followed Christ's

Continued on page 35 …

The relationship … *cont. from page 34*

example. If we are to, today, we must say no to the nation at many points. We can start by saying no to the draft board. If the official asks why nonresistance, we should tell him about Christianity and the God I serve, that the world talks against the government but in the end obeys it, but that the Christian follows Christ and has victory where Christ did. We should tell him about the shoes of Christ, that when we decide to follow Christ we take on the responsibility of acting as Christ would, and would Christ kill or use force? Of course not. We take on Christ's work and whole responsibility of trying to take care of the world. We should explain about the military oath. We cannot swear blind obedience to a man. Our obedience is to God whom we have to serve rather than men. As a citizen we of course have a duty to defend the country. It lowers [national] morale for us not to fight but we more than make it up by serving. In the long run we strengthen it more than we weaken it. It's the little things that count.

This course has been to see the different aspects of our government and understand how the different departments work and to see the government as a whole, related to other governments. We have also seen what the individual can and should do for his government and in turn what the government does for the individual. But we as Christians can see a third aspect. This is the government in relation to God. Socrates' answer to government was to talk against it but in the end

obey. God's answer is to obey the government (Acts 24:16) but where there is a conflict, obey God (Acts 5:29). We can see the limits government should take upon itself. We have a message for the government. We can never tell the government to become weaker, but can point out where we could be stronger. Never can we say, "Disarm!" unless in the long run it would strengthen our country. Always we should point out where to better ourselves such as integration, slum clearance, etc., by group pressure (writing letters) and by talking, or in any other way we can. The key to these five lectures has been: obey government, but God rather than government.

—A student's government final examination essay, written in 1964, reproduced here in its entirety. From 1959 to 1964, government was taught by Leonard Gross.
Photo: 1964 *Witmarsum*

Mennonites To Erect School At Waterford

Construction To Start North Of Convalescent Home

Plans for the establishment of a Mennonite high school to be known as the Bethany Christian high school, at Waterford, were announced today by the Indiana-Michigan Mennonite conference. Construction of the modern, one-story building, to cost an estimated $150,000, will begin March 15.

According to Dr. H. S. Bender, secretary of the board of directors of the conference, the school will be established, primarily, for Mennonite youth in northern Indiana although there are no religious or residence restrictions placed on enrollment.

The school will not be operated in connection with Goshen college, although both the school and the college are under the direction of the Indiana-Michigan Mennonite conference. A high school academy was operated at the college from 1894 until 1935, Dr. Bender said.

The high school will be a first-class commissioned high school with a complete curriculum and additional Bible courses. It will be a day school with no arrangements for boarding.

At the outset, an enrollment of about 100 pupils is expected. Dr. Bender added today that most of these students have already been enrolled.

Newspaper clipping: Mennonite Church USA Archives

I don't remember that the Second World War, or militarism, or the
military reserves, was on the hearts of most of us people at that time, as
a central rationale for beginning our own high school. It was just the
plain fact that Mennonites in Indiana and Michigan thought we ought to
have a school with a Christian emphasis: a Christian school in this sense,
with Christian teaching.

There were people in our Conference who believed in Christian
education. I don't think this was necessarily because the public schools
were so corrupt, but they were secular, you see, and we felt we should
have a religious emphasis in education.

Not everyone saw this as a problem. Some said, "Our children have
gone to Shipshewana, they have gone to Middlebury, they have gone to
all these other schools, and we like it. Why should we have a Christian
school? We have Christian teachers in our public schools too!" They
liked these small public high schools—which meant we had to sell the
Bethany idea. There were articles in the *Bethany Bulletin* and in the
publicity which preceded it, suggesting that Bethany is more than just
having Christian teachers. There was a lot of discussion and argument
in those days about the whole idea of a Christian school.

*Groundbreaking,
March 13, 1953.*

Photo: Russell Krabill
slide collection

In answer to the question as to why
exactly in 1954 Bethany came into
being, Krabill noted that schools were
part of the church's mood at that time.
Other conferences too were launching
out into secondary education—
Franconia and Iowa, with Lancaster
having established a school a decade
earlier. "We ought to have our own
high school!" seemed to be the cry of

the day. Krabill suggested here one philosophical difference between the emerging Bethany and some of the earlier Mennonite high schools as well as the reason for this:

> The philosophy our conference had also contrasted with that of some other conferences. This was probably due to the fact that during the several years before the Bethany Board was actually created, we had men like Paul Mininger and others within conference who did not want the school to be a reformatory or a training school for Mennonitism. Actually, Harold Bender was the person who really sold the Bethany idea. J. C. Wenger was another promoter of the school. He wrote some of the early articles about the school in the *Bethany Bulletin*. The committees giving reports to our conference also promoted the idea of a conference high school in their reports.
>
> We also had some lay people in our conference pushing for such a school. Some Goshen College faculty members supported Bethany; others were skeptical. Paul Mininger (later, President of Goshen College) supported Bethany. He believed in Christian education, and his influence was surely felt. He was a very influential person in our conference. Although Mininger was not a published writer—it was a burden for him to write things—in 1952 he presented the Conrad Grebel lectures on "Foundations of Christian Education," where he advocated the idea of a Christian high school.

The mood of the fifties

Russell Krabill reflected on how Conference anticipated its new school—the relationship of school to Conference. He underscored the difference between a student "reformatory"—which the Board did not want—and a school, where the faith aspect of life is integrated into every subject being taught—which the Board indeed was hoping for. "I think the whole Board would have said what I said, as I look back

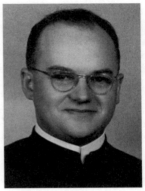

J. C. Wenger
Photo: Mennonite Church USA Archives

'We ought to have our own high school!'

Anticipating how it turned out:
A student perspective

What courses were most useful to me? That's hard to say, for I believe all the courses and teachers I have had have helped me in one way or another. I can say, however, that there have been certain things that have helped me especially.

I appreciate those teachers who made me work and think hard. Those who gave a project and a definite deadline, but who also gave some guidance as to how to go about it, and something to start on. But I also appreciate those who once in a while gave me free rein and made me do something original and creative.

I appreciate those little steps upward; the tasks that seemed enormous and impossible as I looked way ahead to them, but as they drew nearer and I stepped up gradually they became accomplishments. Likewise, I am thankful for the teachers who always gave me something to do which was a little more difficult than what I would have liked.

I am thankful for the teachers who didn't have too much pity on me when I complained and who taught me that most worthwhile things are difficult to obtain.

Continued on page 39 ...

'... when you teach ... there is a Christian way to come at it.'

at those various people," Krabill affirmed.

So it is that Krabill pointed to some unique and strong leaders of conviction and foresight, who were determined that the character and purpose of the new school would avoid retrenchment, staying away from an emphasis on keeping old forms alive, and turning to more of a middle ground, while seeking at the same time an integration of secular and spiritual education. His words are significant in their emphasis on the purpose of the school, enough so to quote *in extenso*:

As I think back to the early fifties, we had people—a few of our leaders, I suppose—who wished the school would be an example of nonconformity to the world. John Steiner, however, as I have already noted, didn't feel that the school ought to be setting the pace on this. He thought it ought to follow the churches and not try to lead out in being different from the status quo. The Board at that time, for example, in keeping with Conference sentiment, held to a dim view on sports, and didn't promote interscholastic sports.

I too have always been conservative in my theology and my church work. Yet I never did believe that the school ought to be the instrument to keep the church in line. In its earlier history, Lancaster Mennonite High School, on the other hand, must have taken a different approach on this than did Bethany. I think there were a number of people in the Lancaster Conference pushing for a school that held to a different outlook.

Saying it positively, I always felt that every Bethany teacher should emphasize the Christian aspect of his or her subject matter. Now maybe the math teachers wouldn't be able to do this as much, but history teachers, Bible teachers, and other teachers could—where you deal with the great concepts of the church. I thought here is a real good place for Bethany to emphasize the Christian aspect of all of these things. Even literature would come in—the way you teach literature. Such was my view. I have a philosophy that Christian education is to bring the Bible and the Lord into every subject. Not to make it a hobby, but I think the occasion comes, when you teach any of these subjects, there is a Christian way to come at it.

We close the interview with some of Krabill's thoughts about Harold S. Bender, crediting him, above all others, for realizing the Bethany idea. Krabill knew Bender well, having been his student, and later a fellow Board member. Something of Krabill's estimation of Bender's stature emerges from the following words:

In 1953 Conference finally elected a High School Board, and because Harold Bender was elected to the Bethany Board, we really got action. Just believe it: One year, the Bethany Board was chosen by Conference, and one year later we opened the school. It's unbelievable! We built a school, we got the faculty—and all that in one year's time! Those 31 meetings tell the story, and Harold Bender did an awful lot of work.

I'd like to say this about Harold Bender. I had him for a teacher in a number of classes at Goshen College, and I knew him well, also having worked with him some. The thing that amazes me is that, considering all the committees he was on, when he came to the Bethany Board meetings, you would have thought that this was the only thing he had going—that Bethany was his baby.

I have one memory about a Board meeting one time. It was in those early days. Bender was sitting at the table, and he had his finger up to do some gesturing and in so doing, he pulled his glasses off. They flew to the floor and shattered. That was in the days before we had these unbreakable lenses. Broke them. Now, if that would have happened to me, I would have been so frustrated I don't know whether I could have collected my thoughts again. He reached down on the floor, gathered up the pieces and went right on with the meeting as if nothing had

Student perspective … *cont. from page 38*

I am glad we had periodic tests, which we needed as an incentive for diligent study. We find it hard to do something we dislike without some kind of compelling force making us do it. Report cards were also helpful in this respect.

I appreciate the teachers who gave their own opinions, and thus taught us how to form some intelligent opinions of our own.

But I also appreciate those teachers who sacrificed some class time once in a while to have fun with their students. I respect these teachers more than those whom I remember as always sober and businesslike.

And the friendships I have developed in these years, among teachers as well as students, are worth more than I'll ever be able to know. Christian friends in whom I could confide have aided my development immensely.

—*Nancy Eash '62 (Myers), "High School in Retrospect" (excerpt from her sociology paper, written in 1962)*

'We built a school, we got the faculty … all … in one year's time!'

Photo: Russell Krabill slide collection

'[Bender] had a vision and ... he put a lot of time and energy into it!'

The financial drive of 1953

Harold Bender, who was the spark plug behind the project for a Conference high school in northern Indiana, approached me in the spring of '53 to see if I would work as a staff person for the committee in planning publicity, and then canvassing the Conference for funds to begin the building. I was very pleased to do this.

Bender himself was acquainted with the experience of the Christian Reformed Church in organizing Christian high schools, and he was convinced that at that point in history a good high school experience would probably be more effective in keeping our young people in the church than our colleges were. This was, so we argued, because they were making their decision for or against the church in their early adolescent years, not after they were in college.

With this in mind I coined the slogan, "If it's Christian, it has to be good," designed several promotional pieces, and began the campaign. I spoke in many congregations, and then during the week visited from home to home making the pitch for support. In this way I collected in cash and pledges in the neighborhood of $125,000 to begin building that fall. That was a lot of money in those days!

It was a rewarding summer, and Bethany has certainly fulfilled our "great expectations." Congratulations on a successful 50 years!

—*C. Norman Kraus (May 2001)*

happened. I simply never will forget that, how he handled that kind of emergency. It is still so vivid in my mind. Well, anyway, I sat with him and I just admired his concentration on the whole thing.

Bender was, in effect, General Secretary of our Board. I don't think he was named to be the Executive Officer as much as he just became one. And what a man! He was on the Committee and he knew what to do. He had a vision and, boy, did he put a lot of time and energy into it![7]

"Hold to the center of the road!"

Although we have no interview with Harold Bender looking back on his involvement and views of Bethany, we do have some of his contemporary correspondence and reports that provide a Bender viewpoint. And we can also report on his level of participation. As already noted, Bender presented the annual Church High School Committee report to Conference on June 4, 1953.

The report obviously was the work of Harold Bender who, through the process of consensus, gathered together the wisdom of the whole committee and its year of work and came up with a well-thought-through, realistic, detailed, and substantive plan: "Accepting the charge of the conference 'to set up a High School,' we have proceeded during the past year, with the counsel of the Executive Committee, to the following actions, which we now report."

The long list of committee actions included: a proposed constitution and bylaws; a proposed site of six acres, already selected, with option to purchase; tentative architectural plans for land and building; cost estimates; tentative selection of a principal (unnamed in the report, but in Bender's handwriting in his personal copy of the report, the name of John Steiner); the names of 111 prospective pupils, all of whose parents were interviewed by Verle Hoffman; no plans for boarding facilities, or transportation, which was to be provided by the parents, with the possibility of pupils coming from afar staying in local homes; firm projections for an annual budget ($20-30,000) and tuition costs ($200 per pupil, with additional children in a family paying half this amount), and thus the need for annual congregational offerings for operating expenses; meeting requirements for state accreditation; carefully noting that all this was tentative, with final decisions to be the work of a new, specially called Conference High School Board; final action in this regard to await the outcome of the financial campaign to be carried out in the summer of 1953 (C. Norman Kraus took on this assignment effectively);[8] and recommending that the school be named Bethany Christian High School (not stated in the report, but given live on the Conference floor).[9]

Bender read through the lengthy list of committee actions, and then concluded his report as follows:

> In conclusion may we say that it is indeed a large and serious undertaking to establish a church high school in our conference district. Much wisdom, diligence, and vigilance will be needed by the school board. Strong and united support from our congregations and conference, spiritually, morally, and financially will be needed. Such a school can mean a great deal for the young people of our district, and therefore for our homes and for our church. For this we need most of all the blessing and grace of Almighty God. In our purpose to have a strong Christian Mennonite High School let us not swerve either to the right or to the left but hold to the center of the road "for Christ and the Church." We bespeak for the future board the earnest prayers and warm generous support of all. They will need both. Respectfully submitted, High School Committee, Amos Hostetler, Chairman, H. S. Bender, Secretary, Ira S. Johns, Ray F. Yoder, C. Norman Kraus.

Of utmost significance is Bender's call for holding faithfully to the center of the road. As Indiana-Michigan Mennonite Conference and its culture were changing, so would the cultural implications of how Mennonite education

C. Norman Kraus took on this [financial campaign] assignment effectively …

Verle Hoffman
Photo from Wenger, J. C., *The Mennonites in Indiana and Michigan*, 1961.

C. Norman Kraus
Photo: Mennonite Church USA Archives

Photo: Royal Bauer collection

A document of sale from Timber Structures, Chicago, Illinois, to the attention of Harold S. Bender, for laminated arches and beams; dated February 17, 1954.

Document: Mennonite Church USA Archives

"History … a Christian way to come at it"
The meaning of history
by Nancy Eash '62 (Myers)

How can history have meaning? We must see all past events in relation to total world context and the present situation. We observe that there is a cyclical aspect to history: that nations rise and fall, that civilizations are fluid, that every action brings a reaction. But from this viewpoint the real meaning of history is not to be seen.

From the Christian perspective, history is linear. It started when man fell and will end at Christ's second coming. Seeing history this way, we realize that the bad in history, which is there because of the part sin played in its beginning, is not hopeless, but there is a hope for the future; not that society will become perfect, but that good will triumph at last and the bad will never completely triumph. For God is always ruling over history *("Heilsgeschichte")*. It is from this perspective alone that we can see the true meaning of history.

Government is a necessary outgrowth of the fallen condition of man. Realizing this, we can see the necessary evil as well as the good in it. We must analyze it to see where it conflicts with our Christian viewpoint. Only on the points where it does conflict can we disobey it. We cannot try to conform the government to our views, but it is our duty to show the government what its boundaries are and how to improve itself within these boundaries.

—A student's government essay exam, written in 1961, reproduced here in its entirety

---

ought to be shaped. A likely reason for Bender's deciding to enter the stage at this particular time probably related to the rapid shift in Conference piety, beginning in 1948, toward the ideal of community. By the early fifties, this new, more positive-sounding approach in "working at human issues" rather than the old, more negative "working at problems, trying to uphold Conference rules and discipline," was well underway. Conference had turned an important corner, and Bender could feel at one with it on the road it was now traveling. Furthermore, Bender's careful articulation and attention to details, along with a style of speaking and writing which invited trust, were further reasons why Conference acted so decisively on the school issue yet that day.

In the afternoon session that same day of June 1953, "Harold S. Bender, Secretary of the Church High School Committee, presented the Constitution and Bylaws of the proposed Bethany School." The committee must have carried out its time-consuming and intricate work to the liking of most Conference delegates, for with a contrasting, almost staccato, movement, Conference passed the following motions:

1. Moved, seconded and carried to adopt this Constitution and Bylaws, … this adoption to be effective at once.

2. Moved, seconded and carried that the election and appointment of High School Board members be made at this conference, their term to begin at once.

3. Moved, seconded and carried that conference authorize the raising of $150,000 over a period of two years, or until completed, to purchase grounds, erect a building, and purchase equipment; conference also decided to issue a warm appeal to all our congregations for a strong and united support of this work.

4. Moved, seconded and carried to approve the fundraising plans reported by the Church High School Committee.

5. Moved, seconded and carried to approve the plan of one annual congregational offering throughout the conference district for the Church High School support, the first offering to be received the fore part of 1954.

6. Moved, seconded and carried that the name of the school be Bethany Christian High School.

The Bethany vision

The following year, on June 2, 1954, Harold Bender preached the Conference Sermon on I Cor. 12:27. He noted the idea of the Church as the body of Christ is to be found

Moved …
that the name
of the school
be Bethany Christian
High School.

The original sign along State Road 15 was lighted and mirrored the gymnasium roofline.
Photo: BCS files

throughout Scripture. As Christ's body, we are more than a mere machine or organization; we are, in our diversity, unified in Christ who is our Head, to whom we give our obedience. We are all members of the body, are all interdependent and vitally related one to another.

Here was in effect Bender's sermonic version of his classic 1943 *The Anabaptist Vision*. For in this message he reaffirmed the idea of a close-knit community of believers, underscoring the worth of each member as Christ's disciple, with the essential quality of community to be found in mutuality, in interrelating closely with one another. Here also was a continuation of the idea of community as developed by Guy F. Hershberger at Conference in 1948 (which in turn was consciously based on Bender's triad of ideas—discipleship, the gathered community, and the ethic of love and nonresistance—as found in what had already become a veritable new Mennonite confession of faith: "the Anabaptist vision"). What Bender did not say (nothing on dress, or restrictions, for example) is as instructive as what he chose to emphasize.

Coming as it did just two months before Bethany opened its doors, it provided in real measure a vital aspect of Harold Bender's vision for this school about to be born.[10] It would be a distinctly Anabaptist institution, embodying the conviction that

Chapel entrance, west end of north hall.
Photo: BCS files

faithfulness lies in the following of Jesus, all of us joining together as the body of Christ present. At that same Conference John Steiner, Bethany Principal designate, spoke on "What a Christian High School Means to Our Conference."

First annual Board report

The next day, June 3, 1954, Bender presented the first annual report of the new Bethany Christian High School Board to Conference. By way of summary,

Bender noted that the BCHS Board was incorporated June 17, 1953. The Religious Life Committee, provided for in the Constitution, would be appointed July 5, 1954. The Board met 31 times throughout the year. A financial campaign would take place in July and early August. Planning for the building, the selection of faculty, solicitation of students, and other normal responsibilities of a school board had taken much time and thought. Bender had words of thanks to all for their solid support:

> We appreciate the warm support from a wide circle of ministers and lay-members as well as the counsel given along the way … We come to the close of the first year with the faculty fully appointed, the school curriculum and organization worked out, the building in good progress, and the student solicitation almost completed. We are encouraged by the progress so far and are confident that we will be able to start the school next September in good order and on a sound basis.

The report continued with details on finances, a note on the completed school catalog, details on the building construction, and the opening date for school, which was set for September 7 at 8:30 a.m., with dedication set for Sunday afternoon, September 12. There were pledges of $75,000 (with $60,000 in hand), with another campaign indicated to complete the $150,000 needed. There was a need to borrow, meanwhile, with the hope that Sunday schools might provide $10,000 for school furniture and equipment. A list of needed books would be circulated, hoping that many of these could be contributed. Eighty-five students were already registered, well distributed over the four years of the high school. Prospects for reaching the goal of 100 students for the first year looked good. With tuition at $200 ($100 for additional students from the same family), it was clear that Conference would need to make up the anticipated deficit. There was assurance that developing plans would meet requirements for a first-class commissioned school. Bender concluded the report in his usual upbeat and gracious manner:

> We close this report with a deep feeling of gratitude to our Heavenly

Anticipating how it turned out:

A student perspective

… This year, for the first time, I saw Christianity as being quite applicable to my studies. In fact, as was stated in sociology, the reason we learn of the secular world is so that we can relate to it as Christians. I believe my gained knowledge in chemistry, English, government and sociology, and German helps me to find a place in the world of society. Yet my high school years have not only been years of intellectual development, but also of social development. I've made many friendships which will last throughout life. I believe that, spiritually, if a young person doesn't reach some sort of maturity in high school, he or she may well never grasp the spiritual realities of life. I think a Christian concept of life, or world view, is important …

—Donald D. Graber '64, "High School in Retrospect" (excerpt from his sociology paper, written in 1964)
Photo: 1964 *Witmarsum*

Bethany Christian High School
First Annual Catalog
May 1954
Goshen, Indiana

Photo: *Bethany Christian High School First Annual Catalog,*
May 1954, Mennonite Church USA Archives

Father for his blessings upon the work, as well as a sincere and warm expression of thanks to our people for their good support thus far. We solicit this continued support in prayers and finances as well as in students, and pledge our best efforts to carry forward to a successful completion the assignment given to us by Conference.

In this fashion, Harold Bender, with quiet confidence, engaging charisma, and abounding energy, brought the task of creating a Mennonite high school to its intended culmination and finish line.

ॐ ॐ ॐ ॐ

And lo and behold, on September 7, 1954, at 8:30 a.m., Bethany Christian High School was indeed finally born. The doors to this spanking-new school swung wide open on that first day, bidding 124 trusting students to enter into an as yet unknowable newness—students, to be sure, who at that same critical moment in their life's sojourn were wondering, hopefully, what sort of an educational experience they might be stepping into.

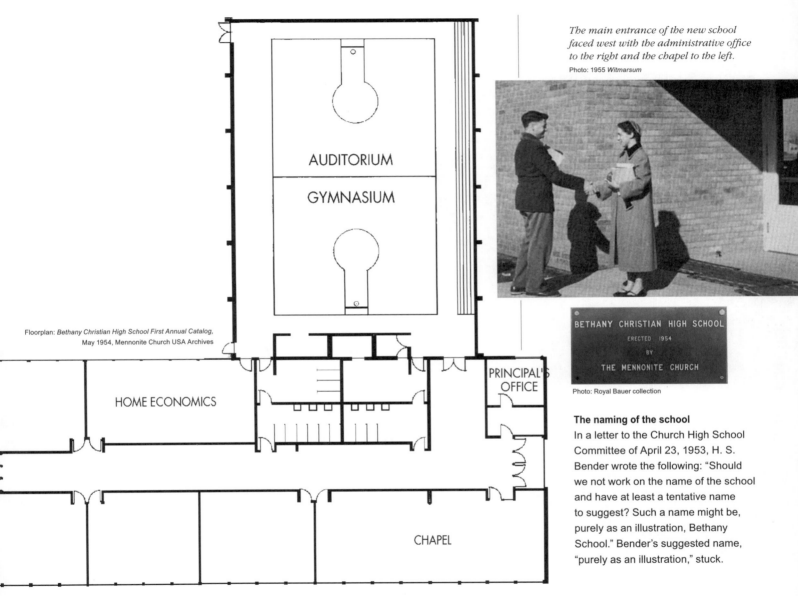

AUDITORIUM

GYMNASIUM

Floorplan: *Bethany Christian High School First Annual Catalog, May 1954*, Mennonite Church USA Archives

HOME ECONOMICS

PRINCIPAL'S OFFICE

CHAPEL

The main entrance of the new school faced west with the administrative office to the right and the chapel to the left.
Photo: 1955 *Witmarsum*

BETHANY CHRISTIAN HIGH SCHOOL
ERECTED 1954
BY
THE MENNONITE CHURCH

Photo: Royal Bauer collection

The naming of the school

In a letter to the Church High School Committee of April 23, 1953, H. S. Bender wrote the following: "Should we not work on the name of the school and have at least a tentative name to suggest? Such a name might be, purely as an illustration, Bethany School." Bender's suggested name, "purely as an illustration," stuck.

Notes

1. Many within the Mennonite Church were still attempting, with some success, to stem the inroads of general society into Mennonite life and culture, that is, till the mid-1960s when the unrest and spirit of the Vietnam Era began in a perceivable manner to erode the realities of a Mennonite cultural separation from the world. Encroaching TV was gradually finding its way into many a Mennonite home, along with a slow but sure, ever-greater acceptance of many North American cultural conventions that Mennonite leaders of an earlier generation would have denounced as "worldly." Thanks to television, coupled with the anti-war sentiment of the times, etc., the (Old) Mennonite Church experienced a cultural transformation, during which time the Church gradually became aware that for a deeper understanding of the Church, one must relate it to the larger, societal questions of the day. For the era in question, however, there was little such awareness on the part of most Mennonite leaders. The social context within which the Mennonite Church found itself—at least up to the early 1960s—was simply not a focal point deemed worthy of much Mennonite reflection, except within the then limited circles of Mennonite higher education. For some of these reasons, this first chapter does not deal directly with the social context within which Mennonites found themselves, but rather deals primarily with in-house agenda.

2. Sources used in this chapter, not otherwise listed, may be found in the following collections of the Archives of the Mennonite Church (AMC): II-5-1:2/30, 31, Hist Mss 6-56, Hist Mss 1-158:12/4, Hist Mss 6-241, and II-5-8: Box 2, File 7.

3. The Community Life Study Committee was composed of A. G. Horner, Ray F. Yoder, Allen B. Ebersole, Oren Detweiler, and Guy F. Hershberger.

4. *Report of the Annual Sessions of the Indiana-Michigan Mennonite Conference,* 1949 (AMC, II-5-1:2/31). One prime example suggesting the nature of this earlier doctrinal era, now being challenged (in 1948) by Hershberger and others, may be found in the Conference proceedings for 1941 when the issue of nonconformity took center stage via a series of addresses on this theme, followed by a resolution: "Inasmuch as there is a present drift in the Mennonite Church in conforming to the world, and, since we have direct teaching from the Bible on this principle: John 17:16; Jas. 4:4; Rom. 12:1,2; John 2:15, 16; Jas. 1:27; I Pet. 3:3,4, and since the drift worldward is not wholesome to a people who claim to be separate, be it therefore Resolved, That we repent of our failure sufficiently to uphold this Doctrine in our teaching and discipline, and that we begin anew to uphold this doctrine by precept and example, faithful preaching and teaching, by reaffirming our former position on the question, Art. 10, Rules and Discipline, that we give ourselves to faithful prayer and united effort as a ministry in maintaining Biblical standards." Section 3 (on Social Activities) of Article 10, for example, reads: "We warn members from indulging in any form of entertainment or amusement that is inconsistent with our faith and practice, or that is a direct violation of the Scriptures, such as, the intermingling of the sexes at bathing beaches and swimming pools, fairs, theatres, moving picture shows, Sunday ball games, regularly organized contesting ball teams, dancing, card games, etc. Eph. 5:11-18; Rom. 12:1,2." (*Report of the Indiana-Michigan Church Conference,* 1941, Hist. Mss, II-5-1: Box 2, File 30, AMC.)

5. Original committee, appointed in 1945: Amos O. Hostetler, Chairman, Carl Kreider, Secretary, Lawrence Yoder, Anson G. Horner, and Homer F. North. *Report of the Indiana-Michigan Church Conference,* 1945 (AMC, II-5-1:2/30). Amos O. Hostetler, an important leader within Conference from the 1920s to the 1970s, quietly yet persistently over the years promoted Christian education for the young people. More than any other person, he was responsible for bringing the Church High School Study Committee into existence in 1945.

6. The committee recruited other brethren to help in the task: John M. Snyder, Wayne J. Wenger, Verle O. Hoffman, Galen I. Johns, and Paul K. Troyer.

7. Interview by writer, February 5, 2001 (AMC, Hist Mss 6-241), and notes from subsequent telephone conversations—excerpted and edited for readability. J. C. Wenger, in 1963, wrote the following about Harold Bender's place in the development of Bethany: "More than any other man, Brother Bender was Bethany's founder. For a number of years the Conference had attempted to establish a Christian high school, but seemed not to be able to get the project launched. Finally, the Executive Committee appointed H. S. Bender to the committee at work on the projected school. It sounds unbelievable, but the fact is that within one year Bethany Christian High School was built and in operation!" *Bethany Bulletin* (Jan. 1963), IX/1. See Everett J. Thomas, "Toward an Anabaptist Vision: A Thirty-Year History of Bethany Christian High School" (May, 1983), 1-4, for further information about Bethany's pre-history (copy in AMC).

8. To prepare for the fundraising work, leaflets were prepared, and a schedule set up to reach out to the Conference congregations before the June 1953 Conference sessions. A speakers' list to carry this out included: Amos O. Hostetler, Harold S. Bender, C. Norman Kraus, Ira S. Johns, Paul Mininger, J. C. Wenger, Paul M. Miller, Galen Johns, Peter Wiebe, and Verle Hoffman. See Harold S. Bender, to "Brother Miller," March 10, 1953, IN-MI Menn. Conf.: Bethany High School—High School Comm., Corres., 1945-53. (II-5-8: Box 2, File 7, AMC.)

9. In a letter to the Church High School Committee of April 23, 1953, Bender wrote the following: "Should we not work on the name of the school and have at least a tentative name to suggest. Such a name might be, purely as an illustration, Bethany School." (II-5-8: Box 2, File 7, AMC.) Bender's suggested name, "purely as an illustration," stuck.

10. What Harold S. Bender accomplished in 1943 with his "Anabaptist Vision," and what Guy F. Hershberger accomplished for Conference in 1948 in granting some positive handles to the idea of community, was truly a return to a normative Anabaptist-Mennonite theology, as it had been articulated over the centuries, whereby discipleship found its fulfillment within the gathered community. Such a return to the idea of discipleship largely brought to an end the doctrinal interlude of the Mennonite Church, extending from the 1890s to the mid-twentieth century, that the Mennonite Church had bought into, and, which, with its emphasis on sometimes sterile and definitional doctrinal categories, stood at odds with a more existential and descriptive Anabaptist approach to faith and life.

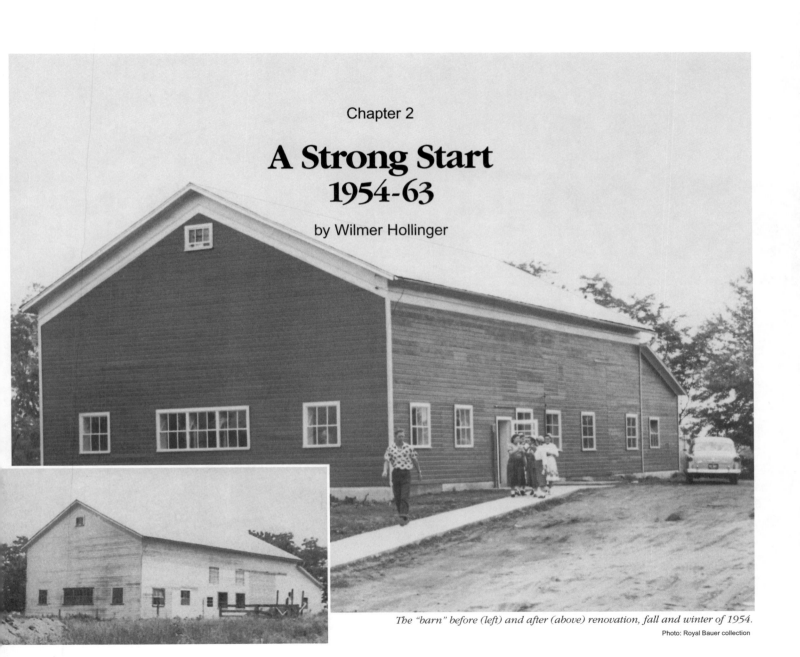

Chapter 2

A Strong Start
1954-63

by Wilmer Hollinger

The "barn" before (left) and after (above) renovation, fall and winter of 1954.

Photo: Royal Bauer collection

Bethany Christian High School, 1955.

Photo: BCS files

The concept of a church high school envisioned by Indiana-Michigan Mennonite Conference leaders for a decade was now a reality. The school would have high academic standards, be state accredited, and have curriculum to accommodate college-bound students as well as students headed for agriculture and industry. The school would also promote the ministry of the Conference churches.

Conference leaders had a general agreement that the school's purpose would be to bring a Christian perspective to education rather than to insulate and protect students from "the world." Conference leaders held these concerns deeply but had not yet turned to the more basic question of a specific theology of education and discipleship: how Bethany might encourage church young people to faithfulness within the church of Jesus Christ remained undeveloped at the school's beginning.

The school opened on schedule in September 1954, although due to a late delivery of some wood flooring, the dedication was postponed until Sunday, October 3, of that year, as the Board wanted the school completed before the dedication. Also the "barn," an older building on the new campus, designed to accommodate

Dedication ceremony with John Steiner at the podium (top, left) and an overflow crowd seated at classroom desks lining the hallway (above).

Photos: 1955 *Witmarsum*. Text of the dedication ceremony excerpted from a 1957 term paper written by Doris Litwiller '56 for Professor J. C. Wenger's Mennonite history class, Goshen College.

several classrooms and the cafeteria, was being remodeled by volunteer labor and would not be finished until the following January.[1]

At the long-awaited dedication, J. C. Wenger, the moderator of Indiana-Michigan Conference, brought the message, and Robert Ewing, the new music teacher, directed a 99-voice school choir. Mennonite secondary education had become a reality in the Indiana-Michigan Conference.

Growing support for the school

Support for Bethany had been growing in the mid-fifties, in part because a larger number of students from the rural churches were attending high school than in the previous decade. Many of their parents objected to the increasing emphasis on sports in the public schools, an attitude due in considerable degree to their objection to sports uniforms, shorts, and jerseys. As for location of the new school, the Goshen area seemed best able to serve the most families in the Conference, although it was clear this location would not well accommodate the areas of Upper Michigan and Southern Indiana. But overall Conference geography did not affect the school so much as did the differences within Indiana itself. In this regard, Principal John Steiner noted in retrospect that expectations of the student families from the Goshen and Elkhart congregations differed from those of supporting rural congregations, which seemed to attract the more conservative families. As it opened, Bethany's challenge was both to hold the support of Conference and also meet the expectations of the local congregations.

But the vision of Amos Hostetler and others for a church high school had finally materialized. Support for the school in the Conference, although mixed, was growing. Clearly, at this point in the school's life, the concern was of necessity the problem of resources. Any Christian philosophy of education for Bethany Christian High School remained somewhat vague.

But the vision of Amos Hostetler ... had finally materialized.

Library study hall.
Photo: Royal Bauer collection

Key personalities

Of the various church leaders probably none devoted so many hours to the school both before and after its opening as did Harold S. Bender, who seemed to have boundless energy and to naturally assume responsibility. Although he was named secretary of the original Board of Directors, by assumption he became in fact executive secretary, serving in this position until his death in 1962. It was Bender who generally contacted prospective teachers, and it was his word that resulted in whether or not they were hired. Letters to the state concerning accreditation often went out under his name, and much of the correspondence to the churches carried both the names of Bender and Board President Amos Hostetler. At times Bender even asserted himself in the day-to-day operation of the school. According to one story, librarian Ruth Roth had carefully arranged the library in preparation for the first day in September of 1954. But when she entered the library on that morning, she found many things rearranged. She discovered that Bender, wanting to make sure everything was "just right," had also arranged the library.[2]

The faculty was a well-seasoned group of people and the key administrators well-qualified. The new principal, John Steiner, although not well known in the area before this assignment, had, according to Hostetler, the right qualifications and convictions. Steiner said the Board never told him what they expected of him, though later he was informed of the importance of both academic and spiritual qualities. Hostetler said they especially needed the other chief administrator, Clarence Holaway, to meet the requirements for a first-class state commission, which it granted the second year of the school's operation.

The first *Bethany Bulletin* listed Steiner as principal and Holaway as business manager. But it seems clear that as late as August of 1954, since Steiner had not yet received his Indiana principal's license, Holaway was acting as principal. As noted above, Bender hired many of the teachers, although Steiner recruited Robert Ewing, Dorothy

Meeting in the home economics room are members of the first Bethany faculty: R. Roth, D. Hershey, C. J. Holaway, J. Steiner, J. M. Nafziger, L. Culp, and R. Ewing. Photo and *Bulletin*: BCS files

**Bender's hiring
of John Steiner
seems providential.**

**If Harold Bender was
the architect
that helped
create Bethany,
John Steiner was ...
the keystone ...**

*John Steiner (1912-1990)
as he appeared in the
1958* Witmarsum *which
was dedicated to him.*
Photo enlargement: 1956 *Witmarsum*

Hershey, and Lester Culp in Kansas.[3] Where full-time teachers were not needed, a number of local people, mostly associated with Goshen College, filled in as part-time teachers.

Bender's hiring of John Steiner seems providential. It resulted from an overnight stay with relatives, the Ira Johns family, on a Christmas holiday trip in 1953.[4]

If Harold Bender was the architect that helped create Bethany, John Steiner was for many years the keystone that held the school together. Steiner had just passed his forty-second birthday when he assumed his new role as principal, a job that demanded much sacrifice. He and his young family moved into an older house east of Goshen, while he worked on extra college credits and adjusted to the new community and the school. His goal was to run a school in which young people would learn to love God and the church. Mildred Steiner said of her husband that he enjoyed his work, that he liked school, and he liked people![5] Hostetler declared it was Steiner and the faculty that really "got the school spirit going—not the Board."

Steiner was highly respected by both students and faculty. His high ideals, his love for students, faculty, and church, affected the entire school spirit. His concern for church unity and harmony were primary; for him, keeping traditional church practice took precedence over personal inclinations.[6] In any case, unless it was very hot, he wore a black "plain suit" that on his large frame added to his awe-inspiring appearance in the eyes of students. But he had considerable spiritual stature as well; he took a personal interest in the spiritual life of his students, seemed to know much about their social life, and even the reasons most had come to Bethany. He was a zealous recruiter for the school and, while being aware that some students came because of home or previous school problems, he shared that information with the faculty only when necessary.[7] In any event many of the students who had problems elsewhere became very good students at Bethany.[8]

In theology Steiner leaned toward fundamentalism, as did much of the Indiana-Michigan Conference in the fifties. His preaching and his teaching reflected something of this theology but, more importantly, a deep love for God and the church. He loved to tell stories in the classroom, often with a humorous twist,[9] and sometimes from the chapel pulpit with a gruesome aspect.[10] Steiner taught several classes; but in the memory of the students, it was not his Bible classes that were significant. In fact students seem to have little memory of what he taught. They simply knew he liked them.

Both students and faculty knew Steiner as a concerned teacher and colleague, but everyone knew he was extremely busy. One student said he seemed almost too busy to teach.[11] He gave the faculty both respect and freedom, allowing them, for example, to choose their own texts from the state-approved list.[12]

C. J. Holaway of Nappanee, the second part of Bethany's highly capable early leadership team, was very near retirement age when recruited by the Conference to be business manager, principal, assistant principal, and then again principal as the time demanded. Whatever his title, he served as the chief day-to-day operating manager of all things academic. He was the school's disciplinarian for normal school activities but was well respected. Also he was considered to be an interesting and understandable teacher.[13]

It seems, however, that students soon learned the difference between Holaway's disciplinary methods and Steiner's. On one occasion, while the Waterford Mennonite Church was meeting at Bethany on Sundays, several Bethany students damaged some school property; their Sunday school teacher asked the students which school

Marion Bontrager taught at his alma mater 1960-62.

John Steiner, the first superintendent at Bethany, was not a welcome visitor when he came to the farm east of Goshen to recruit me for Bethany Christian High School. But he was persistent and understood people.

From unwelcome recruiter John Steiner became one of the most respected and influential persons in my life … [But] should I risk going to a church school again which had no "track record" and wouldn't have an athletic program? … This decision was more difficult for me than surrendering my life to Christ as Lord and Savior … In contrast to today, a church high school was a strange new idea in Northern Indiana … I had to decide! Three days before school began I finally decided to attend Bethany …

The year at Bethany was a watershed year of growth in my life spiritually and personally. The relationship with teachers was special. John Steiner mentored me, treating me like a son. He combined warmth and love with firmness in relating to students. The school's spiritual dimension helped create community among students and faculty I had not known in public school. My view of the Mennonite Church was enlarged. I enjoyed the year at Bethany and felt God rewarded me for the step of faith to follow the Lord's leading …

Looking back, the decision to go to Bethany was a decision about who my primary people would be, church or society. It was a decision about identity and values. It was a decision about what story would be my story: the salvation history story or the American story? It was a lesson in God's faithfulness when God is honored …

—*Marion Bontrager '55*

Eudean Schlabach '55 (Broni), employed as school secretary from 1959-60, stands at the half-door of the superintendent's office.

Photos: left, 1955 *Witmarsum;* above, 1960 *Witmarsum*

Photos: left, 1962 *Witmarsum;* right,1955 *Witmarsum*

'Bethany Christian High School is where I became a person who really loves the Lord.'

Joyce Yoder '56 (Frantz): Growing at Bethany

After I quit school at the end of the first semester of my sophomore year at Goshen High School, my father was really upset with me. So he had Royal Bauer come and talk to me about going to Bethany Christian High School. Of course, he didn't have to do much talking: I didn't want to be a nanny for the rest of my life.

So Mr. Bauer came to our house the summer of 1954 and tutored me all summer. I was ready to enter my junior year at Bethany in the fall of 1954 (thank you, Dad).

At Bethany I really learned to open up. I did some things my parents were not too happy about, like cutting my hair and going to drive-in movies.

One of the things I remember most is music and sitting next to Margaret Yoder, who was always giving me encouragement. I was at my best in anything having to do with bookkeeping. I have been a secretary for better than 30 years at different places, including 23 years at the elementary school in North Manchester.

Bethany Christian High School is where I became a person who really loves the Lord. And I have been faithful to Christ all my life. Thanks to all the teachers who were so kind and loving and understanding.

Photo: 1956 *Witmarsum*

official should be informed; without hesitation they agreed it should be Steiner.[14] Royal Bauer remembers Holaway carrying a whistle that he would blow at times to gain order.[15] According to Marvin Nafziger, Holaway was more demanding in relating to both students and faculty, Steiner more "laid back."[16] During Bethany's early years the official titles of both Holaway and Steiner changed a number of times, but their roles in leading the school were clear.

Testimonies of early teachers and students agree: if one wanted to discuss academic issues or day-to-day school policy, conduct, or discipline, Holaway was the man to see. If one wanted to discuss life issues, spiritual concerns, church-related issues, or severe disciplinary infractions that might involve the student's parents, Steiner was in charge.

C. J. Holaway
Photo: Royal Bauer collection

The teachers

There were many dedicated teachers who for an extremely low salary taught a very heavy schedule. In the six-period schedule by which Bethany operated in its early years, a full-time teacher was expected to teach five one-credit classes, conduct one study hall, be available to sponsor extracurricular activities, and attend all faculty

Lester Culp (pointing) with the Audubon Club, c. 1959. Photo: BCS files

There were many dedicated teachers who for an extremely low salary taught a very heavy schedule.

Royal Bauer in his role as religious counselor with student Frances Hassencahl '59. Photo: Royal Bauer collection

Robert Ewing presents the Freshmen Girls' Sextet with a first-place award. Photo: Mennonite Church USA Archives

Marvin Nafziger as class sponsor, 1955. Photo: 1955 *Witmarsum*

meetings. How did this translate into real life? As an example, Marvin Nafziger recalls teaching one section each of U. S. history, world history, government or economics, bookkeeping, speech, and Bible. Because he taught six periods, he had no study halls. He also served as the school's bookkeeper and sponsored a class. Since his salary was not adequate to support his family, he turned to farming about 80 acres after school and on weekends.[17] Another early teacher was Royal Bauer, who came the second year of the school's existence and served until 1988. He taught English and Bible classes and served a number of years as religious counselor. He was also sponsor of the school paper, *Reflector,* and the school's Christian service organization, known as the "Y." Lester Culp, who came the first year and retired in 1987, taught biology, chemistry, and agriculture; did most of the photography; and also served as sponsor of everything that needed a sponsor. Robert Ewing, who also came at the school's beginning, was kept more than busy teaching and supervising the school's extensive music program. After school he tutored individual instrumental students and took many music students to district and state competitions where they generally were awarded superior ratings.[18]

No historical record of Bethany's early years would be complete without noting the contribution of Sam S. and Rachel Miller. This husband-wife team helped make the school a pleasant, comfortable place. Sam served as custodian, janitor, or superintendent of buildings and grounds, depending on which publication one is

Marvin L. Miller '56: Some musical memories at BCHS

As one of the first students at Bethany Christian High School, I was interested in the music program. Mr. Robert Ewing, our music teacher, had been busy even before the first school year began, contacting all interested prospective students to form a choir and begin rehearsals in order to be involved in the opening dedication services of the school.

While the details of those early rehearsals and presentations are not very clear, I do remember the feeling of joy and excitement at being involved in the choir. The experience gave me an immediate sense of belonging, not only to the new student body but also to an organization of close-knit students who enjoyed singing and praising God together.

Photo: 1956 *Witmarsum*

… a state official described it as … 'one of the best church high school programs in the State of Indiana.'

Rachel Miller serves lunch in the "barn," site of the first cafeteria.
Photo: Royal Bauer collection

Below: Sam Miller clears the walk to the "barn." Photo: 1958 *Witmarsum*

reading. It is fairly clear that Sam's job did not change, only his title. He served from the school's beginning through the 1959-60 school year, while Rachel served as head cook from 1954 through the 1974-75 school year. The students appreciated the Millers; one class took them along on their senior trip and dedicated the 1960 *Witmarsum* to them.

The curriculum

Although Bethany's curriculum lacked the variety of larger schools like Goshen, Concord, and Elkhart, it probably matched or exceeded that of the smaller schools of the time that had not consolidated. In 1954 most local public schools had only small student bodies with a limited number of

Betty Schlabach '55, Marietta Hochstetler '55, Sylvia Steiner '56, Eudean Schlabach '55, Esther Weldy '55, and Joan Frey '55.
"Students will be classified in one of four curriculums … Academic, Homemaking, Agriculture, Commercial." Quote: 1955 *Catalog* Photos: BCS files

teachers. Bethany, however, in its early years, offered in addition to the basic courses, Latin, Spanish, and German, three levels of home economics, several agriculture-based courses, bookkeeping, two levels of typing, plus Bible courses, and an extensive program of a cappella music. Although the state did not consider Bethany's program extensive enough in its first year for a first-class commission, a state official described it as having "one of the best

Original home economics room.
Photos: BCS files

church high school programs in the State of Indiana." Bethany, in fact, did receive a first-class commission in 1956, its second year of operation.

Although in its early years Bethany did not get involved in interscholastic athletics, the school did participate in the state academic contests and testing programs. The reputation gained in these areas drew academically strong students. One junior transfer student said he was first in class rank in his previous school but at Bethany only number six or seven. The original hesitancy that kept some academically strong students from applying at Bethany was soon reversed. Indeed, some local schools became concerned when a number of their better students transferred to Bethany; their academic test scores tended to go down while Bethany's soared.

The students

While some Mennonite students were hesitant to leave their former schools and friends, a fair number did transfer for Bethany's opening year, including 26 seniors, coming from many of the local high schools in Elkhart, Lagrange, and Marshall counties. Several also transferred from the church boarding schools in Hesston, Kansas, and Harrisonburg, Virginia, to be closer to their homes.

Bethany's early years were parallel to a time of world unrest. This was the Cold War era, just a few years after the Korean War. Mennonite students realized their outlook was different from their public school peers. Their peace stance related to the matter of social compatibility: Marvin Yoder (class of '57, teacher 1976-91) recalled that Bethany offered him a more amiable environment than did the public school.[19]

Jerry Burrows '58: The lessons I learned at Bethany

It has been a long time since I received my diploma as a graduating member of the class of 1958 … After graduation, at my father's request, I attended Ontario Mennonite but decided I was not called to the ministry. I went into the U.S. Navy and retired in May 1988 … Two years before I retired, God started to deal with my life … I gave my life to Christ one evening in the Chief Petty Officers' Barracks. Shortly after I retired, I started attending Gulfhaven Mennonite Church … I am now in a rotation leading congregational singing (Robert Ewing would be proud), teaching, leading small group Bible studies and working in the nursery with the little ones …

Many of the lessons I learned and gleaned at Bethany have served me well, especially in the field of human relations. This was a vital asset when I was attached to the State Department in Singapore …

I understand that Dr. Peter Schmidt has passed on to Glory. His taking me under his wing and teaching me to love math has made a difference in my life. He would have enjoyed knowing one of his students was doing atomic and nuclear math while learning electronics. I still use his math on a daily basis in my civilian position with the Department of Defense.

Mr. Ewing was our energetic and enthusiastic director. It was his example of musicianship and dedication that inspired me to continue in the field of music as an occupation of service for the rest of my life. We learned to sing with spirit and joy …

Photo: 1958 *Witmarsum*

Mel Stutzman '56: A memory of "Betsy"
I did have one occasion to ride in Betsy. That was when I was a member of a Gospel team that went on a tour into Michigan to give a number of programs … in the winter of 1955-56. The group consisted of Mr. Ewing, Marlin Miller, and the men's quartets of the three oldest classes. That was a total of 14 people. Betsy proved to be a trusty and unique vehicle for such a trip. It allowed us to all be together so we could practice on the road. And the acoustics weren't that bad either. It was interesting to watch people's expressions when we stopped and all got out, one after the other.
Photo: 1956 *Witmarsum*

Joyce Yoder '56 (Frantz): "Betsy"
Of course we can't forget Mr. Ewing and his … "Betsy": we had a lot of fun in her.

Marvin L. Miller '56: "Betsy"
Another memory of those two years … at Bethany was the trips we small choir members took in Mr. Ewing's hearse, "Betsy." As students we had great fun riding in this unique mode of transportation. He had purchased this vehicle, which had formerly been used for its intended purpose, but which made a great vehicle for transporting the small select choral group to its concerts … Needless to say, the general public got quite a kick out of seeing us disembark from that long black vehicle.

Music program

Music's importance at Bethany was such that for the first several years no other classes could be scheduled during choir period. The first year all but 24 students were in choir, the second year all but 17, who were placed in a study hall. In addition to the choir there were many smaller music groups: octets, sextets, quartets, and in the later 1950s many small choral groups, all coached and resourced by Mr. Ewing. The choir sang in the local churches, led by Ewing, while smaller groups went out as Gospel teams to churches in Northern Indiana and Southern Michigan with another faculty sponsor.

Steve Miller '59, David Bishop '63, Darrel Diener '60, and Leland Miller '63. Photo: BCS files

Sometimes Ewing would take smaller groups to programs in his 1940 Buick hearse (fondly named "Betsy"), which he also used for transporting students to school. Melvin Stutzman '56 recalls crossing the Straits of Mackinac on a ferry to give programs at Wildwood and several other churches in Michigan's Upper Peninsula.

The group consisted of three quartets, speaker Marlin Miller, and Mr. Ewing, all traveling in Betsy.[20] Another student enjoyed pulling into a small town and seeing the faces of the local bystanders as 12 or more people crawled out of the 16-year-old hearse.

> Another student enjoyed … seeing the faces of the local bystanders as 12 or more people crawled out of a 16-year-old hearse.

Mr. Ewing and his 1940 Buick hearse named "Betsy." Photo: 1956 *Witmarsum*

One can page through any *Witmarsum* from the late fifties or early sixties and see the great importance of music, which, amazingly, was not only extensive in scope but always a cappella. This reflected the practice of the Indiana-Michigan churches at this time, which prohibited instrumental music in church and even objected to hymns being accompanied in any circumstance. They did not object to solo or instrumental ensembles in school as long as these did not accompany choirs or smaller groups in worship.[21] In fact during Bethany's first year, the school's only piano was in the gym. Nor was there a special chapel facility; school assemblies and chapel programs were held in the library. By the second year of school, the upper floor of the renovated "barn" housed the chapel, music rooms, and an office for Mr. Ewing.[22]

As with academic competition, Bethany also had considerable success in the district and state music competitions. Ewing could not remember any year when the vocal groups did not get superior ratings at the district level and usually at the state level as well.[23]

Ewing continued at Bethany until graduation of the class of 1959, then resigned because he could no longer give the program what it needed and still support his family.[24] His successor, Freeman Lehman, continued the strong music tradition in the school.

1957-58 Senior Women's Sextet: Rachel Holaway, Ferne Cender, Marcile Kauffman, Carolyn Hershberger, Alice Yoder, and Ruthann Gardner. Right: Freeman Lehman directs the orchestra, 1962-63. Photos: BCS files

Memories of the origin of MSEC Choral Festival

On April 21, 1962, a choral festival was hosted by Iowa Mennonite School, which was the forerunner of the annual choral festival ... The following year, 1963, the first annual MSEC sponsored festival was held at Central Christian High School in Kidron, Ohio.

In my memory I hear the sound of 100-plus voices rehearsing Randall Thompson's "Alleluia" under the direction of Mary Oyer, guest conductor from Goshen College, an exhilarating performance, followed by the individual and combined choirs ...

Programs were given en route to and from the festival at Kouts, Indiana, and Freeport, Illinois, with a visit to the radio station of Moody Bible Institute in the heart of Chicago ... The social interaction, the magic of the music and the bonding of the Spirit will live in the memories of all who participated.

—*Freeman Lehman, faculty, 1959-67*

Photo: 1961 *Witmarsum*

Sports

Even though the school provided a strong intramural program for boys in a number of sports, the lack of interscholastic competition was a source of frustration to some of the athletically inclined students and their families. Despite this, many of Bethany's strong supporters within the church were quite opposed to a competitive athletic program. Steiner, a former coach but ardent churchman, continued to loyally support a policy with which he most certainly disagreed. But this general attitude began to relax as during the early years the boys' basketball teams began to play in the local church league. The 1957 *Witmarsum* reports that the Bethany team won all its games. The dress requirement for sports teams was a serious issue at Bethany in the fifties. The *Witmarsum* from 1955 to 1963 reveals the incremental changes in team uniforms. The early athletic garb for boys was T-shirts and long pants, by 1958 sleeveless jerseys and long pants, and by 1960 the players were wearing shorts and jerseys. There is no evidence of a girls' athletic program in the earliest years of the school.

Extracurricular activities

The Bethany school program offered extracurricular clubs for many interests, with each having a faculty sponsor. The largest and most active was the Young People's Christian Association, commonly

1958 Witmarsum *editor Rosalyn Grieser '58 presents John Steiner with a copy of the yearbook dedicated to him.* Photo: 1959 *Witmarsum*

Young People's Christian Association, 1959-60.
Photo: BCS files

1958 varsity basketball team, front: seniors John Graber, Steve Kauffman, Ed Bontreger, and David Ray Miller. Back: Larry Welty, Larry Weldy, Floyd Troyer, Richard Graber, and Coach Steiner. Photo: 1958 *Witmarsum*

known as the "Y," which was formed in the spring of 1955 to provide opportunities for Christian service, to develop Christian character, and to promote the growth of mind, body, and spirit.[25] The club afforded leadership opportunities for some of the most respected and able students. It had a number of sub-organizations, and its influence and activities, or lack of activities in any given year, greatly influenced school spirit.

With no monitoring, the school encouraged teachers to relate Christian experience to classroom materials ...

Spiritual life

Daily chapel services with a well-developed system of speakers were in place during the first decade. The program periodically included a series of evangelistic meetings or a series of topics which the administration thought vital to Christian life and growth. A recurring emphasis in these special meetings was distinctive Mennonite doctrines and Christian courtship.

Frequent articles in the *Reflector*, usually written by students, expressed Christian concerns. With no monitoring, the school encouraged teachers to relate Christian experience to classroom materials, an approach to religious instruction which suggests no focused philosophy. And although a strong Christian atmosphere prevailed, there were ethical disappointments. One student was ridiculed for reporting the $100 bill she found in a library book. Yet she later discovered these same critical young people ultimately came to be fine Christian adults.[26]

Senior trips and fish fries

An annual senior class trip to Washington, D. C., by chartered bus became a standard event from the school's beginning, sometimes taken in the fall and sometimes in the

Chapel held in east end of north hall.
Photos: BCS files

Parking for senior fish fry north of building, late fifties. Photo: BCS files

Myrna Miller '58 sells candy at Bethany's first concession stand in the main lobby.

Photo: Royal Bauer collection

spring. It was commonly a four-day trip, with students sleeping on the bus going and coming, but of course providing little sleep for class sponsors. Money became a problem, since the tuition package did not fund the trip. Though the first class paid for the trip out of pocket,[27] most of the following classes engaged in fundraising projects and then paid for the trip from their treasury. Early fundraising projects included pancake suppers, chili suppers, bake sales, scrap and paper drives, candy, ice cream, Christmas card sales, and waiting on tables at local church and business banquets. Out of these fundraising efforts emerged what became a strong Bethany tradition: the fish fry. In spring 1956 Ralph Stahly, father of Janice, a junior, suggested that the juniors should try a smelt fry. Stahly, a pastor in the Indiana-Michigan Conference who frequently traveled to Michigan, knew about the large catches of smelt taken along Lake Michigan's eastern shore in that era. On one of his return trips from Michigan he brought the smelt, which class members and their sponsors cleaned and prepared under the supervision of Dorothy Hershey, the home economics teacher.

The class of '58 in Washington, D. C. Photo: BCS files

Guenn Stoltzfus talks with Royal Bauer through bus window, 1960 senior trip. Photo: BCS files

According to class sponsor Robert Ewing, the smelt fry was a great success.[28] The following spring the junior class again decided to try a fish fry but this time contracted with the Jonah Club to provide and prepare the fish. Such was the birth of Jonah Club Fish Fry at Bethany.

As seniors the class of 1958 then held another Jonah Club Fish Fry in the spring. After their graduation the new senior class of 1959 held a Jonah Club Fish Fry in the fall of 1958 and a chili supper that winter. Apparently the junior class, the class of 1960, held a fish fry in the spring of 1959 and so established the tradition of two Jonah Club fish fries per year, one in the fall sponsored by the senior class and one in the spring by the junior class. Other fundraising efforts continued for a few years but were generally underclass projects.

Financial challenges

One of the greatest challenges facing Bethany at its opening and throughout its early years was a lack of funding. The Conference had estimated a cost of at least $150,000 to start the new school. Extensive promotion and solicitation for funds before the school opened netted $75,000. During the summer of 1954, numerous appeals had gone out for funds, but the Board continued to struggle with the debt.

"Between classes" required going between buildings.

As school opened in September, Conference leaders and the Board held another financial drive under the leadership of C. Norman Kraus. By March 1955 the Board was appealing for operating funds. School tuition at $100 per semester was obviously not covering costs, because on May 16, 1955, Steiner reported to the Board that the operating budget had a negative balance of $2,500 and the school was in serious need of more space. He suggested remodeling the agriculture-shop building ("barn") to add three more classrooms. Moreover, at that same meeting the Board learned of an immediate need for $72,000 for the building fund, $2,000 for operating deficit, $7,000 for remodeling, and $1,000 for new equipment, totaling $82,000, of which $7,000 was already pledged, leaving an

Cooks Rachel Miller and Susan Kauffman serve lunch in the original cafeteria located in the "barn," c. 1958-59. Photos: BCS files

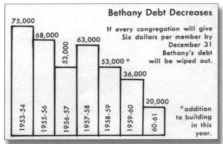

Bethany Debt Decreases

If every congregation will give Six dollars per member by December 31 Bethany's debt will be wiped out.

Year	Amount
1953-54	75,000
1955-56	68,000
1956-57	53,000
1957-58	63,000
1958-59	53,000 *
1959-60	36,000
60-61	20,000

* addition to building in this year.

Chart: August 1961 *Bulletin*

A 1957 graduate, who sat in the front of the classroom, ... observed the school secretary ... tell the teacher that there would be no paycheck for that pay period.

immediate need of $75,000. It was obviously a difficult meeting. The secretary notes it closed at 10:30 p.m.

Students were generally unaware of the school's financial problems. One 1956 graduate of Bethany did note that the school was very strict about having tuition paid on time.[29] A 1957 graduate, who sat in the front of the classroom, on one occasion observed the school secretary come in to quietly tell the teacher that there would be no paycheck for that pay period.[30]

While the faculty members were aware of Steiner's fundraising efforts and knew that he stayed at the school after they all left, they knew little of the extent of the problem; even Marvin Nafziger, who did the day-to-day bookkeeping, was not aware of the school's serious financial circumstance.[31]

Not only was Steiner carrying a lot of the school's money problems, he also had some of his own. To help supplement his income and to raise his visibility and respect in the Conference, both Harold Bender and J. C. Wenger persuaded Steiner to fill the vacant pastorate at Pleasant View Mennonite Church north of Goshen.[32]

But of course this did not help the problem of his being too busy; by the time he reached age 50 he began to show signs of too much stress.

New faculty

The 1959-60 school year saw a larger than usual number of faculty changes. Freeman Lehman replaced Robert Ewing in music and perpetuated the strong music tradition. Marvin Nafziger moved a mile north on

1960 faculty, front row: Margaret Ingold, Freeman Lehman, Phyllis Rensberger, John Steiner, Rosemary Wyse, and C. J. Holaway. Back row: Lester Culp, Dean Hartman, Royal Bauer, Leonard Gross, John Ingold, Delmar Miller, and Melvin Birkey. Photo: BCS files

State Road 15 to teach at Goshen College. A number of younger teachers joined the faculty to meet the need of a growing school.

Teaching loads continued to be heavy. One of these newly hired teachers spoke of his first year as very difficult; his average load was six periods of teaching with either four or five preparations, plus conducting a chapel service about every three weeks. The classes were large with his required courses being one-half his teaching load and running about 40 students per class.[33] Bethany's early faculty were veterans, but the teaching loads weighed heavily on these new and younger teachers.

A number of these new teachers, recently out of college and seminary, also brought with them a new attitude. Being less inclined toward indoctrination, they tended toward an inquiry approach to integrate subject matter and Christian faith.[34] Some parents and church leaders viewed this method with alarm, others with commendation.[35] Steiner himself was deeply concerned about this approach, especially in the Bible classes.[36] The students soon sensed the growing division in the faculty on this issue and, in a school program during the 1961-62 school year, staged an operetta in which they satirized the different approaches of the progressive as well as the more conservative teachers.[37]

Typing, bookkeeping, and shorthand were taught by Phyllis Rensberger, 1959-60. Photo: BCS files

By fall 1959, ...
the enrollment
had doubled as had
the number of faculty.

Summary of first five years

Except for the chronic financial crises, there were few negatives the first five years of Bethany's history. John Steiner was well respected in the Conference, and the school had the growing respect of the Goshen community. By fall 1959, as Bethany began its sixth year, the enrollment had doubled as had the number of faculty. Tuition jumped from the original $100 to $130 per semester. The school

Walter Troyer '60 in the chemistry lab.
Photo: BCS files

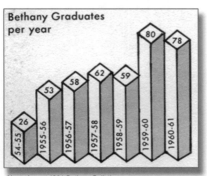

Bethany Graduates per year

54-55: 26
1955-56: 53
1956-57: 58
1957-58: 62
1958-59: 59
1959-60: 80
1960-61: 78

Chart: August 1961 *Bethany Bulletin*

David Ray Miller '58: "I remember when ..."
My mind was taken back to 1958. This was the year that the varsity basketball team bought the school's first blue and white basketball uniforms.

As I remember, a long discussion with the administration occurred before permission was given to wear short pants during a basketball game. I thought we looked pretty snappy in those blue and white uniforms. However, when it came time to take pictures for the annual, we were required to put our long sweats on.

On sports uniforms:
We have come a long way over the years; however, the pants worn today are about as long as the sweats that graced our bodies. What goes around comes around.

Photo: 1958 *Witmarsum*

and the Mennonite community that supported it remained fairly conservative in things social, political, and theological. A large picture of President Eisenhower hanging in the school cafeteria perhaps suggested the school's attempt to be involved with the world, even though not of it.[38]

Entering the sixties

Other changes were taking place. The *Reflector* of December 6, 1960, announced the purchase of a mimeograph machine, its primary purpose being to print the biweekly *Reflector*. But the article noted that teachers could also use it to print tests and music programs. Previously tests were printed with purple hectograph copiers. An individual loaned the money for the new machine and agreed to be repaid with the funds normally spent to print the *Reflector*.

1961 Editor-in-Chief Marjorie Slabach '61 and sponsor Delmar Miller start the mimeograph "presses" rolling on an issue of the Reflector. Photo: BCS files

Student attitudes began to reflect the changing mood of America as the school entered the sixties. The yearbooks of the early sixties portray a decrease in the occasions when girls are wearing coverings. Boys' haircuts change from the flattops of the fifties to longer styles, as girls' hair becomes shorter. Pictures of sports activities also show a change toward conventional uniforms.

As early as January 1960, Steiner requested permission from the Bethany Board to schedule basketball games with other Christian schools. The outcome of this request is not clear, but it is clear that pressure for interscholastic sports was increasing. The issue was not

1962 varsity basketball team with Coach John Nyce.
Photo: BCS files

resolved in school policy until the mid-sixties.

Adding to the changing mood of the school was the retirement of Clarence Holaway in the spring of 1962. Some of the younger faculty welcomed this change, seeing his school policy as outdated.[39] Others, such as Board member Ora Yoder, remarked that "Holaway's discipline will be missed; Steiner really loves the kids but is quite easy on them."

The School Board, aware of the growing need to re-evaluate faculty policy at Bethany, had earlier in the school year begun to work on a retirement policy as well as support for teachers working toward graduate degrees. The Board had also been seeking a replacement for Holaway, knowing that he wanted to retire at age 70. Certainly Bender, and presumably the Board, was aware of some strong faculty dissatisfaction with the Steiner-Holaway leadership team. A faculty delegation had gone to Bender about their concern that during the 1961-62 school year, Steiner was inaccessible, lacked energy, and the ability to inspire scholarship; he seemed in poor health and often came to school late.[40] The Board, or at least Bender, had heard of this, but in confronting the issue over the next months and even years, was never sure of the extent of faculty dissatisfaction.[41] In June, following the close of the 1961-62 school year, Steiner sent a memo to Bender describing his frustration with three or four of his faculty and noting that he could no longer discuss things with Holaway.

In response to all of these pressing issues, the Board, in May and June of 1962, took a number of actions, asking Conference to enlarge the size of the Board and grant permission to have subcommittees do some of the work. It reduced both Steiner's hours and his salary, "so that he could devote more time to pastoral work." It took action to hire a younger educator from Pennsylvania as principal, who was to start in August and also contacted former teacher Marvin Nafziger, now studying in New York City, about returning to Bethany as academic counselor and teacher and to serve as part of the administrative team. Apparently Nafziger answered in the affirmative, but something went awry in the plans with the young Pennsylvanian.

1962 Girls' Athletic Association members Joan Stauffer '65, Sally Troyer '63, Karen Esch '63, Beth Birkey, Ola Bontrager 63, and Nancy Chupp '63. Photo: 1962 Witmarsum

... but it is clear that the pressure for interscholastic sports was increasing.

In 1962 Leonard Gross's government class held a mock trial. Wayne Risser '62 (in hat) portrayed Nikita Khrushchev. Photo: BCS files

1962 salutatorian Susanne King receives her diploma from John Steiner during commencement exercises held in the Union, Goshen College.

Photo: BCS files

Photo: 1966 *Witmarsum*

Dan Shenk '68:
"I remember when ..."
As a Bethany student from 1965 to 1968, I well recall one day in the 1965-66 school year when our boys' phys ed class was clearly getting out of hand. Paper airplanes were flying, and the volume in the room had risen several decibels. Mr. Steiner apparently was in the hall near our classroom at the time. He strode into the room armed with a yardstick, slammed it hard on the teacher's desk with a resounding THWACK, and brought the entire classroom to order in a couple of seconds. He was angry ("righteous indignation") and said only a few words (about how disappointed in us he felt at that moment), but that's all he had to say. My respect for him went up immediately.

The young man and his wife were unwilling to give up their wedding bands. The Board deemed itself unable to hire an administrator who wore jewelry.

In May 1962 a special study committee of the School Board arranged for any faculty member who so desired to meet with one or more committee members. Harold Bender chaired the committee, assisted by Ora Yoder and Annas Miller. The stated purpose of the meetings was to hear from faculty in planning for the successor to Holaway, but reading between the lines of the minutes gives the impression that the Board was trying to assess the depth of the dissatisfaction of the faculty. The outcome of these meetings, in which Yoder apparently did not participate, is unclear, but within the next few months the Board made decisions that set the stage for the next school year.

While several issues facing Bethany in the summer of 1962 called for the Board's attention, it was the issue of school leadership for the fall term that most urgently needed resolution. This task fell to the special study committee chaired by Bender. With the Board's choice for principal no longer available and Steiner on reduced hours by virtue of Board action, Bender thought Holaway might consider one more year of service. Holaway responded that he was willing to help with advice but was not interested in another year as principal.

The proposal that emerged from this flurry of activity was that Steiner would serve as both superintendent and principal. In the fall of 1962 Marvin Nafziger received a call from Steiner inviting him to be part of the administration, in essence principal. He agreed and began taking courses at Indiana University to get certification. Nafziger would join the team as academic counselor and Lester Culp, a charter member of the faculty, would be named as director of student activities. All three could be considered part of the administrative team. This would cover most of the load formerly carried by Steiner and Holaway. In a memo to the special study committee, Bender listed the responsibilities he planned for both Steiner and Nafziger and noted that Nafziger's title would be academic counselor unless the state would not accept his credentials, in which case his title would be assistant principal. Soon after his return to Bethany, he became aware of the deep divisions between some of the teachers and Steiner. Nafziger experienced considerable pressure to help Steiner and the Board keep control of the academic agenda.[43]

The Indiana-Michigan Conference decided to enlarge the Board, and by fall 1962 it had a number of new members. J. Howard Kauffman had been personally approached by Bender and asked about his willingness to serve on the Board. Bender's will prevailed and Kauffman consented.[44]

Amid all the change on the Board and at Bethany, Bender was always the central figure, but during the summer and fall of 1962 his health prevented his presence at some of the meetings. On August 13 Bender attended his last Bethany School Board meeting and on August 15 sent what was probably his last correspondence to the faculty. He told them there would be some "new arrangements" at Bethany and that the Board "solicits and counts on the wholehearted support of the faculty." It was signed "H. S. Bender, Chair of Special Study Committee for the Board." On September 21, 1962, Bender died. His chosen successor was Howard Kauffman, who was given the title, "executive secretary," a title Bender never held but a position he had filled since the Board's incorporation in 1953. Richard Yoder was appointed recording secretary. The school year 1962-63 turned out well, but Bethany's leadership had a difficult year.

Toward the future

The school had opened in 1954, with a projected capacity of 150 students. The numbers had grown steadily, leveling off at approximately 250 students by about 1960. Steiner was an able recruiter but probably stopped trying to recruit in light of the crowded conditions. As Steiner viewed the prospects for the 1963-64 school year, he saw about 260 students enrolling and knew something had to be done.

In 1955-56 the upper floor of the "barn" had been

> ... [H. S.] Bender was always the central figure ...

Directed by Freeman Lehman, the 1962-63 Madrigals were made up entirely of seniors. Front: Sharon Miller, Wealtha Yoder, Karen Esch, Janet Hostetler, Sharon Stutzman, Jennie Morningstar, Ardis Summer, and Sherrill Moore. Back: Wayne Hochstedler, Paul Miller, Lee Weldy, Dwight Landis, Leland Miller, Keith Hoffman, and Dan Miller. Photo: 1963 Witmarsum

Construction begins on the east end chapel and offices addition, summer of 1958.
Photo: BCS files

... serious challenges now lay ahead.

Fifties transportation included a school bus.
Photo: BCS files

renovated. In the summer of 1958, a 60' x 60' addition had been added to the east end of the main building, providing for a chapel and two offices. That same year a 30' x 40' block extension had been added to the north end of the "barn" to provide for more industrial arts and agricultural class space. The old chapel area in the "barn" had been made into classrooms with several restrooms added. But since 1958, largely because of the school's indebtedness, no further building had been done. The American economy was in a recession during these years, so contributions were not coming very freely.

In the summer of 1963, as Bethany stood on the threshold of its second decade, hundreds of students had been blessed by its influence, but serious challenges now lay ahead. The issues of church and administrative leadership and control, the unresolved debate over athletic competition, the pressing need for more space, and the compelling need to provide a better income and retirement plan for the faculty were yet unresolved.

As for an ongoing vision as the school faced a new era, there seemed to be no clear consensus worked out. How would Bethany's purpose ultimately surmount the problems of physical space and economic demands? How would Bethany pursue both academic excellence and pass on a unique Anabaptist faith to its students? Although these questions had, out of necessity, received attention in varying degrees during the Steiner years at Bethany, their resolution would await a future administration.

ॐ ॐ ॐ ॐ

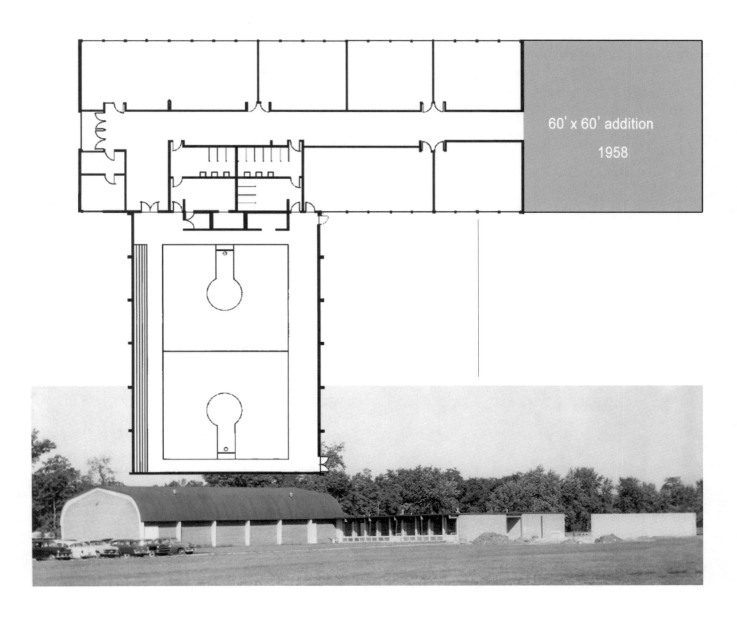

60' x 60' addition

1958

Notes

1. Sources used in this chapter, if not otherwise designated, may be found in the Bethany collection of the Archives of the Mennonite Church (AMC): II-5-8, Goshen, Indiana.

2. Royal Bauer, interview by writer, July 13, 2001.

3. Lester Culp, telephone interview by writer, October 17, 2001.

4. John Steiner, "Sketches," 40, unpublished pamphlet written for his family about 1990.

5. Mildred Steiner, wife of John Steiner, personal interview by writer, July 18, 2001.

6. M. Steiner interview.

7. Marvin Nafziger, personal interview by writer, July 18, 2001.

8. Bauer interview.

9. Marvin Yoder, class of '57 and later faculty member, personal interview by writer, October 11, 2001.

10. Bauer interview.

11. Yoder interview.

12. Leonard Gross, personal interview by writer, August 13, 2001.

13. Melvin and Eva Hershberger Stutzman, class of '56, personal interview by writer, July 19, 2001.

14. Personal memories of writer, who was their Sunday school teacher.

15. Bauer interview.

16. Nafziger interview.

17. Nafziger interview.

18. Robert Ewing, telephone interview by writer, October 19, 2001.

19. Yoder interview.

20. Stutzman interview.

21. Ewing interview.

22. Ewing interview.

23. Ewing interview.

24. Ewing interview.

25. *Reflector,* April 1955.

26. Stutzman interview.

27. Francis Miller, class of '55 student, telephone interview by writer, October 15, 2001.

28. Yoder and Ewing interviews.

29. Stutzman interview.

30. Yoder interview.

31. Nafziger interview.

32. Sketches: 43.

33. Gross interview.

34. Gross interview.

35. Yoder interview.

36. Yoder interview.

37. Gross interview.

38. Personal memories of writer.

39. Gross interview.

40. Gross interview.

41. J. Howard Kauffman, personal interview by writer,
     October 22, 2001.

42. Nafziger interview.

43. Nafziger interview.

44. Kauffman interview.

Chapter 3

A Struggle for Identity
1963-74

by Becky Bontrager Horst

"Students United for Bethany" (SUB) take to the streets of downtown Elkhart, Indiana, in the spring of 1970 to raise money for the school. Photo: BCS files

"Students United for Bethany"
fundraising walk in 1970. Photo: BCS files

The second decade of Bethany's existence, 1963-74, was a restless time for the school, mirroring restless times in American society and in the Mennonite Church. Bethany students and, in some cases, young faculty members, like young people everywhere in the mid-sixties, began to question authority and demand freedom of expression. Financial struggles and administrative turnover at Bethany exacerbated the problems. In a sense this decade was Bethany's stormy adolescent period. Just as teenagers sometimes struggle to find their identity, our school also struggled. Influence from the outside world was rapidly changing the Mennonite Church of the sixties. Bethany's educational task, as originally understood, was not to shelter students from the world but to continually bring together the secular and sacred, giving students a Christian perspective on all of learning. But this was challenging work as secular realities and church priorities rapidly changed. How could Bethany find the path of faithfulness?

During the Bill Hooley administration, Bethany would slowly find a path through the shifting ground of church and world. Echoing John Steiner's earlier stance, Bethany would take its cues from the Mennonite churches in its constituency. Congregations would take the lead in balancing tradition and change and in defining

… not to shelter students from the world but to continually bring together the secular and sacred …

Interscholastic sports began in 1965. Photo: BCS files

1970-71 A Cappella Choir directed by Darrel Hostetler. Photo: BCS files

faithfulness. Bethany would be a denominational school that served and reflected the church.[1] But before this path was found at Bethany came the decade of the sixties, full of ferment and unrest.

Major changes

From 1963-74 Bethany moved through four different administrations. John Steiner's era ended in 1966, Paul E. Yoder served in 1966-68, and A. Don Augsburger in 1968-70. Bill Hooley began his long tenure in 1970, first as superintendent, aided by Principal Wade Bollinger, then by Levi Miller, whose arrival in 1973-74 began a transformation that signaled a new era at BCHS. But meanwhile, in the decade of turmoil covered in this chapter, at least five major changes occurred at Bethany:

1. The center of power shifted from administration to faculty and sometimes to students.
2. The student body composition became more diverse, no longer only ethnically Mennonite.
3. The overall atmosphere of the school changed from formal to informal.
4. The spiritual climate changed from largely unquestioning faith to a mixture of doubt, rebellion, and searching for authentic faith.
5. The birth and growth of interscholastic athletics changed the culture of the school.

Throughout this restless decade, the morale of faculty and students fluctuated, but mostly declined. And the number of students at Bethany rather steadily declined from an enrollment high of over 300 in 1965-66 to a low of 220 in 1969-71. To better understand Bethany's struggles during this era, we would do well to look briefly at the wider context of nation and church.

Restless times in country and church

The mid-sixties to mid-seventies was a time of great change in the United States and in the Mennonite Church. First, a major demographic shift occurred. Baby Boomer young people gained extraordinary power simply due to their numbers. A common warning among the young to "not trust anyone over 30" signaled a clear generation gap. Rock and roll music separated the generations, as did a hedonistic youth culture that insisted, "If it feels good, do it." Second, political and social upheaval dominated American life during this decade. Young people assumed the status quo was wrong, as evidenced by the escalating war in Vietnam, the shooting of war protesters at Kent State University (Kent, Ohio), race riots in Watts (Los Angeles) and elsewhere, and the assassinations of John and Robert Kennedy, Martin Luther King Jr., and Malcolm X.

Yet, at the same time, idealistic hopes for the future blossomed. Civil rights movements (Black, Chicano, and Native American), the women's liberation movement, communal living experiments, and the beginnings of environmentalism all welled up from strong undercurrents of idealism.

Upheaval and idealism also characterized the Mennonite Church in 1963-74. More and more Mennonites moved off the farm, so higher levels of education came to be expected. Radio, television, and athletics brought Mennonites out of the "quiet in the land" mode into mainstream American culture. *The Sound of Music* in 1965 even brought them *en masse* into movie theaters, which were largely thought to be forbidden to church members before that time. Bishop-led authority structures began to crumble as the value of outer signs of nonconformity such as plain coats for men and head coverings for women was questioned. The mark of true Christians was not how they dressed, but how they lived. Different groups of Mennonites variously espoused lifestyles of simplicity, piety, pacifism, or evangelism as litmus tests of faithfulness. Bethany contained all of these groups and exemplified the changes and conflicts that were shaping the larger Mennonite Church.

Photo: BCS files

Radio, television, and athletics brought Mennonites out of the 'quiet in the land' …

The purchase of this new blue van was part of an S. B. A. project, 1970. Photo: BCS files

Photo: 1964 *Witmarsum*

John S. Steiner

Keith Schrag makes a chapel presentation as Marvin Nafziger (left) looks on. Students are: Mamie Ost '64, Eloise Gingerich '65, Fanny Mullet '63, and Bonnie Weldy '63. Photo: BCS files

John Steiner's last years

John Steiner had led Bethany as its superintendent since its first year of existence, working tirelessly and being well-loved by many. Several of his top priorities for Bethany are still evident today: close relationship to the church, academic excellence, respect and love between faculty and students, and a strong athletic program.

Steiner had no development officer or church relations administrator, so responsibility for nurturing close ties with the church fell to him. His annual publicity plan included publication of the *Bethany Bulletin* and arrangements for giving Bethany programs in congregations. In addition to more typical choir programs, Sunday evening services sometimes focused on Mennonite education. A program at Belmont congregation in Elkhart, for instance, on February 16, 1964, included five short speeches:

> "Why Bethany?" – J. C. Wenger, board member and seminary professor
> "Teaching at Bethany: How Come?" – Lester Culp, biology teacher
> "Why Send Our Youth to Bethany?" – Virgil Graber, parent and medical doctor
> "What Bethany Means to Me" – Marcia Middaugh '64, student
> "What of the Future?" – J. C. Wenger on the three most pressing issues facing the school: overcrowded buildings, low faculty salaries, and the popular misconception that Bethany students are "hothouse plants." Wenger concluded his talk by urging congregations to pray, give moral support, send students, and contribute money as they were able.[2]

Steiner was an effective recruiter. He visited many homes, making house calls to talk with prospective students and help them sign up for classes. After they arrived at Bethany, he was their spiritual leader, often preaching dramatic and memorable chapel sermons and praying with students who were being disciplined.

Student life, 1963-66

Student life at the end of the Steiner era primarily echoed the fifties. A motto at the front of the chapel room read "Saved to Serve." The weekly chapel schedule was

Monday: Superintendent Steiner, Tuesday: a hymn-sing, Wednesday: a faculty member, Thursday: YPCA (student organization), Friday: a guest speaker. A student council began in 1963, at the urging of faculty, in order to give students more leadership opportunities, biology and agriculture teacher Lester Culp being the sponsor for many years. Students wore crew cuts and black-framed glasses, curly bangs and full skirts. And the girls still wore white net head coverings in chapel. In the 1963 yearbook seniors stated stereotypical career goals: secretary, teacher, housewife, nurse, and social worker for girls; farmer, mechanic, and scientist for boys. Traditional dating was the norm: Goshen College Lecture-Music Series events were advertised in the student newspaper, and in 1964 the *Reflector* announced four engagements on its front page, three of the girls marrying young men in I-W alternate service.[3]

The biggest events of the 1963-64 school year were long-standing traditions: the junior-senior banquet and the senior trip—this time to the 1964 New York City World's Fair. The all-school social during second semester featured skits by each class and the faculty. Seniors traditionally portrayed key faculty members and faculty portrayed certain students. A new tradition appeared on the scene this year: the annual spring Mennonite High School Music Festival with choirs from Bethany, Eastern Mennonite, Central Christian, Belleville, and Johnstown schools gathering at Christopher Dock Mennonite High School near Philadelphia for the occasion.

For the most part Bethany students were serious about faith and academics, and when they weren't, other students chastised them. Editorials by JoAnne Kraus '65 in the 1964-65 *Reflector* criticized weak singing and poor manners in chapel. Lois Bixler '65 decried classroom behavior. "I can't believe that Christ was ever disrespectful to his teacher," she wrote.[4] However, transfer student Phyllis Hoover '66 expressed appreciation for the more formal atmosphere at Bethany, compared to her former public school, and commended students for their orderly contributions to class discussions.[5] But profiles of two seniors in the February 1966 *Reflector* reveal an increasing cultural divide. The senior girl liked classical music, classic

Enjoying each other's company on the 1964 Senior bus trip to Washington, D. C., are Sharon Stutzman and James Chupp. Photo: 1963 *Witmarsum*

Traditional dating was the norm …

Lowell Hoover '55 attended Bethany in its first year as an older married student. His daughter Phyllis '66, an Imlay, Michigan resident, boarded her junior and senior years, graduating as the first second-generation student. Photos: 1955 & 1966 *Witmarsums*

Crowded hallways. Photo: 1964 *Witmarsum*

1964 Student Council representatives, front: Tom Graber '66, Veronica Beachy '65, Ron Gingerich '64, Marvin Troyer '64, Wanda Lambright '64, and Bob Troyer '66. Back: Don Graber '64, Carl Stauffer '65, Carl Weaver '65, Gloria Miller '66, Glen Yoder '67, and Stan Histand. Absent: Mary Ann Krabill '67. Photo: 1964 *Witmarsum*

books, and plays. The senior boy, however, preferred rock and roll music, basketball, and James Bond books.[6]

Money, facilities, and athletics

In 1963-64 three concerns dominated Steiner's administration: low faculty salaries, an overcrowded building, and the need for an interscholastic athletic program. According to Royal Bauer, who was a faculty member at that time, low salaries were not the only source of faculty dissidence then, but low salaries were the largest problem.[7] Some teachers insisted that they could not live on the pay they were getting. The base faculty salary at Bethany in 1963-64 was only $3,400. In a letter to Superintendent Steiner, faculty member Delmar Miller stated that his sister, with only one year of experience, was earning $5,400 teaching in a public school. By contrast, he was required to take additional courses, although his contract did not allow taking a second job. So he was caught in very difficult financial straits. Several faculty members, out of protest, did not return their contracts in June 1964.[8] The Board agreed to a small consolation: a $100 base-pay raise.

Steiner cared about faculty salaries, but his solution was to bring in more students, an impossibility without a larger building. Steiner was determined to persuade the Board to build an addition to the school, including a library, classrooms, and cafeteria. His report to the Indiana-Michigan Conference High School Board in the fall of 1963 details overcrowded conditions, poor ventilation, and meager storage. With inadequate library and classroom facilities, Steiner knew that Bethany could never become accredited, and it could not grow. That fall, 263 students were crowded into a facility that was approximately half the size of the current school building: only the old north hallway, the gymnasium (present-day chapel) and the "barn." All classrooms were crowded every period of the day.

In a 1972 interview Steiner confessed, "I went out and deliberately filled the school way beyond capacity so that the Board was forced to provide ample facilities for the school." His strategy worked. The Board authorized borrowing $225,000 to begin the building project and to cover operating deficits for several previous years. Ground was broken for the addition in July 1964. Unfortunately, Steiner's strategy caused problems for Bethany's long-term financial health. Faculty salaries remained low, contributions did not increase as much as anticipated, and now there was a building debt to pay off on top of continuing operating deficits. In 1964-65 the deficit was $6,000; in 1965-66 it was nearly $9,000 with total expenditures of $134,000.

Board President Russell Krabill breaks ground for the new west end addition, 1964. Completed addition shown below, 1966.
Photos: BCS files

'I went out
and deliberately
filled the school
way beyond capacity
so that the Board
was forced to provide
ample facilities ... '

The building addition, completed in 1966, gave Bethany wonderful new facilities, including the current cafeteria, offices, science laboratories, and a larger chapel (now the library). Windows on the west side rooms were angled to keep out the afternoon sun and minimize the distractions of passing traffic on State Road 15, an architectural technique borrowed from Harvard University. This was Phase I of Steiner's long-term building plan. Phase II, according to notes scribbled by J. C. Wenger on the margins of his June 2, 1964, Board meeting agenda, would add a new gymnasium at the northeast end of the school and turn the centrally located gym into a chapel. These future plans could serve up to 400 students, which was the minimum standard for Indiana public schools and the "probable future enrollment" at Bethany, according to Steiner's optimistic prediction.

Interscholastic sports begin

In addition to expanded facilities to strengthen Bethany's academic program, Steiner dreamed of adding a full-fledged athletic program. Intramural sports and church league competitions were no longer adequate to draw students and parents who were increasingly involved in junior high school athletic competitions. But the Board was not ready to move quickly. In November 1963 it agreed that, "we should stay with church schools in basketball. And … we advise the Superintendent (Steiner) to hold close rein on any extramural

... the faculty member who would come to personify interscholastic athletics at Bethany ...

Dan Bodiker: Getting hired
In spring 1961, I had just completed my freshman year at Goshen College. The reports around were that summer jobs were going to be hard to find. A college friend from Kansas gave me the name of a person who hired guys for following the harvest. Before you know it, I was on a crew, following the wheat harvest.

In late summer we were in a little town called Lodgegrass, Montana. Another crew of custom cutters was staying in the same town. In fact, that crew had some workers who were from Goshen. We had a chance to visit together at least once. By chance the father of one of those workers was there visiting—a big man with a grandfather's smile. His name was John Steiner.

We talked. I don't remember what we talked about. Years later at a program, John told the group that the type of person that could work long hours and stay with a job like a custom harvester had to do was the type of person that he was looking for in the job that I

Continued on page 93 ...

athletics, keeping the Board informed of all plans."

There is no public record of Steiner's disagreement with the Board's stance, but he soon recruited the faculty member who would come to personify interscholastic athletics at Bethany: Dan Bodiker. Less than two months after its hesitant response, Steiner recommended to the Board that Bodiker be hired as instructor in physical education and coach.

The February 1964 *Reflector* announced Bodiker's appointment to the school. He appears young and svelte on the front page, in a crewcut and striped referee shirt. The same issue gave details about an upcoming debate by interested adults on interscholastic sports at Bethany. Marner Miller and Charles Gardner would argue the affirmative; Leonard Gross and Verle Hoffman would oppose. C. Norman Kraus would summarize the debate at the end. Unfortunately, no formal record of this debate is available, but a student editorial by Jeanette Slabach '64 in the March *Reflector* is revealing. She states that "reactions have been varied, especially among constituents and parents. The majority of students, without really thinking, have decided we definitely want Bethany in the rat race." She foresees a problem of finding enough small schools within reasonable traveling distance for Bethany to play against and proposes that an ideal sports program would be physical education for all. "Especially in Indiana," Slabach continues, "basketball is completely out of perspective ... Bethany is a private school which

New teacher and coach Dan Bodiker, 1965.
Photos: above, 1965 *Witmarsum;* left, 1993 *Witmarsum*

Bethany Braves' Charlie Steiner '67 on the offensive. Photo: BCS files

should emphasize the arts. Where are our drama department, our debating teams, our art classes? Why not develop these things, if not before, at least right along with our basketball team?"[9] Slabach's editorial foreshadows identity debates that would continue at Bethany in the next decade and beyond: the arts versus athletics and religious school versus prep school. Finding the path of faithfulness was getting more and more complicated.

A year later, in February 1965, Board President Charles Gardner wrote a guest editorial for the *Reflector* summarizing both sides of the athletic debate and stating his conclusions:

Pro: Interscholastic athletics would
- Give Bethany a chance for a positive witness in the community.
- Attract boys with athletic ability.
- Build better relations with other schools.
- Develop strong character and self-discipline.
- Build school loyalty and morale.

Con: Interscholastic athletics would
- Create large crowds that would be difficult to control.
- Require too much time from school and home activities.
- Require a larger gymnasium.
- Disrupt student carpools.
- Give too much emphasis to sports.

Gardner's conclusion, affirmed by the Board, was that Bethany should embark on a limited interscholastic sports program as an associate member of an athletic association.[10]

This change marked a watershed in the history of Bethany. All of the consequences that Gardner predicted in 1965 came to pass and more. Sports participation moved the focus of many families' social lives from church-centered to school-centered. On the other hand, sports also created camaraderie and school spirit that helped to carry Bethany through some difficult years ahead. Interscholastic

Bodiker ... *cont. from page 92*
was hired to do.

The second time I really met John was in the spring of 1963. We met in the snack shop at the college Union building. It was just a chance meeting. We talked for ten minutes about the harvest and my plans to go into coaching.

The next spring, I was about to graduate. John approached me with the idea of coming to Bethany to teach. He told me that Bethany was considering getting into interscholastic sports. I would have to be on the ground level of starting that program. At one time in my life I considered going to seminary to prepare for the ministry. I also always wanted to be a coach. The job that John offered seemed to be the best of both options at the same time.

All of the consequences that Gardner predicted ... came to pass and more.

The Gardner family: Susan '67, Thomas '65, Oneta, and Charles. Not pictured: Ruthann '58 and Judy. Photo: BCS files

1970-71 volleyball team coached by
Carolyn Horst. Photo: BCS files

**Howard Kauffman … remembers
Steiner's resignation
as the most difficult part
of his Board tenure.**

Superintendent Steiner teaching Bible class.
Photo: 1965 *Witmarsum*

athletics seemed to weave the web of faith and play inseparably together.

Athletic teams need a mascot and a school song. Before the days of sensitivity toward American Indian stereotypes, faculty members recommended "braves" as the mascot, forming the pleasing alliteration "Bethany Braves." More puzzling is the choice of the Southern Cal fight song for the *Bethany Alma Mater,* which exhorts the pacifist Braves to "fight on" no less than five times. The mascot and song were adopted at the January 1966 Board meeting where questions of patriotism surfaced and sparked a long discussion. Later, the Board adopted the following statement about the national anthem: "Because of the militaristic emphasis of 'The Star-Spangled Banner' and because of our position on nonparticipation in war, we recommend that if any song be sung, the first verse of 'America the Beautiful' be used instead of the national anthem at our home basketball games."

Interscholastic boys' basketball and soccer began in 1965-66. The soccer team played ten games and the basketball team played 16 games. Dan "Bod" Bodiker coached both teams and continued to coach at least three sports per year at Bethany for the next 30 years.

Steiner moves on

After 11 years at Bethany and nine years of pastoring Pleasant View Mennonite Church, John Steiner was exhausted mentally, physically, and emotionally. Meanwhile a group of dissenting faculty members continued to criticize him. One of their main concerns was his theology, which tended toward Fundamentalism.[11] But Steiner had the best interests of the faculty in mind: he was, for example, very concerned about retirement income, as Bethany had no retirement plan for employees. Steiner submitted his resignation to the Board in January 1965. Howard Kauffman, who was executive secretary of the Board at that time, remembers Steiner's resignation as the most difficult part of his Board tenure.[12] The Board asked Steiner to continue one more year, which he agreed to do in 1965-66.

November 14, 1989

Dan Bodiker
Bethany Christian High School
Goshen, Indiana 46526

Dear Dan:

In Old Testament times when the ancient "Fathers" wanted to inspire the Children of Israel they would recount their history to them. And as they heard the old stories of their past they were always moved to action, whether it was in battle, or in praise and thanksgiving to God for all that he had brought them through.

Well, it seems to us that this is just such an occasion in the life of Bethany - a time to recount the history of BCHS basketball in order to inspire current students who may not know the "old" stories - "Remember Aubenaubee!" This morning I recounted that thrilling game to Matt and as I did the emotions from twenty-plus years ago came back full force as I remembered Bethany behind by 20 points with 5 minutes left, the spine-tingling rally that brought us to within one point, that final shot with seconds on the clock, that flew across a massive stretch of court and swished the net. I remember the deafening screams as it became reality to each of us that after our long struggle to bring BCHS to this public occasion - a basketball game with a public school, with cheerleaders, and a "fight" song and everything! - that we had been victorious!!

As with any legend, I'm sure over the years the facts of that night have become a little muddled in our minds. Perhaps you still have the stats. Matt wanted to know who fired (or "flung" as the case may be) that last shot. I told him I wasn't sure who the player was, but surely it was the hand of God who put it through the net!

"Remember Aubenaubee!" has ever since been a battle cry for us in difficult, next to impossible-looking situations. It was as meaningful and memorable as any high school event. We have shared it with our children, and we hope that other BCHS students also have an opportunity to hear the story.

Sincerely,

Martin & Carol

Martin and Carol Honderich, Class of '68
61571 SR 13
Middlebury, IN 46540

cc: Alumni Newsletter

PS: I sha[...] this letter this Gloria Miller Holub and becau[...] brought a[...] [...] she thought I should share it wit[...] alumni.

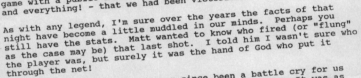

Martin
[Ho]nderich '68
[Pho]to: 1966 Witmarsum

[Ca]rol Helmuth
['68] (Honderich)
[Pho]to: 1966 Witmarsum

Dan Shenk '68:
"Remember Aubbeenaubbee … "

Interscholastic sports at Bethany began with a bang. The very first game in the fall of '65 was between Bethany and Aubbeenaubbee of Leiters Ford. Though it was a home basketball game for Bethany, our gym didn't have a prayer of holding the crowd. So we went to New Paris High School. A member of the Bethany JV team as a sophomore, I recall watching in dismay as the varsity was getting blown out halfway through the fourth quarter. Then something amazing started to happen. Down about 20 points with just four or five minutes left, Bethany began battling back. Lots of quick steals and deadly shooting later, Bethany won 72-71 in one of the greatest comebacks in sports I've (still) ever seen. The crowd, of course, was delirious. Moments after the game a few of us found John Steiner (we hadn't known he was working behind the scenes in support of interscholastic sports). I think I asked, "Well, Mr. Steiner, *now* what do you think about playing other schools?" His huge grin said it all.

Incidentally, that game launched a "battle cry" for the Bethany Braves akin to "Remember the Alamo." Whenever adversity loomed, the chant went up: "Remember Aubbeenaubbee, remember Aubbeenaubbee ..." It's good we didn't have to spell it.

Photo: 1966 Witmarsum
Letter & Goshen News clipping: Dan Bodiker scrapbook

Incredible Comeback Nets Bethany 72-71 Opening Win: Middies Triumph

Bethany Christian High School opened its inter-scholastic basketball career with a 72-71 victory over Aubbeenaubbee in a fantastic comeback win for Coach Dan Bodiker's team Tuesday night at New Paris. In other county action, Middlebury handed Shipshe- [...] Scott a 64-54 loss at [...]

Five games are on tap tonight, with Mishawaka to visit Con- [...] cord, Millersburg to travel to [...] Leesburg and Bristol to visit [...] Howe Military in numer- [...] ous county action, [...] while Milford will host Pierce- [...] ton at North Webster and Men- [...] tone will visit Syracuse.

GREAT COMEBACK
Bethany Christian came from 20 points behind in the final five [...] of play to edge Aub- [...] 72-71 in Bethany's [...] game at the New Paris [...] School Gym. Bethany [...] Braves into numer- [...] during the final per- [...] full court press de- [...] for the first three [...] the final period, as [...] shook loose to hike [...] to 20 points after [...] comfortable 15-point [...] after three quarters. [...] Bethany offense [...] vantage of the [...] and there was [...] newest Elkhart [...] School from cop- [...] [...]ctory. [...] remaining, [...] 71-64, but Larry [...] margin to five [...] throws and [...]

from the field and five free [...] throws. Delvin Yoder was the only other Bethany player in double figures with 13 points, but six other Bethany players entered the scoring column. Russell Parker with 18 led the Braves. Nunn with 18 led the [...] John Overmyer added 14 and [...] John Seponar had 11. Bethany shot .437 from the field on 28 of 64, while the Braves had an even better percentage of .489.

Bethany	G	F	P		A'bbee	G	F	P
Yoder					Parker			
King					Sear			
Schrock					Seponar			
Stantler					Nunn			
Trenb'm					Overm'r			
Bontr'ger								
S. Yoder								
Miller								
Totals	29	19	33		Totals			

Aubbeenaubbee [...] 14 18 38 [...]
Preliminary: Bethany [...] 18 18 20 [...]
Officials: Duane Conrad, New Paris, and Norris Boomershine, Goshen.

Paul E. Yoder served as superintendent from 1966-68. Photo: 1968 *Witmarsum*

There were many
discipline problems ...
many students
were not there
by choice ...

John Steiner's last year was a good one. The building project and interscholastic athletic programs were underway and faculty morale had improved.[13] In a tribute to Steiner published in the March 1966 *Reflector,* faculty member Royal Bauer expresses his appreciation for Steiner's willingness to listen to his dissenters and allow them to change their minds while still "saving face."[14] Steiner moved on to jobs at several public schools, and Bethany searched for a new chief administrator to continue its pursuit of faithfulness in Christian education and to pull it out of debt.

Paul Yoder administration, 1966-68

Paul E. Yoder had served as a teacher and administrator at Western Mennonite School in Oregon before being called to Bethany. Yoder's administrative style was not easily transferred from Western, where he was well known as an excellent biology teacher, to Bethany, where he was unknown. Bethany faculty members had looked forward to having a stronger voice in a new administration than they had had under Steiner's leadership. Yoder did expect faculty to take responsibility, but primarily in terms of implementing policies that he posted with little or no faculty discussion. Yoder was essentially a shy man who felt most comfortable working in his office.[15] He did not feel comfortable dealing with discipline problems, and as early as October 1966, he began taking cases to the Board for counsel.

There were many discipline problems. The student body was large—291 in the fall of 1966 when the new addition was dedicated. And many Bethany students were not there by choice but because their parents wanted them to "get straightened out" or to "become a Christian." Several had even been expelled by their local public schools.

Students were becoming more and more assertive and rebellious, while faculty felt increasingly powerless and alone. Yoder had no principal to handle discipline, so his job was impossibly large. Guidance counselor Dan Schrock resigned after the 1966-67 school year, and Board member Don Augsburger served as part-time counselor in 1967-68.

A special meeting to discuss morale

By March of 1967, both faculty and student morale had sharply declined. The Board called a special meeting of faculty members and their spouses to discuss the situation. According to Bill Hooley, who was secretary of the Board at that time, those who attended broke into six small groups with Board members in each one. Among the conclusions of that meeting:

- The school needs a mission statement.
- Good school spirit continues around athletic events.
- Faculty wants more voice in determining schedule, policies, and textbooks, and they want to receive copies of communication that goes out to parents.
- Bible courses and chapel need strengthening.
- Better patrolling of hallways and more consistent disciplinary action are needed.[16]

The path of faithfulness would require administrative leadership to articulate and practice a clear vision for Christian education and engage the full participation of faculty.

More diversity in the student body

Meanwhile, the Bethany student body did not stand still. Hair was longer and shaggier now and skirt lengths varied from mini to maxi. The 1966 yearbook speaks of "conscientious youth dedicated to the will of Christ, ever struggling to find a place in a world torn by war and prejudice."[17] The theme of the spring 1966 junior-senior banquet had been "Southern Plantation," with Mrs. Pasley of the Elkhart NAACP as a special speaker. Theresa Ventura was Bethany's first Hispanic graduate in 1956; Georgia "Kitty" Thompson was the first African-American grad in 1958. Although there was some diversity in Bethany's student population in its early years, more was desired. In the fall of 1968 Dr. Virgil Graber urged fellow Bethany Board members to think seriously about integration. "How could we

Later, in the seventies and eighties, the Mennonite Church's High-Aim program would bring many black and Hispanic students to Bethany, enriching the school through cultural diversity.

1978 High-Aim students. Photo: Royal Bauer collection

Don Augsburger at work. Photo: 1969 *Witmarsum*

Bethany needed to raise $9,000 in just a few days in order to make loan payments and payroll.

Business Manager Melvin Birkey also ran the bookstore. Photo: BCS files

bring twenty-plus Negro students to Bethany?" he asked. Later, in the seventies and eighties, the Mennonite Church's High-Aim program would bring many black and Hispanic students to Bethany, enriching the school through cultural diversity.

Most students in 1967-68 were focused on more immediate concerns at Bethany. In a *Reflector* editorial, Rhoda Shenk '69 paints a grim view of school morale: "Students criticize the administration for criticizing the students. Hard feelings are flourishing."[18] But she goes on to praise several individual teachers and acknowledges some improvements, specifically stronger athletics and the decision to allow girls to wear formals at the junior-senior banquet. Athletics provided a significant boost in morale at Bethany during this difficult year; the boys' basketball team was runner-up in the county tourney and the soccer squad posted a record of 5-2-1.

Augsburger takes the helm, 1968-70

Don Augsburger believed strongly in Mennonite education and had been a behind-the-scenes leader at Bethany for several years before he became interim superintendent in 1968. Augsburger began as a Board member in 1965. In April 1967 he had been the speaker for Spiritual Life Week, and in July he wrote the superintendent's report on Bethany for Indiana-Michigan Conference. The Board asked for Yoder's resignation in February 1968. During his second year as superintendent, Augsburger contacted prospective superintendent candidates. In May the Board Executive Committee called a special meeting to address a financial crisis and, as chair of the Board, Augsburger was there. Bethany needed to raise $9,000 in just a few days in order to make loan payments and payroll. The committee produced a five-pronged strategy:

1. Business manager Melvin Birkey would try to collect $6-7,000 in outstanding tuition.
2. Augsburger would write a letter to parents.
3. Annas Miller would pursue a short-term loan.
4. Someone would check with Indiana-Michigan Conference to see

if any congregational contributions were available.

5. Someone else would make an appeal to the alumni association.

Within a week, the money came in. In June 1968 Augsburger (at the time executive secretary of the Board) was handling the hiring of new faculty and in July he gave a tentative "yes" when an enthusiastic Board offered him the position of superintendent. He organized a faculty conference in August to help the year to start off right, and by November, faculty interviews with the Board revealed much appreciation for his administrative leadership. But Augsburger never intended to keep his position as Bethany's superintendent for long. During the two years that he served at Bethany, he remained pastor of North Goshen Mennonite Church and also taught several education courses at Indiana University, South Bend, Indiana.[19]

Faculty leaders step forward

The faculty appreciated Augsburger's leadership while he was at the school, but he was gone much of the time, and Bethany had no principal to handle student discipline or day-to-day decisions while he was away. Several veteran faculty members provided important

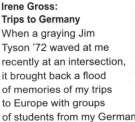

Irene Gross:
Trips to Germany
When a graying Jim Tyson '72 waved at me recently at an intersection, it brought back a flood of memories of my trips to Europe with groups of students from my German classes. Those memories go back 30 years.

It was July 1972 when, as a young teacher and inexperienced tour guide, I accepted the challenge of organizing what would become the first of many trips to Europe. Jim's class was the first class I saw through to graduation. By the end of their junior year, he and seven other students started making plans with me for a month-long trip through several European countries that was to be the culmination of four years of persistent German study.

To cover the rental fee of a minibus, we sponsored several fundraising projects. To keep the costs down, we spent many nights in homes or in churches, and ate mostly sandwiches. Cramped in the VW Microbus with sleeping bags crashing down on top of them at sudden stops, the group bonded, and nothing could dampen the students' enthusiasm. Nothing

Continued on page 100 ...

The 1971-72 advanced German class was the first to travel to Germany; teacher Irene Gross, lower left. Photo: 1972 Bulletin

Alfonso Valtierra '62 (here cajoling John Bauman '68) returned to teach Spanish and history, 1967-70. Photos: BCS files & 1962 Witmarsum

Hollinger's strategy was to identify students with natural leadership ability and form a bond of respect with them … Irene Gross … promoted faculty camaraderie …

Wilmer Hollinger

Lester Culp

Darrel Hostetler

Faculty photos: 1969 & 1970 *Witmarsums*

leadership in his absence. Lester Culp continued to lead the student council. Wilmer Hollinger worked with student leaders on senior trips and in other venues. Hollinger's strategy was to identify students with natural leadership ability and form a bond of respect with them. Irene Gross, who came as the German teacher in 1970, promoted faculty camaraderie and took groups of German students to Europe every other year.

Darrel Hostetler joined the faculty as music teacher in 1967 and became an outspoken advocate for students. They dedicated the 1970 yearbook to him, and when Hostetler's young son died of cancer during the 1969-70 school year, the choir sang at his very moving funeral service.

Gross *… cont. from page 99*

could intimidate them, not even a sauna and skinny-dipping experience in Sweden.

For me, that memorable first trip was also a learning experience for all subsequent trips. Each of the trips was a unique experience, full of surprises, but always rewarding. However, never again would I be talked into lentil suppers, car washes, and bake sales. Traveling by van, although allowing for more flexibility, was often more than my nerves could stand in hectic European city traffic. In future years we traveled by train and spent our nights in youth hostels.

During my career as a German instructor at Bethany, the trips to Europe stand out as a great opportunity for me to open up a wider world to my students. Most of all I hope it taught them that years of sometimes tedious study of a foreign language helped to break down communication barriers and confirm the commonality of the human experience.

Above right: Darrel Hostetler works with an instrumental ensemble. Photo: BCS files

From left: Don Grieser '73, Nancy Conrad '75, Becky Stichter '74, and Keith Hooley '73.
Photo: Royal Bauer collection

Social-political climate reflects chaotic times

Although soccer and basketball games continued to offer important social rallying points at Bethany during the Augsburger years, its social climate was powerfully influenced by movements outside the school itself. Anti-war and civil rights protests climaxed, and Martin Luther King Jr. and Robert Kennedy were both assassinated in 1968. Reflecting this unrest, the theme of the 1968 junior-senior banquet was the title of a Bob Dylan song: "The Times, They Are A-Changin'."

Spiritual climate affected by powerful movements

The spiritual climate at Bethany during Augsburger's term in 1968-70 was also powerfully affected by movements beyond the Mennonite Church. Folk and protest movements influenced the music choices and theology of some students. Bethany's own folk trio, the Sons of Jubal, often sang at the Partly Dave coffeehouse in downtown Elkhart. Many students were drawn to charismatic worship at the new Zion Chapel, begun by Goshen High School teacher Vic Hildebrand, and some experienced dramatic, life-changing conversions. The topics of spiritual healing and speaking in tongues sparked much discussion, soul-searching, and Bible study among Bethany students. A James Krabill '69 *Reflector* editorial refers to confusion caused by various views on healing, yet he calls students to "grow in respect for others' ideas and the contributions they are making in our lives."[20] Faith debates and discussions abounded, but those in leadership still longed for more spiritual impact. Board members wished for more of a "Christian community" feeling at Bethany.

The vision that Augsburger laid out in the November 8, 1968, *Reflector* called for larger enrollment, including Christians from other faith traditions, more flexible curriculum, and deeper spiritual involvement.

Galen Johns:
To be or not to be

Photo: 1969 *Witmarsum*

One moment that rivets itself in memory is the request that came in 1970 for me to consider becoming superintendent at Bethany. As secretary of Indiana-Michigan conference, I had had my office in the building from 1968 to 1970. I also worked part-time in public relations while Don Augsburger was superintendent.

Bill Hooley was secretary of the Board when they were searching for someone to replace Don. In that role, he asked me to consider becoming the next superintendent. The Board was aware that I had neither a teaching nor an administrative license. They said they would hire a principal to take care of legal and academic requirements. My job would be to be the lead administrator (except for the academic program), serve as a liaison with the church, and be the main disciplinarian.

That request set off a wrenching struggle within me. I was not used to saying "no" to the church. But it just did not seem to me that I was qualified to fill that role. The quandary wasn't made easier when Wilmer Hollinger, representing the faculty, encouraged me to say "yes."

How I struggled! I was indeed committed to do what God wanted. Furthermore, God usually called me through the church. But this time, it just did not seem comfortable.

One day I told Bill I would have an answer the next morning. That night was a night of prayer, but a miserable one. I tried to discern if there was some kind of "Gideon's fleece" that

Continued on page 102 ...

Johns ... *cont. from page 101*
could guide me. None was found. When the deadline arrived the next morning, all I could do was depend on my gut feeling that this was not to be my role.

Imagine my relief when, following my response, Bill said that he and his wife had reconsidered the invitation that had first gone to him. They had decided that if I said "no" to becoming superintendent, that he would say "yes." Bill's great contribution to Bethany has been an affirmation that God can lead through a negative response.

Students carried out a blitz of fundraising activities, spearheaded by seniors Jane Miller and Evy Kreider ...

Debbie Bontrager '70 observes as parent Vesta Kauffman works on a quilt for the SUB auction, 1970. Photo: BCS files

Students United for Bethany (SUB) a minor miracle

A general malaise continued to plague Bethany administrators, faculty, and students, but a remarkable event in the spring of 1970 foreshadowed the positive change that was to come. Despite Augsburger's strong leadership, enrollment continued to fall, dropping to 248 in the fall of 1968, then in the fall of 1969, 220, where it hovered for the next five years. Debt from the new addition and accumulated operating deficits continued to weigh down the administration and Board. At one point, Augsburger wondered aloud if the school should close. Several student leaders took this as a challenge and, with the help of an all-night prayer meeting, began planning a huge fundraising project. Augsburger took their plans for SUB (Students United for Bethany) to the Board in March 1970. With violent anti-war protests in mind, the Board approved a statement that critiqued "negative demonstrations," but supported this positive action by students. Just a few weeks later, students carried out a blitz of fundraising activities, spearheaded by seniors Jane Miller and Evy Kreider: a walk-a-thon along U. S. 33 from Island Park in Elkhart to Bethany, with rest stops at Sunnyside Mennonite Church and Stutzman Motor Sales—students picking up trash along the way, especially between Dunlap and Goshen; car washes at ten locations with ten students at each one; an auction, rummage sale, and bake sale; and work projects in homes and businesses.

The community responded wholeheartedly to this student-led initiative. More work projects were offered than there were students to do them. SUB raised a remarkable total of $40,500—an enormous amount in 1970 dollars. It also raised school morale to unprecedented heights, at least temporarily. Jane and Evy spoke for all Bethany students who participated when they wrote, "Through Project SUB we rediscovered who Bethany is and why we need and want it."[21]

Bill Hooley begins his servant leadership

Unfortunately, the euphoria of SUB did not last. Bethany remained in debt, enrollment remained low despite extra recruitment efforts in the summer of 1970,

Bill Hooley at his desk.
Photo: 1971 *Witmarsum*

and it would take several years before Bill Hooley would hit his stride as the new chief administrator of Bethany.

Hooley first declined the invitation to serve as Bethany's superintendent, but during the calling process, he felt God turning him around.[22] Hooley was well prepared spiritually and experientially for the task. His background was in Christian education, and he had served in student life administration at Goshen College and as secretary of the Bethany Board. Many faculty and Board members continue to speak of Hooley as the most sincerely Christ-like man they know.

Bill Hooley's goals for the first year of his administration, were that:

- 1970-71 be a growing year for Bethany.
- Unity and pride in the school increase.
- As a result of this school year, students will be more committed to the values of Jesus.[23]

It is difficult to determine whether or not these goals were met. The soccer team won the Northern Indiana conference championship in both 1970 and 1971, a feat that certainly helped increase unity and pride in the school. And when the "barn"

1971 championship soccer team. Photo: 1971 *Witmarsum*

caught fire on an April morning in 1971, it brought out the best in a group of sometimes contrary male students who rescued most of the shop equipment. Bill Hooley's leadership style was not flashy. He favored quiet incremental changes that accumulated over time. He likens his own style to the way he filled a tire rut in front of his mailbox

Photo: 1973 *Witmarsum*

Larion Swartzendruber: The 1971 "barn" fire

In April 1971, my first year of teaching at Bethany, I had a drafting class on the second floor of the "barn." I left them for a few minutes to walk downstairs to the woodshop to check on some students who were working there. As I rounded the corner, one of them shouted, "Fire!" and I looked up to see smoke curling down from under the eaves of the roof. I ran to my office to call the fire department.

This was before the days of 9-1-1, so as I fumbled around trying to find the number, the students immediately started evacuating the shop. There was just a frenzy of activity. Four or five of them worked together to carry the big workbenches out the back door into the parking lot, then they ran back inside to get the partially finished grandfather clocks, tools, and even the tool cabinets. The radial arm saw was fastened to the wall, so Chuck Garber '73 got on top of a table and just pulled with all of his might while everyone else pulled too and they ripped it right out of the wall.

After the guys cleared out the woodshop, they went to work on the metal shop, rescuing all the welding tools. As we were carrying out the acetylene and oxygen tanks, the firemen arrived and started yelling at the boys to get out of there. They were pretty upset that these kids were still in a burning building handling tanks of flammable gas. But later they praised them for being so careful with the tanks, capping them first before they moved them.

The first fire truck to arrive was the Elkhart

Continued on page 104 …

Swartzendruber ... *cont. from page 103*

Township truck driven by LeRoy Mast '67, a Bethany graduate. Eventually Goshen and New Paris trucks joined them.

This all happened during the lunch hour, so the entire cafeteria full of students saw it. Wilmer Hollinger asked everyone to drive their cars across the athletic field to get them out of the way so the fire trucks could get in. It was just a few weeks before the fish fry, so all of the napkins and other paper products were stored in a closet upstairs in the "barn" and they all burned.

The students who cleaned the equipment out were guys that some people thought didn't care very much about anything, but afterwards Senior Glendon Lambright came up and put his arm on my shoulder. He said, "It's really a shame that after you came in here and put so much energy into getting this place fixed up and really had some nice things going here, that this kind of thing would happen." That really touched me.

at home. Each day when he got the mail, he dropped a handful of gravel into the rut. After several months, it was filled.[24] Hooley approached his leadership task at Bethany in much the same manner. His early years were occupied mostly with debt liquidation work and summer graduate work at Western Michigan University. His was not an aggressive style of leadership, nor did he treat it as self-aggrandizing. It was some years before he changed his title from superintendent to principal. When Hooley was away doing graduate work, the day-to-day operation of the school was left to Assistant Principal Wade Bollinger.

Wade Bollinger
Photo: 1973 *Witmarsum*

Life team, front: Jay Ganger '75, Ruth Cocanower '76, Brenda Hostetler '75, and Cindi Miller '75. Middle: Elaine Helmuth '75, Mary Hostetler '75, Sally Oyer '75, and John Davidhizar '75. Back: John Culp '75, Stan Martin '76, faculty sponsor Al Peachey, Rex Bontrager '75, and Karla Hochstetler '75.
Photo: 1973 *Witmarsum*

Larion Swartzendruber in the classroom.
Photo: 1971 *Witmarsum*

Student behavior declines

Unfortunately, Bollinger's years, from 1970-73, were characterized by weak discipline and generally poor relationships with faculty. So another downturn in student behavior and overall school morale ensued, reminiscent of 1966-68. Power shifted to students, who began to run wild during noon hours and passing periods. They respected faculty for the most part, so classroom discipline was not a serious problem, but faculty felt little support for enforcing discipline outside of class.

Student misbehavior began innocently enough. Girls disciplined for wearing skirts that were too short (not more than three inches from floor to hem when kneeling) complained that their skirts weren't too short; their knees were just too low. And

Photo: 1974 *Witmarsum*

when a fiercely cold winter in 1970-71 prompted a group of girls to break the dress code and wear pants to school, administrators chose to ignore the infraction. Wearing pants was better, in their opinion, than wearing miniskirts![25] Behavior worsened year by year. By November 1971 an anonymous *Reflector* editorial castigated the student body for messing up restrooms, spilling soft drinks outside the concession stand, and being unkind to students who were new or on the margins.[26] Food fights occurred in the cafeteria. Alcohol and drug use became more frequent, and so many students were smoking cigarettes that smoking was allowed in the bus restroom on the 1971 and 1972 senior trips. By 1972-73, students were disrupting class, leaving school, and doing permanent damage to restrooms.

The reign of freedom and confusion

During these years, several faculty members tried to promote values of Christian community, but their efforts only seemed to shift the power balance to students who were hardly equipped to handle it. In 1971 music teacher Darrel Hostetler proposed

Judy Zimmerman '70 Herr: Senior trip and a mattress (a hotel in Washington, D. C.)
Among the four girls in our room, someone had brought along a small iron ... After all, we did not want to look wrinkled! But there was no ironing board. Never mind, we

Photo: 1970 *Witmarsum*

could use one of the beds to iron on. The very last morning of our stay, I needed to iron a blouse. I did so and was getting dressed when I smelled something funny. I picked up the iron and noticed ... there was a small burned area ... on the bed. The iron had burned through the sheet and made a charred mark on the foam mattress.

What to do? Being honest and innocent, we did not think of trying to hide what had happened. Instead, I went to Don Augsburger, one of the chaperones ... and he went to talk to the manager. I explained what had happened and that it had been an accident. The manager inspected the bed and said that I would need to pay $50, the cost of replacing the mattress. Fifty dollars was a lot of money in those days, especially for high school students. I'm sure my face betrayed my shock and dismay. But imagine my surprise when Don responded, "All right, we'll pay the $50, but we'll take the mattress with us."

So I returned from my senior trip $50 poorer and the owner of a slightly damaged mattress. The manager seemed as surprised as I was at Don's response. Don told me afterwards that the hotel probably would have taken my money and just turned the mattress

Continued on page 106 ...

Zimmerman Herr ... *cont. from page 105*
over and continued using it. Rather than let them take advantage of a naïve girl from Indiana, he called their bluff! The mattress was loaded onto the bus ... for the ride back to Bethany.

1973 Reflector *staff members: Joan Steiner '73, Bonnie Gingrich '74, Danile Stoltzfus '73, and Myron Yoder '73.*

1973 *Witmarsum*

that everyone in the Bethany community should call each other by first names. His dream was for student-teacher relationships to be characterized by friendship, like Jesus and his disciples. And Bible teacher Jim Derstine spoke out against all hierarchy, calling for "brotherhood" and mutual decision-making. Although both of these proposals were based on Christian principles, student leaders at that time were not of the same mind as their high-minded teachers. They seemed to interpret the proposals in terms of student power and freedom. Some called for sweeping changes in the educational system and asserted that adults who didn't go to school in the 1960s "just can't understand us."[27]

Spiritual climate declines

The spiritual climate of Bethany had reached an all-time low. As early as 1971, a few students began calling for chapel to be voluntary. The 1973 yearbook states that "for many, chapel is the bleakest 20 minutes of their day."[28] In December 1972 a chapel speaker, Ruth Ann Miller, told about her own faith walk and encouraged students to become sincere Christian believers. Groups of students gathered afterwards to discuss the talk, some of them quite upset by this message, and others welcoming it. "No one wants something shoved at them—even if it's delicious cherry pie," asserted one student. Another countered, "Haven't you ever been so excited about something you really *wanted* to share it?"[29] A student whose parents were missionaries in Mexico expressed disappointment in the low level of faith she found at Bethany. She expected students to be more church-oriented, she said, but found them confused instead.[30]

Too much freedom, not enough leadership

By spring of 1973, both Board and students knew that it was time for a change. Wade Bollinger's contract would not be renewed. And *Reflector* Editor Joan Steiner '73, youngest child of former Superintendent John Steiner, spoke for many students when she wrote, "I hate to admit that I think the students of Bethany have more freedom than what they are capable of handling, but it's true."[31] Fortunately, change was coming soon.

Levi Miller Photo: 1974 *Witmarsum*

Levi Miller era, 1973-76

Bill Hooley took a leave to work on his doctoral dissertation during the 1973-74 school year, and Levi Miller, who had been principal at Iowa Mennonite School for 12 years, was hired to fill the gap left by both Hooley and Bollinger. Miller was the right man for the job. His firm leadership coupled with a sense of humor, creative conflict resolution, and natural friendliness slowly began to turn the school around.

The first year was rough as Miller took on a senior class that was used to being in nearly total control. He did his best to bring a broader perspective to students. A *Reflector* profile of Miller by Karla Roth states, "It is unfair for the students to think only of 'us.' Bethany includes the faculty, parents, pastors and alumni who may feel more of the long-range effects than the current students. Others have to live with the reputation we give the school."[32] The same issue of the *Reflector* reports that 70 percent of the 171 students polled came to Bethany for reasons other than Christian atmosphere or a Christian education. The writer calls for students to respect each other in order for Bethany "to be fun again."

Miller implemented some creative solutions to persistent problems. For instance, when repainting the boys' restroom doors did not stop graffiti from appearing, he ordered the doors taken off the stalls. They remained off and the graffiti stopped.[33]

> Every passing period found him observing and verbally sparring with the students in his good-natured way as they passed from class to class.

Darrel Hostetler: Remembering Bethany

Photo: 1969 *Witmarsum*

First names for teachers? I came to Bethany with some clear ideas of a Christian school. These emerged during six years at Iowa Mennonite and one in a public school setting. I learned from IMS students that calling me Darrel or Mr. Hostetler had little to do with whether they respected me. When there was respect, however, having me be vulnerable enough to be addressed as Darrel helped to form a closer relationship.

Bible teaching. I came to Bethany as a music teacher and will likely be remembered primarily for my work with choirs and music classes. The late sixties, however, was a crucial time for Bethany's Bible program. My sense then and now is that my work as Bible teacher was more significant in the long-term good of the school than my more visible efforts in music. My first concern was that the study of the Bible be seen as a serious discipline. Then students could begin to gain tools for study so that the Bible would make an impact on their hearts and hopefully change their lives throughout their adult years. Jim Derstine, Ray Gingerich, and others joined me in these efforts.

Drama production. Drama productions are now well established at Bethany. My vision of presenting *Amahl and the Night Visitors* in my early years was met with a fair amount of skepticism. With little experience in drama,

Continued on page 108 ...

Hostetler ... *cont. from page 107*

I took overall responsibility for the acting and the music. I had great confidence in the talents of our students, feeling that their strengths could compensate for my weakness. I think my confidence was well placed. *Amahl,* given on alternate years, became a highlight of the music program.

Insert: Lola Albrecht '71 as Amahl. Above: Amahl and the Night Visitors *cast on stage.* Photos: 1970 *Witmarsum*

Sometimes he simply used a firm and consistent hand, as when seven students were sent home from senior trip for smoking. Suddenly, breaking rules brought consequences. Miller's main strategy for changing hallway misbehavior was simply to be present whenever students were in the halls. Every passing period found him observing and verbally sparring with students in his good-natured way as they passed from class to class. Faculty rallied to help patrol the halls, and gradually student behavior improved.

With Miller's arrival, power began to shift back into the hands of faculty and administrators. Now administrative energy could gradually be focused on more important things like debt reduction, curriculum development, faculty hiring, and improving spiritual life. The decade of restlessness and searching for identity was drawing to an end. Bill Hooley's stable and focused administration could now do its gently transforming work to carve out the path of faithfulness.

ॐ ॐ ॐ ॐ

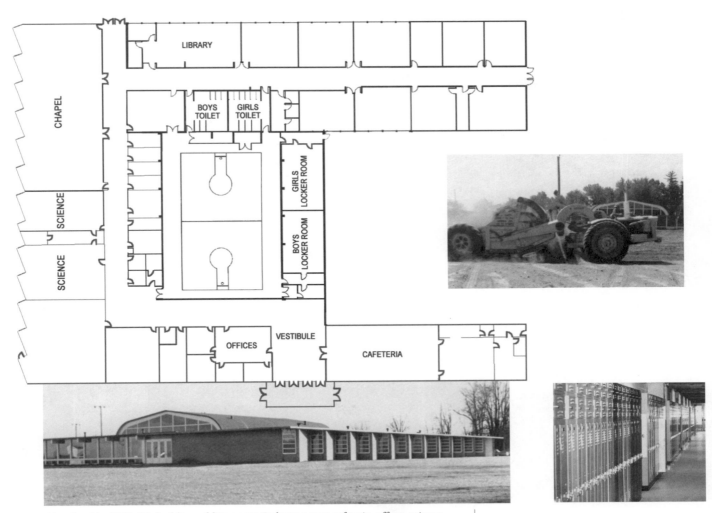

Completed in 1966, this building addition gave Bethany a new cafeteria, offices, science laboratories, and a larger chapel. Windows on the westside rooms were angled to keep out the afternoon sun and minimize the distractions of passing traffic on State Road 15. New lockers were installed and the driveway graded and graveled. Photos: 1966 *Witmarsum*

Notes

1. William D. Hooley, interview by writer, August 3, 2001.

2. Sources used in this chapter, not otherwise listed, may be found in the following collections of the Archives of the Mennonite Church (AMC): II-5-8 and Mss. 6-56, No. 2215.

3. "Engagement Announcement," *Reflector,* March 10, 1964: 1.

4. Lois Bixler, "Hear Ye: Disrespectful People," *Reflector,* December 2, 1964.

5. Phyllis Hoover, "Bethany Compares Favorably," *Reflector,* April 28, 1965: 2.

6. "Senior Profiles," *Reflector,* February 2, 1966: 3.

7. Royal Bauer, interview by writer, October 17, 2001.

8. Although Bethany teachers came with commitment and enthusiasm, their contracts asked of them a continuing heavy load.

9. Jeanette Slabach, "Bethany and Basketball," *Reflector,* March 10, 1964: 2.

10. Charles Gardner, "Inter-school Sports?" *Reflector,* February 24, 1965: 2.

11. Galen Johns, interview by writer, August 15, 2001.

12. Howard Kauffman, interview by Wilmer Hollinger, October 22, 2001.

13. Wilmer Hollinger, interview by writer, August 15, 2001.

14. Royal Bauer, "Through the Eyes of a Faculty Member," *Reflector,* March 30, 1996: 2.

15. Hollinger interview.

16. Hooley interview.

17. *Witmarsum,* 1966: 11.

18. Rhoda Shenk, "What's *Right* with Bethany?" *Reflector,* January 19, 1968: 2.

19. Hooley interview.

20. Jim Krabill, "The Spirit and the Christian," *Reflector,* February 25, 1969: 2.

21. Jane Miller and Evy Kreider, "Project SUB," *Reflector,* April 10, 1970: 1.

22. Hooley interview.

23. William D. Hooley, "Administration Close-Up," *Reflector,* September 29, 1970: 1.

24. Hooley interview.

25. Hollinger interview.

26. "Letter to Editor," *Reflector,* November 19, 1971: 2.

27. Tim Baker, "Cave Thoughts," *Reflector,* October 20, 1972: 2.

28. *Witmarsum,* 1973: 73.

29. Paul Landis, "Faculty Freelance," *Reflector,* December 15, 1972: 3.

30. Jeanette Slagel, "Cindy de Mexico," *Reflector,* February 23, 1973: 1.

31. Joan Steiner, "Editorial," *Reflector,* March 30, 1973: 2.

32. Karla Roth, "The Other Point of View," *Reflector,* December 21, 1973: 1.

33. Levi Miller, interview by writer, September 11, 2001.

Left and above: A furnace was located in each room, as shown in these photos taken in the first home economics classroom, c. 1950s.

Below: Merlyn Miller '59 heads up the cafeteria line located in the "barn" as Mary Birkey takes lunch count. Photos: Royal Bauer collection

Right: These 1958 students brought food in metal lunch boxes. Photo: BCS files

Left: Galen Otto with commerce class, c. 1950s. Photo: BCS files

Above: The main entry faces State Road 15. Administrative office windows are visible. Right: the split door leading into the office area, c. 1950s.
Photos: Royal Bauer collection

Phys ed uniforms double as basketball attire for this 1958-59 junior girls' basketball team, front: Martha Miller, Mary Swartzentruber, Donna Troyer, and Dorothy Troyer. Back: Julie Byler, Shirley J. Miller, Norma Shaum, and Shirley Kauffman. Photo: BCS files

Above: 1958-59 Gospel team hits the road.

Below: Ruby Bontrager '58 provides music at a 1956 all-school party. Photos: BCS files

Some things haven't changed! Above: 1962 fish fry traffic congestion.

Below: 1959 fish fry pie room. Photos: BCS files

Neal Slabaugh (1955-58), Dan Stutzman (1956-58), Archie Byler (1958-59), Robert Yoder (1958-59), and Arnold Roth (1959-62) were bus drivers for Bethany Christian High School. Photo: BCS files

According to the 1955 Witmarsum, *"[B]asketball became a major sport ..." during the first season of Bethany's existence. Two boys' teams were chosen by Coach Steiner and entered in the Church League. Varsity—claiming a 9-2 record—moved up to play Goshen College teams in a double elimination tournament by the season's end. Varsity players, front: Marvin Miller '56, Marion Bontrager '55, Lewis Hochstetler '55, and Marlin Miller '57. Back: Coach Steiner, Morris Litwiller '56, Richard Hershberger '57, Francis Miller '55, David Troyer '57, Daniel Wenger '57, and student manager Galen Eash '57.* Photo: 1955 Witmarsum

As a part of Lester Culp's agriculture class, these 1958-59 male students are getting "field" experience. Photo: BCS files

Junior class officers Janis Yoder, Roger Beachy, Margaret Baumgartner, and Jonathan Billheimer graduated in 1962. Photo: BCS files

1962 senior men's quartet: Lloyd Kauffman, David R. Miller, Jonathan Billheimer, and Leroy Cross. Photo: BCS files

In a 1961-62 shop class are "unidentified", Titus King '64, Paul Byler '64, and Charles Kauffman '61. Photo: BCS files

Below: An icy sidewalk between buildings provides lunchtime recreation, c. 1961-62. Photo: BCS files

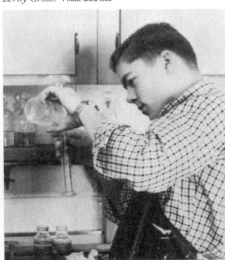

Above: Carl Weaver '65 takes advantage of a noon science lab, c. 1964. Photo: 1964 *Witmarsum*

Left top: David Leinbach '66 begins his driver's ed class in the school parking lot under the watchful eye of instructor Ron Friesen. Photo: 1964 *Witmarsum*

Left bottom: Seniors Tom Graber, Jerry Slabaugh, and Curt Grieser clean a skylight in preparation for a 1966 open house. Photo: 1966 *Witmarsum*

Ruth Yoder '66 and John Birkey '66 in a scene from the 1965 speech class production of Our Town, *directed by Royal Bauer.* Photo: Birkey collection

1968-69 service committee members: Joe Schrock '69, Lois Brenneman '70, Jim Krabill '69, Bonnie Mierau '69, Barbara Leinbach '69, and Becky Lehman '70. Photo: BCS files

Calvin Frye '70 at a student desk, c. 1960s. Photo: BCS files

Proofreading Reflector *copy: Nancy Baker '71 and Joy Bair '73.* Photo: BCS files

1979: New windows are installed. Photo: BCS files

1983: "greased pig" chase. Photo: BCS files

1995-96: Sumo wrestler Willie Kanagy is cautioned by the referee. Photo: BCS files

Right: The first boys' tennis team of 1992, front: David Wieand '93, Wesley Schrock '95, Jeffrey Miller '94, Ryan Troyer '93, and Phil Swartzendruber '93. Back: Ryan Gingerich '96, Matt Lind '95, Charles Love '96, Matt Thomas '95, Jeffrey Bontrager '93, and Kenneth Brett. Not pictured: Seung-Eel Lee '93. Photo: Goshen News

Below: Anna Newburn '01, Becci Steury '01, and Mike Nachtigall '01 canoe the Elkhart River during a 1997-98 environmental science class project. Photo: BCS files

1995 <u>Fun Fest</u> committee, front: Linda Yoder, Pat Weaver, and Susan Garboden. Standing: Karen Miller, Arianne Hochstetler, ChloAnn Stalter, Dan Bodiker, Karen Sommers, Marlys Stutzman, Dave Shenk, Ruthie Yoder, Janette Yoder, Cheryl Nester-Detweiler, Ray Gyori-Helmuth, and Larion Swartzendruber.
Photo: BCS files

1998-99 archaeology in Virginia interterm: Archaeologist Paul Schuster of Ferry Farm (George Washington's boyhood home in Fredericksburg, Virginia) instructs Sarah Buller and Anna Baer '00 in an archaeology dig. Photo: BCS files

Above, front: 1997-98 auto mechanics interterm instructor J. D. Smucker. Row 1: Anthony Slabaugh '01, David Snider '99, and Nick Gingerich '01.
Row 2: Kenton Delagrange '00, Eric Saner '00, and Nathan Ghrist.
Row 3: Greg Perrin, Rob Tribble, and Josh Miller '01.
Back: Kevin Witmer '00.

Left: Studying in the hallway, c. 1997-98, are Lena Buckwalter '98 and Angelique Birky. Photo: BCS files

1999-2000 middle school boys' soccer, coached by Shannon Wetzel-Gall.
Photo: BCS files

1999-2000 middle school orchestra members Colin Yoder, Ashley Bontrager, Kristin Fath, and Julia Klassen are directed by Brian Mast. Photo: BCS files

Christine Stutzman with middle school students Ashley Wittrig and Darin Schwartzentruber. Photo: BCS files

1999-2000 middle school girls' volleyball teams, coached by Cynthia Good Kaufmann, clockwise from front: Coach Good Kaufmann, Jennifer Manley, Danielle Anderson, Angela Gingerich, Elizabeth Buschert, Jessica Buller, Charity Grimes, Jennifer Klassen, Emily Morgan, and Maya Kehr. Photo: BCS files

Above: Kyle Reinford '02 portrays Joseph in the 2002 musical Joseph and the Amazing Technicolor Dreamcoat. *Right: Eileen Becker-Hoover is part of the clean-up crew during a 2001 donkey basketball game.* Photo: BCS files

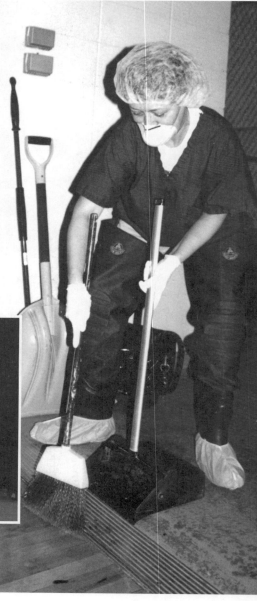

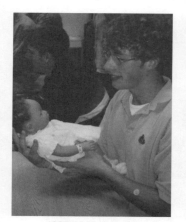

1999-2000: David Martin '00 holds computerized "Baby Know It All," with Chris Kingsley '00 in background. Photo: BCS files

1999-2000 nutrition class: Joyce Rose of "Cooking Together" instructs Jordan Buller '02 in Chinese-style cooking. In background are Scott Stably '02, Ted McFarlane '02, and Bess Miller '00. Photo: BCS files

Tim Nice '02 and Ted McFarlane '02 perform a sax duo for the 2000 Spring Arts Day. Photo: BCS files

Chapter 4

A Vision Renewed
1974-80
by Sally Weaver Glick

Learning lessons in teamwork.
Photo: 1979 *Witmarsum*

Top: Eddie Mendoza '76 and Mable Bontrager '77.
Bottom: 1977 frosh pyramid. Background: 1975
aerial view of BCHS facilities.

Photos: BCS files & 1977 Witmarsum

Though the calendar read 1974, in the world at large the ethos of the sixties was only now coming to an end. The Vietnam War was winding down in a series of broken cease-fires. The Watergate scandal had culminated in President Richard Nixon's resignation. A worldwide energy crisis was causing inflation to skyrocket, dramatically increasing the cost of fuel and food. The Beatles had broken up, and embroidered bell-bottom blue jeans were out. Change was on its way.

As in the world around it, the chaos of the sixties had worked its effects on Bethany. While Levi Miller's arrival had begun a turnaround, the school was still struggling with low morale, an uncertain identity, and students who were ready to challenge authority. The relationship between the school and the Indiana-Michigan Conference of the Mennonite Church was shaky, with many congregations uneasy with what they saw happening there. Inflation was turning Bethany's always troubled financial situation into a crisis. But here too change was on its way.

The period of 1974-80 was a transition time for the school, a time during which strong leadership helped the school to clarify its mission, mend its relationships, and re-establish its identity as a mission of the Indiana-Michigan Conference. Administrative and teaching faculty came together as a cohesive team,

Together they formed
a community that ... sought
to integrate the whole person,
heart and mind ...

Everett Thomas Photo: 1973 *Witmarsum*

joining with students to explore the meaning of Christian faithfulness in high school life. Together they formed a community that continually sought to integrate the whole person, heart and mind, in this era's expression of the interweaving of the threads of Christian discipleship and high school academics.

To continue or to close the doors

In the fall of 1974 Bethany began its twenty-first year of operation. Bill Hooley was back as superintendent after a year's leave for study and research. Levi Miller was principal, continuing the work he had begun the previous year of turning around student discipline. As student behavior improved, so did faculty morale. After the low point of the early seventies, the school finally seemed to be on an upswing. But even as the administration and faculty began to feel more optimistic, uncertainties threatened the school's existence.

The turmoil and confusion of the late sixties and early seventies had left their mark. Trust in the school's mission had eroded as the constituency's concerns over student behavior and the lack of a clear identity had culminated in low confidence in the school. BCHS Board minutes of November 1974 note a negative attitude toward Bethany in some congregations. They also note ongoing financial problems. The 1964-66 expansion of the school had never been paid off, resulting in Bethany's continuing struggle with a debilitating debt load. A troubled economy and soaring inflation had caused overall debt to swell to $185,000. Caught between low tuition rates and escalating operating costs, the school was borrowing money to meet operating expenses. The administration and the Board began to seriously question whether Bethany should continue. Bethany was a mission of Indiana-Michigan Conference. If the Conference could not, or would not, support Bethany, perhaps the time had come to shut down.

On December 17, 1974, a group of concerned individuals gathered in the Bethany chapel. The Board had invited the advisory council members, the representatives of Conference congregations, to come and to bring their pastors and other interested congregational members. The Board presented the school's situation and asked the question, "Should the school continue?" Bethany English teacher Everett Thomas was present at the meeting; he described the scene in a 1982 essay on the school.

> Interested parents, graduates, students, teachers, Board members, and pastors filled the chapel for an ad hoc meeting one evening to ask whether it was time to close the doors. But instead, speaker after speaker, often recent graduates or current students, voiced their strong determination to get the school back on track. The group left with a commitment to raise $18,550 in the next three months, and to pursue longer-range plans for eliminating the debt load. Bethany would continue, but rebuilding trust and raising money would be a slow process.

Renewed vision: matters of the heart

Rebuilding trust would not happen overnight, but Bill Hooley was ready to take on the challenge. By the fall of 1974, Hooley had served three years as superintendent of Bethany, plus the year of research and writing of a dissertation. "I was 31 when I came to Bethany. It took time to build confidence and trust with pastors, Board, faculty, students. And it took time to develop my own vision and goals."[2] The research for his dissertation had provided data he could draw on, and the time away had given him the opportunity to clarify his ideas. Now he was returning with a renewed sense of direction, ready to share this with the school and with the church at large.

For Hooley the school was a mission of the church, accountable to Conference. In a November 1974 *Gospel Herald* article, he posed several questions about the shape of this mission:

> Do Mennonite high schools have the responsibility of training the sons and daughters of Mennonites who cannot adjust in a public school setting and

If Conference could not, or would not, support Bethany, perhaps the time had come to shut down.

1974 graduates Lamortto Wofford, Anita Helmuth, and Veronica Henderson.
Photo: 1975 *Witmarsum*

For Hooley the school was a mission of the church, accountable to Conference.

"Words to live by" from Prov. 11:14 and Dan Schrock, guidance counselor. Photo: 1975 Witmarsum

'A Christian educator
in a church high school
is concerned about more
than the mind;
he attempts to deal with
matters of the heart too.'

Singing in chapel. Photo: 1974 Witmarsum

are labeled delinquents? Are Mennonite high schools intended to prepare each student for an assignment with the Mission Board or some other church institution? Are Mennonite high schools supposed to protect and safeguard our Mennonite youth from the world so that the traditions of our fathers can be carried forward without fear of deviancy?

While acknowledging that some might answer "yes" to these questions, Hooley held that each was "a limited and therefore a distorted view of our church high schools." Instead, he described the basic task of the church high school, the one that differentiates it from public high schools, as being one of dealing with Christian values, attitudes, beliefs, and commitments. It is an academic center, with a high priority given to learning, but "a Christian educator in a church high school is concerned about more than the mind; he attempts to deal with matters of the heart too."[3]

In Hooley's vision for the school, Bethany would be a place which encouraged students to develop their whole person, mind *and* heart. It would provide them with opportunities to reflect on and own for themselves Christian values and commitments. Rather than being sheltered from the world, they would encounter the world in the company of faculty who would help them examine and process what they experienced there. Bethany's role as a mission of Conference would be clear: a vision of church and school working toward a shared goal of preparing students for a life of Christian discipleship.

Hooley used every opportunity to give voice to his vision for Bethany, writing articles for *Gospel Herald* and the Conference paper, *Gospel Evangel,* speaking in congregations, and meeting regularly with pastors in groups of four or five, also offering ample opportunity for conversation. After years of struggling with identity confusion, both Conference and school responded positively to this clearly articulated vision and the renewed clarity of the school-Conference relationship.

Hooley and Miller: heart and spine

Bill Hooley was a leader strongly committed to nurturing others and strengthening relationships—between students and faculty, between teachers and administrators, between the school and Conference. The Christian discipleship that students were learning was also the foundation for Hooley's understanding of his personal task at Bethany: "How do we live out the life of Jesus? How do I as principal model such an approach? Not just talk about it, but how do I live it out in relationship to students, faculty, Board, and conference congregations?"[4]

Hooley found an ally in Levi Miller, and the two quickly became a good working team. Hooley describes Miller as "quiet, low-key, ordinary as an old shoe— with amazing strength and ability to confront students." A number of former teachers also mention Miller's clear standards and ability to zero in on what a student needed.[5] He was able to find good solutions to awkward situations, bringing a sense of humor that could catch people off-guard. And he was able to bring a diverse faculty together, with a sense of "let's get something done." Wilmer Hollinger, former history and government teacher, describes the Hooley-Miller team as working well together, with Hooley providing the gentle guiding hand and Miller able to bulldog changes through.[6] Or, to draw on Thomas' 1982 essay on the school: "While Hooley put a heart back into the school, Levi Miller gave it a spine." Hooley was happy to delegate day-to-day supervision and discipline to Miller, who did it so ably, and focus his own energies on bringing to life his newly clarified vision for the school.

Leadership transitions

The Hooley-Miller team was together for only two years, but their collaboration put in place strong patterns that carried the school through several transitions until the naming of Thomas as principal again established a solid administrative team. Miller left the school in 1976, called to other church work at Rosedale Mennonite Missions. For the next several years the principal (by 1983 Thomas was called "assistant principal") changed every year or two. Ed Herr had been teaching and coaching at

Loretta Birky '59 (Chupp) was employed as receptionist/ bookkeeper from 1975-92.

Photos: 1959 & 1976 *Witmarsums*

'While Hooley put a heart back into the school, Levi Miller gave it a spine.'

Royal Bauer (standing, left) helps Bill Hooley join the third tier of a faculty pyramid during the all-school social. Photo: 1975 *Witmarsum*

1975-76 Board members, front: Willard Conrad, Flossie Yoder, Phyllis Stoltzfus, Edith Kauffman, and Russell Krabill. Back: Orris Yoder, Dennis Weaver '70, Roy Yoder, Herb Maust, and Alice Roth. Not pictured: Franklin Newcomer and Wayne Sommers. Photo: 1976 *Witmarsum*

... Hooley also had an ally in Herbert Maust, who was president of the Board from 1971-80.

Roy S. Koch Photo: 1976 *Witmarsum*

Bethany for a year when he replaced Miller as principal in the fall of 1976. He was able to maintain the established discipline and to build up the athletic program, but he eventually decided the position was not quite the right fit for him and, after two years, moved on to an athletic director position elsewhere. For the 1978-79 school year, Mike Lambright came on a one-year sabbatical leave from Christopher Dock Mennonite High School in Pennsylvania. He was also able to maintain the established discipline, but being at Bethany such a short time, he could not leave much of a mark. Everett Thomas, well known to the Bethany community, replaced him. Thomas had taught English there from 1972 to 1977, before leaving to pursue seminary studies. He returned to fill in for Devon Schrock in January 1979; Schrock had been hospitalized after a farming accident. Then in the fall Thomas became assistant principal, joining Hooley, Roy Hartzler (director of curriculum and faculty development), and John Zook (guidance counselor) to create a strong administrative team.

During this whole time period, Hooley also had an ally in Herbert Maust, who was president of the Board from 1971-80. Working together for such an extended period, they came to know each other well and could support each other firmly. They did not always agree but respected each other and were able to work out their differences for the good of the school.[7]

Reducing the debt

Having heard a definite "yes" to the question of whether Bethany should continue, the school moved into high gear to eliminate the debt. In January 1975 it began a three-year-long debt-liquidation drive. Roy S. Koch was hired part-time as director of public relations. Having been Conference minister for the previous five years, he was in a good position to rebuild relationships between the school and Conference congregations and to seek financial contributions. He also pursued individual donors, writing letters and meeting one-on-one with possible contributors.[8] His enthusiasm for the school was contagious, and positive attitudes toward Bethany blossomed even as morale improved on campus. Slowly and fairly steadily the debt shrank.

Students also took part in the debt-reduction efforts. Inspired by the successful efforts of the 1970 Students United for Bethany (SUB), a group of seniors organized SUB II in early 1975. This particular group—Steve Christner, Ron Chupp, Don Kaufman, Gerald Miller, Steve Miller, and Robin Slabaugh—caused a few raised eyebrows among administrators and Board members, since some of these students had reputations for exactly the sort of troublemaking that Conference congregations were concerned about. Two had even been suspended from school for a time. Their fellow students assumed that these would be the ones to cheer at the thought of the school closing. Robin Slabaugh admits that they were perhaps a surprising group to jump into planning SUB II:

Participating in the SUB II bake sale are Grant Maust '77, Mike Schwartzentruber '76, and David King '76. Photo: 1976 *Witmarsum*

> But when we heard about the school possibly closing, we didn't want to see that happening. We had too much fun there—we didn't want it to close. And most of us had been troublemakers earlier. We figured that had been hard on the school's reputation and that we may have cost the school some support. My brothers were involved in SUB. And I knew what they had done, so we began planning.[9]

The group organized three days' worth of rummage sales, auctions, bake sales, car washes, and a 15-mile sponsored walk-a-thon from Elkhart to Goshen. The whole school took part in the fundraising activities April 17-19, 1975, bringing in $20,400 for the campaign.

**This particular group ...
caused a few raised eyebrows
among administrators
and Board members since
some of these students
had reputations ...**

The windmill (or … The BCHS obsession with money)
by Judy Weaver '77

The thing that bothers me is that I can't quite decide whether it was a dream or not. I counted my money today, and it was all still there, so it could have been a dream, but I don't know—it all seemed so real at the time.

I remember waking up, too. I yawned and stretched and opened my eyes. Then I sat up and looked around, and that's when I noticed something unusual. I was sitting in the middle of a turkey farm. Not far off was a small brick windmill. Well, naturally, I thought the whole situation was a little weird, but I decided to make the best of things. Since the turkeys were rather dull company, and I'd always wanted to see a windmill close up, I stood up and sort of strolled over to it.

It was a normal windmill, with vanes that turned round like a wheel, made of brick, with a little door, a few windows, a domed roof, and a soccer field out in back. Anyway, I raised my hand to knock, but before I did the door was flung open, and a tall grinning fellow pulled me inside.

"Well, hello, there! Would you like to join us? Or better yet, make a large donation and dry up."

I guess I was a little dazed. I said, "Huh?"

He said, "I am Mr. Rock, and that door over there is the one you go through to promise your very large donation." He started kind of pushing me towards the door.

"Wait, Mr. Rock," I said, "I've never been in a windmill before. Can't you tell me something about it first? What do you process here, and what is your position—what do you do?"

"Oh, that …" He put his hands in his pocket and looked thoughtful. "Process … hmmm, let's see now … once in a while, on the side, we send a kid or two through … that teaches 'em! Actually, that's what I'm here for, to make sure they get there. I'm their rock, their advisor, and all that. It's very important, so you can be sure your extra large donation will be well spent."

Just then a woman in a sweatsuit went jogging past. She called to me as she ran, "Make it a super large donation. My work is very pertinent!" She jogged out the back door.

Before I could demand an explanation, a young fellow in corduroys came up and shook my hand. "Uh, hi there!" he said. "Uh, so you're from the turkey farm. What work do you need done? Washing walls, bathing turkeys? Only $5.00 an hour per worker …" Mr. Rock pulled me away from him and pointed out a man who was wandering by. "There's the man you need to speak to. He's always cooking up ways to get donations …"

"Wait! Stop it! Hold everything!" I yelled, because I was getting very confused. "I'm getting very confused! Let me see the person in charge. Who's in charge of this mill?"

"Why, the Miller, of course" said the young fellow, and dragged me by the arm over to the door Mr. Rock had pointed out. I was shoved inside and the door latched behind me.

I found myself standing in front of a sort of small, round, benevolent-looking character, who was seated at a desk. He was smiling. He pushed a pen and some paper towards me and said, "Well, hello there! Would you like to join us? Better yet, make an extremely large donation and dry up … till next year. I'm the Miller and everyone likes me."

"Mr. Miller, sir, I'm confused," I said, "Everyone keeps asking me to donate money. I didn't know mills worked like this. Why don't you just make flour or bread or something?"

"Because," he answered, "we haven't got any dough. Now about your ridiculously large donation …"

(Faculty and administrators at the time of writing included Dan Schrock, guidance counselor; Linda "Pert" Miller '68 Shetler, physical education; Roy Koch, director of public relations; and Levi Miller, principal.)

Revisiting tuition policies

Eliminating the debt was one mode of dealing with Bethany's financial woes; re-examining tuition policies was another. Committed to keeping tuition affordable, the Board in 1969 had cut tuition by a third, relying on tax deductible patron contributions to make up the difference, an approach that at first worked well, with parents and others contributing enough to cover the drop in tuition income. But over the years contributions went steadily down, while operating costs rose. In November 1976 the *Reflector* reported that in 1965-66 operating costs had been $430.37 per student. Contributions had covered 68 percent of those costs. But in 1974-75 operating costs were $1305.11, while tuition was only $150. Contributions covered just 37 percent of operating costs. Over 60 percent of Bethany parents were not making patron contributions in addition to tuition. The tuition policy was clearly no longer functioning in the way intended.

Students relax in the northwest corner of the cafeteria during their disco "daze."
Photo: BCS files

The Board was still strongly committed to keeping tuition affordable, but something had to be done. In 1976 the Board doubled tuition to $300, or $500 for those coming from non-Conference congregations and then in 1977 raised it again to $400 and $650. Until this time the only financial aid program available was the High-Aim program, designed for minority students. Now, while raising tuition to a more realistic level, the school also began a student assistance fund in February 1977, intended for any students whose financial circumstances were such that the higher tuition would mean they might not otherwise be able to attend Bethany.

As the efforts to get the financial situation under control continued, the school kept students and parents up to date with the progress made. Regular reports appeared each month in the *Reflector* throughout the campaign. This was sometimes more information than most students apparently wanted. While relieved to hear that the debt was dropping, they often got impatient with all the emphasis on money-raising. The 1976 April Fool's edition of the *Reflector* includes an account of the last $129,000 of debt being paid off in a surprise move by a single donor. It also has a brief satire on the debt campaign written by Judy Weaver '77 (see page 130). This

The blizzard of January '78 cancelled Bethany classes for more than a week. Photo: 1978 *Witmarsum*

> 'If BCHS effectively serves
> the church it is because
> of a team effort.'

A '57 graduate, Marvin D. Yoder returned to
Bethany, teaching Bible from 1976-93.

Photos: 1957 & 1976 *Witmarsums*

latter article evidently struck a responsive chord with students, for it was reprinted in the *Reflector's* twenty-fifth anniversary retrospective on February 9, 1979.

A creative and committed faculty

While the administration played a vital role in holding up the vision for Bethany, that vision could not take on flesh and substance without the work of a committed teaching faculty. Hooley had inherited a number of strong, dedicated teachers when he became superintendent, and he was always on the lookout for more. As he wrote the Board, "We need the resources of the most creative minds available to consistently evaluate existing programs and curriculum and to propose new alternatives." Hooley was able to draw a number of experienced and well-trained teachers to Bethany and to discover others just starting out who would go on to become strong teachers. The Board supported him in this search by working to bring salaries within 10 percent of public school salaries in the area, making teaching at Bethany a more attractive option.

Hooley was deeply convinced of the importance of all Bethany staff working together to carry out the school's mission. As he wrote in a 1979 report to the Board, "The effectiveness of BCHS never depends solely on one staff person even though selected staff may be more crucial than others. If BCHS effectively serves the church it is because of a team effort."

In his first years at the school, Hooley had been aware of a separation between teaching and administrative faculty. Throughout the seventies he worked to eliminate that separation, creating a cohesive administrative and faculty team that could join together to solve whatever problems arose.

Supportive orientation of new teachers helped to build this sense of being part of a team. During a teacher's first year at Bethany, Hooley would spend an hour weekly with him or her. He saw this time as an opportunity to give the new teacher a thorough orientation to Bethany, to develop a close working relationship, and to encourage the growth of that individual. Diane Schrock Hertzler, former music teacher, recalls coming from a good public school experience and being "floored" by the encouragement given new faculty at Bethany and the way it helped build an *esprit de corps*.[10]

Retreats were another occasion for sharing the vision and for sustaining a strong sense of working together for a common goal. The annual fall retreat normally involved a full day with an outside resource person and then a time of focusing on school business during the forenoon of the second day. Former faculty members describe these retreats as being spiritual experiences, "pulling and challenging us with a view beyond ourselves" and "firing us up for the year ahead."[11] Social activities also helped the faculty to have fun together. The overnight winter retreat at Camp Amigo or Camp Mack was a relaxed time, with families along and no agenda to work through. And at other times of the year there would be chicken

Bit by bit relationships grew and ties were strengthened, building the staff's identity as a team while working for the nurture and education of the students.

Faculty members Al Peachey, Everett Thomas, Larion Swartzendruber, and Rick Stiffney provided barbershop music for the 1974 junior-senior banquet.

Photo: Al Peachey collection

Audio-visual department: André Gingerich, Steve Stutzman '78, and Ken Hollinger '79.

Photo: 1976 *Witmarsum*

Photo: 1978 *Witmarsum*

1976 Chamber Choir directed by Diane Schrock (shown above), front: LeAnn Mishler '76, Lisa Hoover '76, Suzanne Gross '77, and Bev Gingerich '76. Center: Miriam Lehman '76, Anne Hostetler '76, Kit Bowen '76, and Philip Martin '77. Back: Dave Schwartzentruber '77, Duane Leatherman '76, Maureen Moore '77, Carol Weaver '76, David King '76, and Keith Miller '77. Not pictured: Ruth Ann Cocanower '76.

Photo: 1976 *Witmarsum*

barbecues, or birthday celebrations, or spontaneous get-togethers. Bit by bit relationships grew and ties were strengthened, building the staff's identity as a team while working for the nurture and education of the students.

Beyond the classroom

While day-to-day classroom experiences were one important setting for nurturing and educating students, others took place beyond the classroom.

Bethany teachers put in many extra hours helping students and each other with extracurricular activities. Schrock Hertzler describes "a synergy that carried

he faculty beyond their contract assignments ... Faculty enjoyed being together and they enjoyed working with students. They pitched in to make things happen, whether that was assisting students with chapels or measuring the long jump at track meets."[12]

Faculty caught the vision of working with the whole student—mind, heart, and body—and gave that vision life in many forms. They sponsored a range of clubs: Spanish, German, photography, home economics, art, audio-visual, library, Audubon, Run for Your Life, and the Student Body Association. They worked with students on chapels and in discussion groups and joined them in life team

Faculty caught the vision of working with the whole student—mind, heart, and body—and gave that vision life in many forms.

Photo: 1976 *Witmarsum*

Linda "Pert" Miller '68 Shetler taught physical education and coached at her alma mater from 1972-81. She is pictured (left) with the 1976-77 varsity volleyball sectional champs, front: Gloria Steiner '77, Carmella Reyes '77, mascot Keri Yoder, Mable Bontrager '77, Mary Troyer '78, and manager Donita Schwartzentruber '79. Back: Becky Maust '77, Betty Helmuth '77, Maureen Moore '77, Diana Boyts '79, Joyce Yoder '78, and Coach Shetler.

Photo: left, 1977 *Witmarsum*

Shown with a 1973-74 Art Club project are officers Sharon Shumaker '75, sec.-treas.; Dee Ganger, pres.; and Mary Hostetler '75, v.-pres.

Photo: 1974 *Witmarsum*

For interterm in 1975, Merrill Krabill '75 (right) chose to perfect his ping-pong game.

1981 classmates Rachel Hochstetler (left), Karla Yoder (third from left), and Jane Miller (fifth from left) are shown at the Society of Brothers during their 1979-80 interterm. Photos: 1975 & 1980 *Witmarsums*

presentations to Conference congregations. Music continued as a strong thread, with many students playing in orchestra or singing in chorale, or in the concert and chamber choirs. Sports involvement was also strong, with intramural activities taking place at lunchtime and after school. In addition faculty members put many hours into coaching interscholastic sports, which in this time period included girls' track, volleyball, and basketball; and boys' track, baseball, soccer, basketball, and, after 1978, cross country. In 1974 the school became a full member of Indiana High School Athletic Association, which allowed teams to participate in sectional tournaments.

As if that weren't enough to keep everyone busy, the faculty's creativity and enthusiasm also led to experimentations with new extracurricular activities. Some of these flourished for a time and then faded; others have become traditions. Bethany's first attempt at an interterm, a time for "educational experiences not normally available in the traditional classroom setting," took place in 1975.[13] Acquiring the idea from other Mennonite schools, Bethany experimented with a two-week interterm in January of that year. Students chose among activities such as ping-pong and badminton, independent reading, serving as teachers' aides in schools, remodeling Hotel Elkhart for use by Mennonite agencies, or taking a trip to the Society of Brothers. Interterm for one student, Lester Snyder, involved making a documentary of the hotel remodeling.

Interterm soon became an institution, though there was some tinkering with its spot on the calendar. It began as a two-week experience but in the 1977-78 school year was reduced to one week and moved to March. Later it was moved to the fall. Faculty members reflecting on their interterm experiences described them as a lot of stress and work, especially with the effort to keep the activities affordable.[14] But they also found the experiences very enriching and rewarding for themselves as well as students. Each year the faculty tried to provide options with a good mix of skills, activities, and interesting places, striving for choices that were both educational and enjoyable. The continuing success of their efforts has made interterm one of Bethany's best traditions.

The year 1975 also saw the first Bethany Arts Festival. Everett Thomas was looking for a way for students to present artwork and drama and hit upon the idea of having a weekend arts festival.[15] Artwork and the products of the woodworking classes would be on display and members of the drama class could present their work. Eventually music was added as well, with ensembles playing in the halls. Participants in the festival strolled around, listening to music, watching dramas, and examining displays of artwork, woodwork, and writing. Each year an art project to be kept at the school was selected. After flourishing for a number of years, the festival faded away, to be reborn in another form at a later time.

Another bright idea that took shape, flourished, and then faded was Perspectives Week. In addition to the annual Spiritual Life Week, in the spring of 1978 the school spent a week exploring Anabaptist roots, under the theme "Seeds of Identity." As part of the week's events, Bethany produced the opera *Martyrs Mirror*, an effort that involved the participation of many students and faculty. In 1979 the theme was "The Call to Shiloah," a wide-ranging look at the concept of obedience to God and his way. While *Martyrs Mirror* was again produced in 1981, Perspectives Week as an overall concept did not last.

Bryan Kehr '78 and Carolyn Dueck '78 portray the Jan Wouters family in the 1978 production of Martyrs Mirror.
Photo: 1978 *Witmarsum*

Elaine Clymer: Memories of Bethany
One course I developed was Sociology for Living. In this course we discussed relationships, marriage, reproduction, and parenting. In those years these were new subjects for Mennonite schools. In our class we practiced the art of parenting by having "egg babies." Students were paired as "mother" and "father" and were given an egg to care for. The parents had to make little baskets to carry the egg and were responsible for their baby at all times. If they were involved in an activity where they couldn't take their egg, they had to find a baby sitter. If they dropped their egg and it cracked or broke, they were guilty of child abuse. Students had to write a report on what this experience taught them. Many found new meaning to the word "responsibility."
Photo: 1979 *Witmarsum*

Carl Miller '78 Photo: BCS files

… Maust characterized the student body as 'genuinely cooperative and supportive,' noting also that 'a real sense of unity has developed in which faculty and students now work together.'

Students admire a new van purchased with 1979 Student Body Association-sponsored work day monies. Photo: 1979 Witmarsum

Rather than understanding the task 'to be in the world but not of it' as a call for separation, they understood the task as a call to engage with the world but not to adopt its assumptions and actions.

Students and faculty: working together

With a clarified vision, changes in admissions policies, and overall improvement of morale, the faculty and Board began to note definite shifts in student attitudes and character as well. The student rebelliousness of the sixties was vanishing. In his 1977 annual report to Conference, Board President Maust characterized the student body as "genuinely cooperative and supportive," noting also that "a real sense of unity has developed in which faculty and students now work together."

Over the next several years, the annual reports continue to laud the positive morale and the good working relationships between teachers and students. Such relationships allowed students and teachers to reflect together on the intersection of high school and faith issues. One vision for the school saw it as a shelter, a place where children of Mennonite families could learn the expectations and beliefs of their heritage while being protected from the rough winds of the wider world. While some Indiana-Michigan congregations still looked for this, others had a different perspective. Rather than understanding the task "to be in the world but not of it" as a call for separation, they understood the task as a call to engage with the world but not to adopt its assumptions and actions. They then looked to Bethany, not as a safe haven meant to protect their children but as a place where the students could begin to encounter the broader world in company with teachers and others who could help them reflect on and process that encounter from a Mennonite perspective. Classroom discussions, chapels, interterm, Spiritual Life Week, Perspectives Week, Peace Society … all were opportunities for this kind of reflection and growth to take place.

Not a reform school

In the fall of 1973 Bethany put into effect a new admissions policy, a policy whose cumulative effect had a major impact on the student body in the late seventies. During the turbulent sixties, some parents and congregations had looked to Bethany as a last resort for coping with problem children. In contrast Hooley was convinced that such reform efforts did not serve either the school or the student well. The Board and faculty agreed that while the school might be able to help a few difficult students, the school's primary identity was not that of a reform school. With the new policy Bethany would no longer accept any student who had been expelled from another school. And, more significantly, Bethany would not accept students who did not wish to attend there.

Hooley describes this as one of the more important administrative decisions he made.[16] In his perception the policy helped build a sense of pride in the school, reduced vandalism, and led to a more unified student body. Others agree about its importance. In interviews alumni and former administrative and teaching faculty mentioned this policy repeatedly as a key element in changing the dynamics of the

Ed Herr: The Ed Lewis story

Photo: *Witmarsum*

When I arrived at Bethany Christian High School, as the boys' basketball coach in the fall of 1975, I met Ed Lewis. Ed was a junior High-Aim student from Chicago. He was also a 6' 3" basketball player with the reputation of being somewhat difficult to coach. I was also warned to make certain that he kept his grades up to be eligible to play. So I made sure I got to know Ed. Before basketball practice began, in talking to

Continued on page 140 ...

Lori Miller Photo: 1978 *Witmarsum*

Roy Hartzler Faculty photo: 1978 *Witmarsum*

Ed Lewis '77 and Mario Cordero '75.
Photo: 1976 *Witmarsum*

Herr ... cont. from page 139

Ed, I told him there were just two ways to play the game, his way and my way. His way was called "intramural basketball" and my way was "varsity basketball." Ed decided he would play my way. He worked hard, had a good attitude, and always supported me as a coach and friend. He ended up as a good player.

As the season moved on I began to notice that Ed had trouble catching hard, quick passes and that when he read, his eyes were close to the book. I asked him if he had ever had his eyes checked. His answer was, "No more than in the Chicago public schools and they never found anything wrong with my eyes."

I talked with his boarding family, who also felt he needed to have his eyes checked. They contributed some money along with some other people, making it possible for Ed to go to the eye doctor. Ed did need glasses, so we collected some more money and he received glasses.

You could say having glasses was a real "eye opener" for Ed. His studies became easier because he could see the print better than he had for many years. He became an excellent basketball player and in his senior year was the second leading scorer in Elkhart County.

Ed also became more confident and self-assured as he began reading and studying for the first time in his life. One of my proudest moments came when Ed, in the spring of his senior year, asked if he could speak in chapel. It was an honor to listen to him explain how Bethany had touched his life, thanking the school and God for helping him and agreeing that hard work does help lead to success.

school. Earlier there had been a division between those students who wanted to be there and those who were made to come. Often those who did not want to be there caused turmoil and disruption for everyone. Now students were at Bethany because they had chosen to be there, a fitting approach for a school belonging to the believers' church tradition.

Several guys lend a hand—servanthood style—to one of God's smallest creatures, a "bug." Photo: BCS files

Makeup of the student body

Whether due to the changes in admissions, overall Conference policy, the improving morale, or general demographics, during the 1974-80 time period Bethany's enrollment soared. In 1973-74 there were 228 students at the school. For the 1979-80 school year, 262 students enrolled and another 23 applied but were not accepted because of space limitations. About 90 percent of the student body came from Indiana-Michigan congregations, with other Mennonites and Conservative Mennonites adding another 2-3 percent, and the remainder coming from other denominations. Not too surprisingly, given the makeup of the congregations the school served, the Bethany student body was largely white, rural, Midwestern, and Mennonite. More surprising is that Bethany actually had a broader diversity than neighboring Goshen High School, thanks to programs such as High-Aim and International Christian Youth Exchange (ICYE). In 1978, for example, Bethany's minority population was 8 percent, while Goshen High School's was at 2 percent.[17]

The High-Aim program was begun in the late sixties as a way of bringing minority students from urban Mennonite churches into Mennonite high schools and communities. It was an important learning experience, not only for the minority students coping with the shift from an urban setting, but also for Bethany students and host families whose contacts otherwise were mostly white and rural. Susan Mark '76 Landis recalls the friendships and challenges she received from High-Aim students as important for her own discipleship development.

> I received real challenges to my assumptions about peacemaking when someone who had been caught in the midst of physical violence—in an alley between two angry young men—pushed me with questions about what a peacemaker should do. I also learned the beginnings of white privilege when I was allowed to take excused absences from school for planned family vacations, but High-Aim students, either lonely for home or without transportation, were given unexcused absences for coming back from Chicago a day late … It forced me to think about race issues, nonviolence, and justice in a way I never would have otherwise.[18]

Links to the wider world also came in other ways. ICYE was created after World War II to encourage young Christians to learn from Christians in other countries. Throughout the seventies the program brought one or two foreign students to campus each year, while the same number of Bethany students spent a year in another country in exchange. These were not the only students with international experience. Awareness of other lands came from children of missionaries on furlough, children of international students at the nearby Associated Mennonite Biblical Seminary, and children of Goshen College faculty returned from sabbatical-year travels.

Respecting diversity

Whether through international, racial, theological, or personality differences, students were well aware of the challenge of diversity. In a September 1975 *Reflector* editorial Michael Schwartzentruber '76 wrote:

Links to the wider world also came in other ways.

Photo: 1976 *Witmarsum*

Photo: 1980 *Witmarsum*

ICYE students Shigeru Toda, Japan (top), and Outi Sarsa '80, Finland.

**Leonard Gross:
The High-Aim story**
During the turbulent and radical sixties, new ideas of justice and equality were beginning to surface within American society that also had a direct impact on the Mennonite world of education. In 1968

Leonard Gross
Photo: 1961 *Witmarsum*

Mennonites envisioned a program called High-Aim that would include urban African-Americans and Hispanics as students at Mennonite institutions.

Bethany embraced High-Aim from the outset, and over the years accepted dozens of students, most of them coming from distances that necessitated their staying in local homes, at least during the week. For several years our family housed High-Aimers Kit Bowen, Terry Bowen, and Wesley Parker, all from Chicago. We came to love our extended family and remain in contact with them to this day. They graduated from Bethany and have since found meaningful vocations.

In the Bethany annual, *Witmarsum '79*, the High-Aim program was featured as a two-page spread of photographs listing ten High-Aimers, with the text reading: "The High Aim program was started in 1968 in order to give minority youth from urban areas the opportunity for a Christian education. High Aimers face quite a challenge adapting to a school where the vast majority of the student body is both white and coming from a Mennonite family. Different members of this program have experienced both satisfaction and dissatisfaction with it. What is certain is that all of us have a chance to grow through

Continued on page 143 ...

Bethany is not just made up of people from Indiana and Michigan, but it is made up of people from all over the world. We have diversity in as many forms as it comes. We have people in different sizes and shapes, different colors and nationalities, rich and poor. We are all individual. I must not put you down and you must not put the next person down because they are different ... To learn we must first accept each person as they are. We must not try to change them to our molds, or we'll only create a barrier ...

Michael was not the only one with this awareness. A *Reflector* editorial calling on students to appreciate and respect each other was practically a rite of fall. Editors urged their fellow students to value their differences and to use them as "building blocks, not walls," to borrow the words of 1974 editor, Rita Yoder '75. Diversity was a resource to be drawn on, sometimes difficult, but also valuable and rewarding.

Wilmer Hollinger found that students in the late seventies rose to the challenge, learning to work well with diversity of many different types. He names the class of '76 as a good example of this. Diverse groups were represented in the leadership group, which was made up of Mike Schwartzentruber (president), Kit Bowen (vice-president), Susan Mark (secretary), Pat Shumaker (treasurer), and Rachel Martin (business manager). The diversity made it more difficult to work together, so that decisions often took longer. But when the leadership group was able to agree, they were able to bring a lot of others along with them, melding the class together into a whole.[19]

Integrating Christian values

There was no shortage of opportunities for faculty and students to explore faith issues in the academic

Anita Yoder '78 Photo: 1978 *Witmarsum*

setting. Classroom discussions were one natural forum. Brenda Hostetler '75 Meyer also recalls chapels that led to such lively discussions that classes were suspended and interactions continued in the halls.[20] Traces of ongoing discussions also show up in the *Reflector* in letters to the editor and in articles covering current campus issues. The 1977-79 *Reflectors,* under editors Anita Yoder '78 and Thomas Charles '79, allowed plenty of opportunity for such reflections, with issues appearing biweekly instead of monthly. There was space for these discussions to develop into actions and experiments. One such outcome was the cheerleading experiment of 1978-79 (see page 144).

Peace Society brought a longer-lasting result, one that grew out of discussions of what it meant to be peacemakers. Initial impetus for the group came from a 1978 interterm visit to Washington led by Nina Lanctot and Irene Gross. The group explored a variety of ways people deal with issues of peace, Christianity, and government. They visited people with strong convictions and lifestyles: Mark Hatfield, Marian Franz, Sojourners, and the Berrigans at Jonah House.[21] Inspired by these interactions, some students began meeting in the spring and continued over the summer. By fall the group expanded to include other students and faculty. According to an August 1978 *Reflector* article, "This group brought together people who were searching for answers about peace, and people who had convictions and wanted to act on them." The group met monthly to look at the biblical reasons for being a peacemaker, to learn more about particular situations around the world and at home (e.g., hunger, or South Africa, or recycling at Bethany), and to come up with possible responses.

Heart, mind, *and* body

Athletics was another area that repeatedly provided opportunities for reflection on how best to integrate Christian values and high school life. In addition to the

Peace Society brought a longer-lasting result …

1979-80 Peace Society members, front: Donna Parcell '82, Jenny Miller '82, and Lori Zook '81. Back: sponsor Marlin Groff, Lisa Roth '82, Ann Minter '82, Deb Augsburger '80, Diane Yoder '82, Cathy Smeltzer '80, Linda Dintaman '82, Stacy Haines '82, and sponsor Irene Gross.
Photo: 1980 *Witmarsum*

Gross *… cont. from page 142*

Gross *… cont. from page 142*

relating to people of different backgrounds."

For financial and other reasons the High-Aim program slowly dwindled in scope, coming to an end in the 1980s. Its demise notwithstanding, the success of the High-Aim program is evident—as seen in the lives of Kit, Terry, and Wesley, and of many other High-Aimers who walked Bethany's halls.

Cindy Hartzler '80 (Hartzler-Miller): The short-lived cheerleading squad experiment

Scene: An after-class discussion in the girls' locker room in early autumn 1978. Several students lament the cheerleading

Photo: 1978 *Witmarsum*

tradition of popular girls wearing sexy skirts and applauding for boys. Shouldn't we tone down the sexuality of the attire, involve boys on the squad, and cheer at girls' sports events too? And why not make enthusiasm the criterion for participation instead of gymnastic talent? Wouldn't it be more fitting for upside-down-kingdom-type Christians?

With the support of Pert Shetler, physical education teacher and cheerleading sponsor, and the rest of the Bethany faculty, we pursued our bold vision. Twenty-one students participated, including students who, like me, never considered themselves to be "cheerleader types." We practiced chants, we decorated lockers, we organized pep sessions, we created a master schedule to cover nearly every interscholastic competition. We wore a modest uniform: painter's pants and royal blue sweaters.

But there were glitches. Few boys showed interest in joining the squad. The plan to cheer at girls' games and at track meets fizzled out. We worked hard and had fun, but we were not especially graceful or synchronized. Indeed, from the

Continued on page 145 ...

Bethany was not exempt from "Hoosier Hysteria."
Photo: 1977 *Witmarsum*

A spirited pep rally. Photo: 1979 *Witmarsum*

cheerleading experiment, other issues appeared in the *Reflector.* Letters to the editor questioned how fans should behave at an Anabaptist-Mennonite high school and how appropriate the use of "Braves" was for a mascot. Interscholastic sports also came in for their share of questioning. Participation in these competitions between schools had begun in 1965, but some still wondered whether they involved too much time, too much money, and too much emphasis on competition and winning.

In November 1974 and again in December 1977, the *Reflector* published lengthy spreads exploring this issue, with a number of students and coaches providing their perspectives. Whether pro or con, the framework for the discussion was, "How best can we live out our Christian values in this area?" The goal was not to woo spectators or to win at all costs, but to participate in sports in a way that was consistent with the purpose of the school. Interscholastic sports were seen as consistent with these goals when kept in a proper balance with academics—and when athletes were developing their skills and learning to work with their

... the framework ... was, 'How best can we live out our Christian values in this area?'

teammates, showing good sportsmanship, and demonstrating good interactions with other area schools. Athletics fit the school's commitment to developing the whole person—heart, mind, *and* body.

Evaluating the school

From the beginning Bethany has emphasized both academic excellence and Christian discipleship. Knowing how to evaluate these two threads is not as obvious as it might appear at first glance. One source of evaluative criteria has been the State of Indiana, which granted Bethany a first-class license during its second year of operation. This was the top certification and meant that the school met all the state requirements for institutions of secondary education and that the state would review its license only every several years. With this recognition the school had reached a benchmark of validation of its claims for academic excellence.

In May 1976 the state moved the school to a continuous commission. This meant that the school was still accredited, but that some of the state requirements were in question and the license would be reviewed annually. The Board was naturally concerned about the shift, but Bill Hooley called for another perspective.[22]

The state requirements covered a range of issues, from teacher certification to curriculum to physical plant concerns, such as how many square feet the school had, the number of urinals, and the type of lighting. While many of these requirements were good, they did not really touch the heart of education. And they left no leeway for special circumstances. In the state's eyes, for example, a teacher like Irene Gross

Hartzler-Miller ... *cont. from page 144*

perspective of some Bethany supporters, we were just plain embarrassing. When it comes to athletics and cheerleading, we were told, Bethany shouldn't try to be so different from the public high schools.

Hooley wanted the school to be critiqued by the church, not just the state ...

Clockwise from left: Donna Minter '76, Bonnie Miller, Gretchen Metzler '77, Diane Leatherman '77, Ronda Miller, Shigeru Toda, Valerie Davis '76, and two unidentified students. Photo: 1976 Witmarsum

Tim Ovaska '78 and Mike Troyer '78 clean gutters for the 1977 work day. Students voted to use the proceeds toward a new heating system fund.

Photo: 1978 *Witmarsum*

Bethany was debt free for the first time in its history ...

was under-qualified, since she did not have a teaching certificate. It had no way to recognize that she was nonetheless an excellent teacher and countless students could testify to the love of languages and knowledge of German that she gave them. Hooley was not willing to lose a teacher like Gross simply to meet state criteria.

Hooley wanted the school to be critiqued by the church, not just the state, and over a range of categories pertinent for a church school, not primarily on the basis of the school's physical plant. He was pleased when in 1979 the faculty agreed to a year-long extensive self-study, using materials provided by the Mennonite Secondary Education Council. Mennonite Board of Education suggested 15 biblical themes for evaluating schools, which faculty members used to assess the school's curriculum, its written philosophy of education, and their own expectations about teaching at Bethany. Committees met to examine such areas as the school's organization, instructional program, faculty life, student life, and resources. The work and the resulting 100-page report provided a solid foundation to draw on as the school moved into the eighties.[23] By looking to the denomination as well as the state for evaluative criteria, the school sought a balanced approach to the evaluation of its two threads, the sacred and the secular.

Getting ready for the eighties

In June 1979 Bethany celebrated its twenty-fifth anniversary, just five years after the school's continued existence had been deemed uncertain and precarious. But those five years had seen dramatic changes. Bethany's twenty-fifth year, 1978-79, was a high point for the school in a number of ways. In June 1978 the debt-liquidation drive came to a successful conclusion. Bethany was debt free for the first time in its history, a moment celebrated by banner headlines in the *Reflector* and *Gospel Evangel*. During that summer the Board purchased 15 acres east of the school, realizing that if the school ever wanted to expand in any way, it would need this land. The school year began with a capacity enrollment of 265, the highest it had been in 11 years, with waiting lists of young people who had to be turned away.

Relationships with Conference congregations were thriving, and student and faculty morale was high.

The picture was bright, but there were also signs of trouble ahead. As soon as the debt was liquidated, the school plunged into long-overdue improvements. The nationwide energy crisis was causing heating bills to soar, and Bethany's building, with little insulation, lots of glass, and individual propane heaters in each classroom, was not designed for such a situation. In the summer of 1978 the north wing was insulated and re-roofed. In the summer of 1979 an extensive retrofitting began. Smaller double-glazed windows replaced the large plate glass windows; the project also included insulated walls and a new vestibule and central heating. This left the school in much improved physical condition, but with the creeping return of financial problems. Income was up significantly, with the higher enrollment and the raises in tuition. Contributions from patrons and congregations were strong. But the school was having difficulty raising capital funds, and cash flow was not good—problems that would lead to increasing difficulties in the eighties.

Despite the hints of another cycle of financial trouble ahead, the school was in good shape for facing the eighties. Bethany had made the transition from the low point of the seventies. The students, faculty, and Conference had caught Hooley's vision for the school, leading to a clarified sense of mission and identity. Relationships between the school and Conference were much better. The faculty was functioning well as a team, and students were eager to work with them. Day-to-day problems would always arise, financial difficulties would reoccur, but the school was ready to face them together.

Kim Shank '79 demonstrates her bubble-blowing prowess. Photo: 1976 *Witmarsum*

Notes

1. Sources used in this chapter, not otherwise listed, may be found in the following collections of the Archives of the Mennonite Church (AMC): I-5-8, Box 2, 2-5-1, Box 3, I-3-3.5, Box 32, I-5-8, Box 5, and II-5-1, Box 3. (See also Robert Baker, "Boarded Up," *Gospel Evangel,* Jan.-Feb., 1975: 7-8.)

2. William D. Hooley, personal interview by writer, August 3, 2001.

3. William D. Hooley, "Mind and Heart in a Mennonite High School (1)," *Gospel Herald,* November 12, 1974: 879-880.

4. Hooley interview.

5. Royal Bauer, Levi Miller, Allen Peachey, Dan Schrock, group interview of former administrators and teachers by Becky Bontrager Horst and writer, September 11, 2001.

6. Wilmer Hollinger, personal interview by writer, June 8, 2001.

7. Herb Maust, personal interview by writer, August 15, 2001.

8. Roy S. Koch, personal interview by writer, July 23, 2001.

9. Robin Slabaugh, personal interview by writer, November 11, 2001.

10. Irene Gross, Roy Hartzler, Diane Schrock Hertzler, Allen Peachey, Patricia "Trish" Yoder, group interview by Bryan and Anita Yoder Kehr and writer, August 18, 2001.

11. Gross, Hartzler, Schrock Hertzler, Peachey, Yoder interview.

12. Gross, Hartzler, Schrock Hertzler, Peachey, Yoder interview.

13. *Reflector,* May 28, 1974.

14. Gross, Hartzler, Schrock Hertzler, Peachey, Yoder interview.

15. Everett Thomas, personal interview by writer, fall 2001.

16. Hooley interview.

17. Ethnic demographic statistics are not available for this time period. These percentages are based on examination of the schools' yearbooks.

18. Susan Mark Landis, e-mail to writer.

19. Hollinger interview.

20. Lyn Schlabach Buschert, Bryan and Anita Yoder Kehr, Brenda Hostetler Meyer, Paul and Kathy Meyer Reimer, group interview with BCHS alumni, by writer, August 24, 2001.

21. Nina Lanctot, personal interview by writer, November 11, 2001.

22. Hooley interview.

23. Bethany Christian High School, Goshen, Indiana, Report of Self-Study, April 3, 1980, from BCHS office.

Anita Yoder Kehr

Bzp T. Kehr

How Firm a Foundation

by Bryan and Anita Yoder Kehr

Bethany hallway, 1983. Photo: BCS files

What does it take to pursue faithfulness in the midst of financial crisis? The experience of Bethany Christian High School in the 1980s provides one answer to that question. The threefold nature of faithfulness in a Christian school—the faithfulness of faculty, administration and board members, as well as the desire to nurture faithfulness in students—became clarified and distilled during this period of fiscal trial. The eighties began with serious financial concerns from shortfalls in the operating budget and a crippling debt load remaining from the retrofitting project. Remedies to the school's indebtedness included potentially demoralizing reductions in program and employment levels as well as increases in tuition. However, because of the school personnel's strong commitment to Bethany's mission, the eighties also inaugurated a period of stability, consolidation, and professional growth and development for the school. The faculty united in support of the administration's vision of Christian education, and the average tenure for teachers actually lengthened. A three-part study, *Making a Good School Better,* provided a blueprint for defining the school's mission, reviewing the curriculum,

Above, left: Tug-of-war during school opening get-acquainted activities.

Photo: BCS files; enrollment chart: Nov./Dec. 1986 *Bulletin*

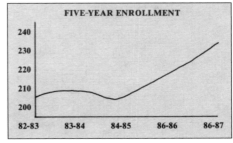

... the eighties ... inaugurated a period of stability, consolidation, and professional growth ...

Left: Jim Buller's '71 BCHS senior picture. Above: Jim—as a mathematics teacher at Bethany ten years later—talks with John Kolb '84.

Photos: 1971 & 1981 *Witmarsums*

An era of transition demanded a renewed vision for the next leg of the Bethany community's journey of faith.

guiding professional improvement for faculty, and developing new ways to nurture the spiritual formation of students.

The faithfulness and commitment of faculty and administration yielded fruit. Students now attended Bethany because they wanted to be there. And by the end of the decade, with enthusiastic community support, Bethany built a gymnasium of sufficient size to host the entire range of high school athletic events, renovated the old gym to become a chapel and performance center, and added new music rooms. Energy, excitement, cohesion, and commitment marked Bethany Christian High School during the eighties.

However, in the early nineties both new and recurring obstacles began to impede Bethany's growth. With the end of the capital campaign and the resignation of Everett Thomas as development director, Bethany again entered a period of fiscal unsteadiness as its operating deficit increased rapidly while the enrollment cycle began a downward trend. Just before the Persian Gulf War of 1991 erupted, the Northern Indiana community noticed that Bethany did not fly the national flag, which created an extended controversy in the *Goshen News*. The dedication for the entire building project took place in January 1991, but within two weeks of that happy event, Bethany student Kari Nunemaker was abducted and murdered. Moreover, the curricular innovations that strengthened the program of the school also required more commitment from faculty. The rate of faculty turnover increased again, in part because of the added responsibilities and in part because of an aging faculty. An era of transition demanded a renewed vision for the next leg of the Bethany community's journey of faith.

Deep waters

Bethany began borrowing money regularly in the early eighties to meet operating expenses and to pay debts. Although the retrofitting project of the late seventies began only after the school had received pledges of $45,000 toward its completion,

the school had only received $9,600 by 1980. And although the project received a federal grant of $47,000, substantially reducing the principal of the loan, and even though significant savings in energy won the school a National Energy Award in October 1983, the project's loan at 11 percent interest created a heavy burden of monthly payments. Inflation, economic recession, and declining enrollment, partly due to the area's smaller high-school-aged population,[1] also exacerbated the problem.

The budget shortfalls became severe enough to affect the program of the school. Elective classes with low enrollments were largely eliminated. (One group of students, however, found a way to continue the elective of their choice. In 1981-82, after the drama and speech class was removed from the curriculum, nine seniors joined together and hired their own drama instructor, Don Yost. While they received no credit because the school had not hired him, they did receive the teaching they sought.) The industrial arts program experienced severe enough cuts so that by the early nineties only one section of general shop remained from a program that had once included welding, building trades, small engine repair, and mechanical drawing.

The faculty faced corresponding reductions in their contracts. As the number of classes decreased, so did their workload. Administrators also shared the cost-cutting burden and decreased their own contracts. By the 1983-84 school year, 77 percent of the professional staff served on a part-time status. The financial future of Bethany did not seem promising.

Above: Maria Lehman '82, Joe Lehman '82, and Lisa Roth '82—three of nine seniors who paid for their own drama class after it was cut from the 1981-82 curriculum.

Left: 1980-81 Peace Society members Linda Hochstetler '82, Starla Graber '81, and Todd Friesen '81 wrap newspapers for recycling.
Photos: 1981 & 1982 *Witmarsums*

Inflation, economic recession, and declining enrollment ... also exacerbated the problem.

Bill Hooley
Photo: 1982 *Witmarsum*

These conversations ... also nurtured a sense of partnership between congregation and school.

Sanctified distress

Despite this rather bleak picture, the strong partnership between church, home, and school provided a solid foundation for making creative long-term plans to strengthen and enrich Bethany. In his 1981 report to the Board titled "Proposal for Balancing Program and Resources," Superintendent Bill Hooley outlined steps that he and the administrative team were taking to address the fiscal challenges. Members of the Bethany Advisory Council received questionnaires to assess attitudes relative to Bethany in their congregations. John Zook, who served as director of admissions and counselor, and Hooley (then superintendent) hosted a series of breakfasts to which they invited local pastors. Subsequent to these breakfasts, during the fall of 1981, Hooley and Zook asked the pastors to give specific help in addressing the long-term challenges of the school. They responded to a range of questions, including projections of their congregation's financial support to Bethany as well as the number of students their congregations might send. How might Bethany attract a higher percentage of local Mennonite students? Should it more actively recruit non-Mennonite students? How could the school's academic and extracurricular program be balanced with resources? How might Bethany initiate a tuition partnership program with congregations? These conversations between school administrators and church pastors yielded more than a collection of suggestions and ideas; they also nurtured a sense of partnership between congregation and school. In his summary Zook observed that

- The philosophies, purpose, and programs of BCHS are congruent with the values of nearly all the local Mennonite pastors, and
- BCHS at this time enjoys the goodwill and moral support of virtually all the local pastors.[2]

The Bethany administration also invited parents, students, faculty, and staff to become partners in addressing the short-term and long-term challenges facing the school. Parents received a questionnaire in the fall of 1980 to help the administration develop long-term plans to strengthen Bethany's viability. Hooley gave a chapel talk in October 1980 outlining the challenges facing the congregations and school, and he invited students to participate in finding solutions to the problems. In late October Hooley met with all of the faculty and staff to give details of the fiscal situation and a plan to adjust the program to balance with resources. Following the group meeting, he held conferences with all faculty and staff to discuss with each the proposed adjustments and their individual impact. He also asked each person to become part of the solution to the current problem. And to explore ways to boost enrollment, Hooley appointed a committee including Zook (administration), Diane Schrock and Dan Bodiker (teaching faculty), and Jeff Strasser and Linda Hochstetler (students). In all of these settings, Hooley stressed his commitment to maintain a sound, high quality educational program that also nurtured faith.

Jeff Strasser '83; Linda Hochstetler '82
Photos: 1981 *Witmarsum*

Strengthened, helped, and caused to stand

By the early eighties Hooley had gathered a team of deeply committed teachers and administrators to serve Bethany. "I was always in recruitment mode," he noted, "looking for people who could serve Bethany well."[3] Partly as a result of the participatory approach to meeting the challenges, faculty members embraced their partnership with the administration in carrying out the school's mission, in spite of the financial restrictions. A group of faculty colleagues—Irene Gross, Roy Hartzler, Diane Schrock Hertzler, Al Peachey, and Trish Yoder—remarked on the spirit that impelled them in the early eighties.[4] They felt affirmed, inspired, and freed to teach in order to fulfill the vision of Christian education and nurture at Bethany.

In fact faculty stability marked the eighties. Twice-yearly faculty retreats developed both their relationships with one another and their professional skills. A fall retreat immediately prior to opening, aimed to inspire and prepare the faculty

Photo: 1985 *Witmarsum*

... faculty members embraced their partnership with the administration in carrying out the school's mission ...

Top: Trish Yoder taught PE and health and coached girls' volleyball and basketball from 1981-88. Bottom: John Zook served as guidance counselor, 1978-97. Photo: 1981 *Witmarsum*

Above: Trish Yoder (second from right) shares her personal journey before a faculty meeting, one of the ways faculty built camaraderie. With Yoder are Everett Thomas, Eileen Becker-Hoover, and Diane Schrock.
Photo: 1982 *Witmarsum*

Left: Retreats were also a part of the Bethany faculty family tradition. Taking part in table games at Brunk's Cabin in 1965 are (clockwise from left) Marilyn (Vernon, Spanish) Yoder; Paul Nisly, English; Royal Bauer, librarian; Evelyn Bauer, art; "unidentified"; Laura Metzler, secretary; and Moses "Moe" Miller, custodian.

Below: In 1965, homemade ice cream was a part of retreat tradition. Wilmer Hollinger holds the dasher while Ron Friesen scrapes it and Vernon Yoder takes a taste.
Photos: 1966 *Witmarsum*

for each new school year. A second, mid-year retreat served a purely social function as faculty and their families came together for recreation and respite.

The Bethany faculty became a close-knit group with a continuing sense of camaraderie. Among Mennonite Secondary Education Council (MSEC) schools of this period, Bethany's faculty had the lowest annual rate of turnover, 5 percent from 1982 to 1987, compared with an 18 percent average for the other MSEC schools.[5] Hartzler and Schrock Hertzler recall the biennial MSEC gatherings as times when the Bethany faculty became aware of their extraordinary cohesiveness; both admit—reluctantly—to some degree of smugness during those meetings.

In the early eighties, because of a talented, committed faculty, and in spite of the financial constraints, the administrative team began to dream about ways to make a good school even better—a task that would include support and nurture of the faculty. Through formal study and visionary thinking, administrators also guided the development of a mission statement, a reworking of the curriculum, an enrichment of teaching styles and methods, and a restructuring of the school's organization.

Beginning in 1981-82 the administration instituted a systematic process of curriculum review, for the first time integrated into the ongoing activities of the school. Hartzler served as the first appointed faculty member to oversee the process of examining, subject by subject, the Bethany curriculum. The appointment and support of faculty members to lead this effort reflects the nature of the Bethany culture. In contrast to many school systems, where specialists develop curriculum and teachers implement it, at Bethany a teacher became part-time administrator and served as a facilitator to engage faculty members of each curricular area in reviewing and revising curriculum. Later, faculty members received stipends to work on curriculum review and development during the summer. The partnership promoted creativity and dreaming, and also produced ownership in the courses offered at Bethany. It also significantly increased the workload of faculty members whose subject area was being examined in a given school year.

The first two years of the review yielded two changes in the curriculum to clarify and expand the academic expectations of students. In June 1983 the school approved a seven-class schedule instead of a six-class schedule and, in June 1984, it adopted a standard of 19 minimum graduation requirements, encompassing basic practical skills for the world of work as well as for citizenship and Christian discipleship.

In addition to this, the administrative team took three successive leaves during the mid-eighties for the "good of the school." Zook received the first leave of absence from regular duties in the 1984-85 school year. It was during this year that the faculty adopted the "Ten Guiding Principles for Bethany Christian High School," written by Hooley (see page 161). With these as evaluative standards, Zook led the Bethany community in analyzing the school's overall mission and asking all faculty members to "revise their course activities, objectives, and plans so that we do indeed have a unified and concerted effort that will help us achieve our learning goals and mission."[6] The Bethany mission statement's primary purpose of

Above: Roy Hartzler taught chemistry and physics from 1976-97. Photo: 1981 *Witmarsum*

Below: 1982 graduates. Photo: 1983 *Witmarsum*

The partnership promoted creativity and dreaming ...

Diane Schrock Hertzler (left) leads a frosh SALT group for Eric Yordy, Joe Berry, Rhonda Hochstetler, and two unidentified students, all from the class of 1990.   Photo: 1988 *Witmarsum*

The Bethany mission statement's primary purpose of 'encouraging and enabling each student to become a more informed, skilled, and compassionate disciple within the church of Jesus Christ' now became the controlling force for the curriculum.

Mary Swartley
Photo: 1984 *Witmarsum*

"encouraging and enabling each student to become a more informed, skilled, and compassionate disciple within the church of Jesus Christ"[7] now became the controlling force for the curriculum.

Another specific result of this study was the implementation of the SALT (Serving And Learning Together) and PEPPER (Persons Engaged in Private Enriching Reading) programs. These programs—SALT for freshmen and sophomores, PEPPER for juniors and seniors—brought small groups of students and faculty together to engage in activities, based on Zook's work, to foster personal development and group interaction skills.

Mary Swartley examined the classroom instruction at Bethany during the 1985-86 school year. To gain another perspective, she visited 20 schools that the U. S. Department of Education deemed exemplary. Through chapels, interaction with faculty and students, and a written report, Swartley conveyed ways of developing effective pedagogical skills and thus a more effective school.

Hooley took the third leave during the study for the betterment of the school during the 1986-87 school year, focusing on structures that would best promote faculty development as well as the overall health of the school community. Hooley's study put in place structures for regular feedback between the teachers and principal, made recommendations to increase faculty members' time to prepare for classes, and included a system to help faculty identify professional and personal goals. These recommendations emerged from the desire to promote faculty development and monitor the health of the school.

Curricular review and innovations continued throughout this period, with faculty given contracted time for the work. In 1987-88 an ad hoc study group reviewed Bethany's work with students needing special help. The group's recommendations included a commitment to strengthen the existing program of support without beginning a special education program, at least in the immediate future. In 1993-94 Marisa Yoder and Roy Hartzler developed a new program for hands-on environmental education. Yoder later won the National Conservation

Ten Guiding Principles for Bethany Christian High School
by Bill Hooley

1. **Centrality of Christ**

   Christ's teachings and life shall guide our personal lives and set a standard for our teaching, school activities, and administrative structures.

2. **Centrality of students**

   Serving students is our primary purpose; therefore, the school program shall be designed to be responsive to each student's needs.

3. **Every student a learner**

   All students can learn and grow; the time and energy of teachers shall be given appropriately so that each student can achieve maximum growth and productivity.

4. **Community of cooperation**

   Faculty and administrators shall model a community of cooperation, mutual support, and accountability. Learning experiences shall be designed to help students experience and become committed to a community of cooperation.

5. **Educating the whole person**

   Schooling shall encourage intellectual, personal, spiritual, social, and physical growth. All students shall be known well enough by at least one faculty member that they can be challenged and guided in each of these areas.

6. **Integrated learning**

   Teachers shall design learning experiences that integrate their own subjects with other academic disciplines as well as with life in general.

7. **Students as workers**

   Each student shall be an active worker rather than a passive recipient of knowledge, and classroom learning experiences shall be structured accordingly.

9. **Future look**

   The curriculum shall lean toward the future rather than the past. The past shall be used to understand the present and to respond appropriately to the future.

10. **Teacher as coach and model**

    Teachers shall not only be specialists in an academic subject, but shall also be skilled in creating a healthy, effective learning environment in which they serve as coaches and mentors.

    —Adopted December 20, 1984; condensed by Becky Bontrager '71 Horst

Above: Rhoda Keener works with juniors Matt Fisher '89 and Pete Carpenter '89. Inset: Rhoda Shenk '69.

Photos: 1988 & 1969 *Witmarsums*

The 1981-82 Chamber Singers became a small congregation in the fall production of Martyrs Mirror. Photo: 1982 *Witmarsum*

Secondary Teacher of the Year Award from the National Association of Conservation Districts in recognition of the course's innovative approach to experiencing and learning about the physical world.

A foundation laid for faith

The students of this period, while exhibiting the normal developmental cycles of high school students, were in general highly motivated and committed to Bethany. The admissions policy implemented in the seventies mandated that students would not be admitted unless they themselves wanted to attend Bethany, a policy which in turn fostered deeper commitment to the school. Students continued to receive a quality academic education at Bethany, now enhanced by regular curriculum review. The new SALT and PEPPER programs enabled more direct faculty mentoring of intentional small groups.

Along with these innovations, some programs were ending. Life teams, small groups of students who developed and performed inspirational programs in Indiana-Michigan churches, gradually decreased in number and finally were discontinued in the 1989-90 school year. The Student Body Association (SBA) Banquet, which usually featured a meal prepared with the help of exchange students, ended as well, this time after one meal at which students rebelled against the food offered. A second, and final, production of the opera, *Martyrs Mirror,* took place in November 1981. Once again the program involved the cooperation of the entire school community— students, faculty, and administration—as well as the local church community, this time with Yellow Creek Mennonite Church providing the venue.

A shift away from classes in the "practical arts" took place during the eighties, at least partly based on financial constraints. In November 1983 Lester

Culp's farm management class hosted a "Farm Day," which included "a special chapel service and a tractor drive-in. All teachers and students were invited to express solidarity with the concerns and issues faced by farmers."[8] Later in the decade, this class would become a casualty of budget cutting. Other classes—industrial arts, home economics, and agriculture—were cut because their enrollments fell below the criterion of seven students, a standard implemented by administration and faculty as a way to make sound economic decisions about curricular offerings. For example, by the early nineties Bethany offered only one high school woodworking class.

Some programs continued and expanded. Interterm remained an annual highlight that each year gave students opportunities to engage in a wide variety of learning experiences both on and off campus. Faculty continued to provide leadership for this program and to find ways to do as much as possible while costing students and their parents as little as possible.

The annual Spring Arts Festival, established in the late seventies, provided a venue to recognize a whole range of student work, from fine-crafted woodwork to

John Zook: The corn picker

In March 1984, a Bethany interterm group led by Dr. Carl Yoder and me went to Mendenhall, Mississippi, to work at Mendenhall Ministries. The organization was founded by John Perkins to meet some of the physical, social, and spiritual needs of the impoverished African-American population of Simpson County. Racism and segregation still reigned there, even though federal law had mandated integration of the county schools. In fact, because Robin Bryant '84, an African-American student, was part of the interterm group, students were warned by local folks not to cross the tracks into the white section of town.

Some students dismantled the interior of an abandoned building in order to make it suitable for a new school facility. Some students husked corn that had been handpicked the previous fall on a small farm owned by the Ministries. After husking those piles of corn, several students who came from farming families came to believe that a mechanical corn picker would be a great asset to the farm. Upon returning to Bethany, the interterm students were successful in raising money and buying a two-row picker at Goshen Implement Company for $2,000. Later in the spring, Kevin Kauffman '85, Carl Bontrager '86, and David Bornman '86, with the assistance of a parent, delivered the picker to Mendenhall.

With some of the 500 bushels of corn they husked on their 1984 Mississippi interterm (left to right): Lisa Nunemaker '86, Sharman Miller '84, Susan Schmidt '85, and Greg Newswanger '84. Photo: Fall '84 *Bulletin*

In Goshen, with the used corn picker they purchased, are Carl Bontrager '86, David Bornman '86, "unidentified", Lisa Nunemaker '86, and Greg Newswanger '84. Photo: Fall '84 *Bulletin*

Devon Schrock taught English and served as
Reflector *advisor, 1977-99.*
Photo: 1981 *Witmarsum*

*During Spring Arts Festival '84,
woodworking instructor Wilbur
Hershberger (right) talks with Larion
Swartzendruber, who taught the class
from 1970-75.* Photo: 1984 *Witmarsum*

**Spring Arts Day soon became
a celebrated annual tradition
at Bethany.**

paintings and photography, to small-group performance. However, with many of the woodworking classes failing to meet enrollment requirements, the practical arts displays gradually diminished. But planning soon began for a new way to emphasize the arts.

Mary Swartley, business teacher, and J. D. Smucker, choir director, had both experienced a special arts day at Christopher Dock Mennonite High School in Eastern Pennsylvania. The day-long event focused on musical and dramatic performance and writing, while maintaining a visual arts component. A faculty committee, including Swartley, Smucker, and Devon Schrock, English teacher, began to research the possibilities and lay the foundation for the first Spring Arts Day, to be held in 1991. The regular schedule was suspended for the day, and students competed as classes (freshmen, sophomores, juniors, seniors) in a variety of categories, including drama, poetry, and readings as well as vocal and instrumental music. Spring Arts Day soon became a celebrated annual tradition at Bethany.

Bethany students also entered another new arena of competition. In 1987 Rhoda Keener coached the first Bethany teams to compete in the Hoosier Academic Superbowl. Bethany won state titles in three subject areas and that year established a winning tradition that would claim more than 15 Academic Superbowl State Championships throughout the eighties and nineties.

There was also change and expansion in athletic competition. New additions to the program included boys' golf (spring 1989), softball (spring 1990), girls' tennis (spring 1991), and boys' tennis (fall 1992). The tennis courts were built with the aid of an anonymous gift during the spring of 1992. The track program ended after the

89 season when the old cinder track became a parking lot in consequence of the building addition (see below).

Bethany students experienced unprecedented athletic success in the eighties. Some highlights include a 1980 volleyball sectional championship, a 1983 cross country team that was undefeated in dual meets, a sectional baseball championship in 87, the capture of multiple Northern Indiana Soccer Conference Championships, and regularly competitive basketball teams. From 1980 to 1993 the school awarded 20 teams an "outstanding" designation, defined as having a winning record of 70 percent or better. Those outstanding teams included the boys' cross country team (1983), girls' cross country (1986), boys' basketball (1986-87, 1987-88, 1988-89, 1989-90, 1990-91, 1991-92), boys' soccer (1986, 1987, 1990, 1991, 1992, 1993), girls' basketball (1987-88, 1988-89), baseball (1987, 1988), volleyball (1989), and girls' tennis (1991).

Perhaps partly as a result of this success, the idea of building a gym, which had circulated for many "homeless" years of traveling near and far to "home" basketball games, began to take on new life in the Bethany community. The building program became the central marker of Bethany's vitality in the eighties and into the very early nineties.

Expansion as a rite of passage

A full-sized gymnasium, now dubbed the "Mennolands," did indeed come into being. And, in addition, Bethany expanded by two acres west of the "Big Four" railroad tracks (where tennis courts were eventually built) and developed softball, baseball, and soccer fields east of the tracks. New rehearsal rooms gave added space to the growing music program. The old gym became a chapel and performance center, while the old chapel became a new and larger library. After more than 35 years, Bethany no longer needed to borrow or rent facilities to hold its basketball contests, musical concerts, and graduations. The expansion of Bethany's building did more than add space; it served as a rite of passage.

The dream of having a full-sized gym had lived among students and alumni for

The 1987 Academic Superbowl team.
Front: Mark Yoder '90 and Eric Yordy '90.
Back: Heather Kropf '90, Coach Rhoda Keener,
and Lisa Stauffer '90. Photo: BCS files

Bethany students experienced unprecedented athletic success in the eighties.

Jay Little '84 runs for the cross country team. Photo: 1984 *Witmarsum*

many years. However, during the 1985-86 school year, the administration took the first step in fulfilling that dream by setting up a facilities study committee, comprising both professional and nonprofessional, both Bethany and other-than-Bethany people: Vernon Birky, Cecil Bontreger '64, Harvey Chupp, Luetta Friesen, Dwight Grieser '61, Bill Hooley, Suzanne Kauffman, Herb Maust, Wilmetta Maust '59, Robert Miller, Al Peachey, Sandra Riegsecker, David Schwartzentruber '77, Miriam Stauffer, Phyllis Stutzman '60, Larion Swartzendruber, and Burl Troyer '62. The committee's purpose was to assess the long-term facility needs of the school. In 1986 Everett Thomas became director of development and with other administrators began to seek the counsel of local pastors with regard to expanding facilities. Early in 1987 the Indiana-Michigan Mennonite Conference heard a report and reviewed a building proposal to give feedback in the early planning stages. The project's momentum increased when in May 1987 Bethany received its gift of the two acres west of the railroad tracks. At its June 1987 meeting the Bethany Board formally passed a resolution to build, if enough money could be raised. Bob and

By the eighties cheerleaders had become athletes too.
Photo: 1984 *Witmarsum*

In only their third year of competition, the 1986 girls' cross country team lost just one meet all season. Photo: 1987 *Witmarsum*

ue Miller served as co-chairs of the capital fund campaign, which began with an initial goal of raising 80 percent of the amount required. An anonymous donor challenged alumni to contribute to the project by promising to match donations up to $250,000 dollar for dollar. Another anonymous donor gave $500,000 as an endowment for the project. The project received enough money by September 1988 to allow the seeking of bids. Groundbreaking took place in November 1988.

A setback to the project came with a January 2, 1988, announcement that the anticipated cost of the building project had leapt from the initially projected $1.5 million to $3.1 million, due to incorrect cost projections. However, successful fundraising continued with increasing community enthusiasm. In May 1989 Jane Stoltzfus '71 Buller spearheaded an "alumni fundraising weekend" that brought in $35,000. The effort began with a variety show and ended with a dinner, an auction, and entertainment. The auction sold new and used items, but the highlight was the sale of Bill Hooley's beard. Hooley, who had worn a well-groomed, mustache-free beard for as long as nearly anyone could remember, had it shaved off during the

Hank Willems '89 controls the ball as he heads toward the goal. Photo: 1987 *Witmarsum*

Members of the 1987 baseball team explode in celebration after their sectional victory.
Photo: 1988 *Witmarsum*

1988-89 was the second consecutive winning season for girls' varsity basketball. Photo: 1989 *Witmarsum*

Jon Shenk '92 follows through on his golf swing. Photo: 1990 *Witmarsum*

Wilmetta Yoder '59 Maust served as secretary from 1977-94. Photos: 1959 & 1981 *Witmarsums*

The goal ... was realized in just two years through the constituency's great generosity.

Mary Mullet '60 Stutzman served as secretary from 1980-86. Photos: 1960 & 1981 *Witmarsums*

sale, where it attracted lively bidding at four different times and eventually raised a total of $6,050. The weekend of the first Spring Fest spurred alumni contributions well past the $250,000 challenge goal.

Phase I of the building project—the gym and its lobby and restrooms as well as the new athletic fields—was dedicated on Sunday, November 5, 1989. Five days prior to the dedication, Everett Thomas announced at the annual associates dinner that the full $3.3 million had been raised, meaning that Phase II—the renovation of the existing building—could proceed. The goal that had seemed nearly unattainable was realized in just two years through the constituency's great generosity.

The "real" dedication of the facility, however, came with the first interscholastic boys' basketball game held in Bethany's very own gym, large enough to host all of its athletic events, on November 17. Toilet paper rained down from the sold-out stands after junior Phil Friesen scored the first Bethany basket of the game against archrival Westview. Although Bethany lost the game 77-70, celebration reverberated. (One year later Bethany returned the favor by handing the Warriors a loss in the first game played in *their* new gym.) LeRoy Lambright, sports editor for the *Goshen News,* commented in his November 18, 1989, column that the

> grand opening of [Bethany's] sparkling new gymnasium [is] perhaps the most significant addition to the community of Waterford since a few daring Mennonite fathers had the foresight to create Bethany in the mid-50s. It's a giant step forward from the original candlelight gym in which Bethany athletes have at least practiced and sometimes played games in the past.[9]

With the money raised, Phase II began immediately, and its dedication took place in January 1991. Renovation of the old structure, which resulted in a much larger media center and a beautiful auditorium, would now infuse Bethany arts and academics with new life.

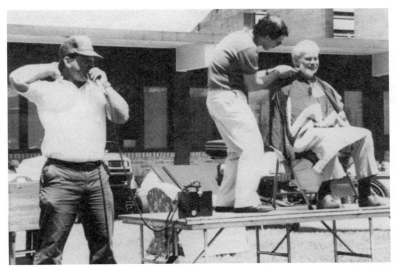

Auctioneer Dale Nunemaker '68 sold Bill Hooley's beard four times during the 1989 alumni auction, raising $6,050 toward the building. The beard is being removed by Goshen barber Tim Miller. Photo: Fall 1989 *Bulletin*

Participating in groundbreaking ceremonies in November 1988 for the new gymnasium are speaker Orville Yoder, Mennonite Board of Education assistant executive secretary; banker Ralph Gunden, Goshen Mayor Mike Puro; architect LeRoy Troyer; Indiana-Michigan Conference Minister Del Glick; fundraising chairs Bob and Sue Miller; Principal Bill Hooley; and Board President Norm Kauffmann. Photo: 1989 *Witmarsum*

Everett Thomas:
Building the church for tomorrow

In 1985 the Bethany Board decided it was time to address the problem of the school's inadequate gymnasium. As the Board planned, other facility issues emerged which needed attention. With everything added together, the total came to $3.3 million instead of the $1 million originally anticipated.

Fundraising began in earnest in 1987. The School Board resolved to delay groundbreaking until contributions or pledges covering 80 percent of the cost were received. Even so, by October 30, 1989, nearly 1,500 supporters gathered in the new gym to celebrate the accomplishment of the first phase of the project dedicated to "Building the Church for Tomorrow."

During an amazing two-month period in early 1988, we received nearly $2 million! Principal Bill Hooley and I would go to lunch with a supporter and get a check for $50,000. The next day we'd receive a letter from the Mennonite Foundation with notice that another contributor had given us $100,000. The next week we would receive a call that someone else would pledge $25,000. At the same time, we were receiving hundreds of smaller contributions and pledges from across the church. (See the brass donor tree in the current gymnasium lobby.) Those months in late winter and early spring were a kind of harvest. It felt like we were walking through an orchard with hands outstretched trying to catch all the ripe and glistening fruit dropping around us. Bethany's faithful service of more than 30 years yielded an abundance of goodwill and enabled the school to look ahead to many more.

**Jill K. Landis '94:
From Braves to Bruins**

I can't recall what sparked the conversations about changing the mascot. Was it cultural awareness, personal experience, or increased sensitivity? I was a sophomore at the time and a member of the committee that researched and later proposed the mascot be changed. My most vivid memories do not come from the boardroom ... but rather the process after the decision was made.

Our committee, assigned with the task of suggesting alternative mascots, called a spring convocation of the entire student body. Names, designs, and logos were cast onto the overhead screen, while "ughs," "ahs," and laughter trickled throughout the room. Bethany Beacons ... Bethany Bruins ... the choice was obvious.

As the decision to become "Bruins" went into effect, changes began to appear. An accidental "Braves" slipped out during cheers or team huddles and "Go, Bruins" at first sounded odd, but quickly the new name became familiar. Athletic teams benefited from the change by sporting new uniforms. Newspaper articles filtered through the *Goshen News*, and people from the community responded to the alteration with affirmation, wonderment, or confusion.

Though deciding to change our mascot didn't affect other community schools—no one else followed suit—it did something to us. More than anything, I think, changing our mascot offered a first-hand look into an aspect of Mennonite identity: one wrapped in alternative actions, concerned for the experiences of others, and willing to work toward change, even something as simple as changing from "Braves" to "Bruins."

Photo: 1993 *Witmarsum*

Looking ahead

The general success of the athletic program and the completion of the building project led to a renewed discussion about the propriety of the Bethany mascot: the "Braves." In October 1991 Isaac Wengerd '92 wrote a *Reflector* article raising the issue. The article reported interviews of several faculty members, including Athletic Director Al Peachey, who also expressed discomfort with the name Braves. The January 1992 School Board meeting created an ad hoc Bethany Mascot Study Committee, which reported its work at the May Board meeting, and at its June meeting the Board viewed a Mennonite Central Committee video, "Your Chiefs Are Peacemakers." It then acted formally to endorse a mascot change. At the beginning of the 1992-93 school year, Willie Kanagy (assistant principal, 1989-98) and Hooley gave a chapel presentation and discussed the issue with students, who were asked to select representatives to a mascot selection committee. In November 1992 the committee brought three options to the student body: the "Blazers"/"Trailblazers,"

Above: Everett Thomas unveils a banner announcing the gymnasium project is "On Time & Debt-Free!" as building chairpersons Bob and Sue Miller make the announcement.

Above right: Bethany's new gymnasium construction underway.

Photo above: 1990 *Witmarsum* Right: BCS files Campaign chart: Fall 1989 *Bulletin*

he "Bruins," and the "Royals." Students voted their preferences, and in January 1993 he School Board affirmed the vote of the student body to change the mascot to "Bruins."

Bethany also explored other kinds of expansion to its program. From the early eighties the question of whether to establish a middle school emerged periodically. Each time, after a period of study, the idea was laid to rest. In the early nineties an ad hoc study committee went so far as to conduct a survey of area congregations. The majority of the committee did not recommend the establishment of a middle school, and the Board agreed not to pursue the project. However, David Helmuth, a minority voice on the committee who could not attend the Board meeting when the committee reported its findings, sent a letter to Board President Lovina Rutt (January 4, 1993) in which he said, "I acknowledge that as a member of the last 'middle school committee,' which reported to the board ... I did interpret the gathered data differently than that of the majority point of view ... I believe a middle school is needed in order for BCHS to continue to be viable for the future."

1989 dedication service. Photo: BCS files

The original gym is renovated into a beautiful auditorium. Photo: BCS files

Rain of toilet paper. Photo: 1990 *Witmarsum*

New challenges

With the completion of the building project, the Bethany community hoped for continued growth in enrollment. However, as predicted by demographic studies from the mid-eighties, a lower pool of available students actually began to cause a

The flag, Part I: Coming down

One ordinary school morning in the mid-seventies the custodian, Ira Stoltzfus, came into the office to get the flag to hang on the pole in front of the school. As he was getting the flag, he

Ira Stoltzfus
Photo: 1973 *Witmarsum*

made some comment, half to himself, about the necessity of this daily chore. But Principal Levi Miller heard him and immediately responded, "I'd forget about putting the flag up; you don't have to do that any more." Ira looked at him quizzically to be sure he was serious, and then, seeing that he was, quietly put the flag back in the cupboard where it then remained. Bethany Christian lived with an empty flagpole for years and the pole became a daily reminder that Bethany Christian did not fly the flag.

It seems incredible now that there were no faculty comments, no student questions, and no board discussion at the time. It appeared to be a nonissue both within the school and in the community. It was more than a decade later that the school became embroiled in controversy because it did not display an American flag nor sing the national anthem before boys' basketball games.

—Bill Hooley

Donor tree in new gym lobby. Photo: BCS files

1992-93 season—Jason Birky '93. Photo: BCS files

1992-93 season—Karmen Riegsecker '92. Photo: BCS files

New gym gets mascot wall. Photo: BCS files

drop in enrollment. Then operating costs started to escalate, resulting in operating deficits. And in the year following the triumphant dedication of the gymnasium, the Northern Indiana community debated why or why not Bethany should fly the United States Flag.

The Iraqi invasion of Kuwait on August 2, 1990, led to an uneasy autumn season of increasing military preparedness (Operation Desert Shield). On November 30, 1990, before the actual onset of the Persian Gulf War on January 16, 1991, the opening salvo in the flag war was launched with a letter from Robert L. Hartsough of Ligonier, in which he decried the absence of the U. S. Flag and national anthem at a Bethany basketball game. Letters in support of and against Bethany's policy occupied the *Goshen News* for the next month and became the "Top '90 Letter Topic," with 17 individuals writing letters to the newspaper about the issue.

Another, very different kind of blow challenged Bethany in the next year. The completion of all the building additions and renovations was celebrated on Sunday, January 20, 1991. But the euphoria was followed quickly by tragedy. Kari Nunemaker, a Bethany sophomore, was abducted on January 28; her body was found on February 5. In the period between her abduction and discovery, the school community prayed and feared together. When the time came, they mourned and

Genevieve Miller '56 Kehr was head cook from 1977-88. Photos: 1956 & 1981 *Witmarsums*

1985-86 international students. Photo: 1986 *Witmarsum*

... the Northern Indiana community debated why or why not Bethany should fly the United States Flag.

**The flag, Part II:
Controversy**
The spirit of national patriotism bloomed during the Persian Gulf War of 1990-91. As a basketball team, we were not prepared to confront it so boldly in the context of sport. Three particular events in that season stand out in my memory.

The first one came in our third game of the season when a neighboring school came to play at the "Mennolands," the nickname of our gym. The visiting school brought fans with a boom box who loudly played and sang the national anthem while the teams warmed up, perhaps to make up for the anthem that Bethany does not play before sporting contests.

The second incident followed soon. This time the surprise came from an area Christian school where many of their fans held small flags on short sticks that they waved with enthusiasm while we were shooting free throws or in-bounding the basketball near them. This they did to make up for the flag that does not fly in front of Bethany's building.

The third incident happened after much discussion about Bethany's flag-and-
Continued on page 176 ...

Above: Justin Shank and Ken Keesling '95 work on benches for the Garden during interterm. Below: Friendship Garden. Photos: BCS files

The Friendship Garden ... became a tangible way for the Bethany community to remember and to grieve.

grieved together. Kari's death shocked the entire Elkhart County community. The Bethany community had experienced tragedy earlier in the eighties with the deaths of students Wendell Bontrager and Marcus Hershberger in an airplane accident, but the violent and inexplicable nature of Kari's abduction and murder led to a prolonged period of questioning and mourning. For the second year in a row, a news story with Bethany connections dominated the local media. The sanctity and security of the school community had been violated. The Friendship Garden, created in the courtyard of the school a year later, became a tangible way for the Bethany community to remember and to grieve.

While Bethany enjoyed the fruits of a stable faculty during the eighties, the late eighties and early nineties saw more turnover. Wilmer Hollinger noted that during his 20-year tenure at Bethany, his interaction with students in the mid-eighties was most satisfying in terms of cooperation, interest, and engagement. However, his faculty responsibilities also grew with activities like interterm, SALT, and PEPPER, and he was ready to leave after the 1985-86 school year. Some faculty members retired, including Royal Bauer, Lester Culp, and Mabel Nisley. Other long-time faculty left for more personal reasons. Marvin Yoder, who had provided an unprecedented period of stability for the Bible program, left

A litany for Friendship Garden
by Devon Schrock

From many diverse ways and places we gather here:
We come to dedicate this plot of ground,
This place of trees and shrubs and flowers and rocks,
This garden where life now lies hidden,
awaiting the spring.

Here we recall voices calling in the hallways of Bethany our
  school;
We hear the sound of laughter at lunchtime;
The quiet confidential talks while we sat leaning against our
  lockers;
and we remember also the tears we shed for her.

We come to dedicate this Friendship Garden as a place of
  friendship,
This Friendship Garden which prods our memories
and calls forth pain
as we remember one who has been a very special friend
and is now gone from us.
The plaque reads:

WATER GARDEN
in memory of
Kari Nunemaker
BCHS student
Dec. 2, 1974 - Jan. 29, 1991

Kari disappeared January 28, 1991.
Her body was found on February 5, 1991.
Her funeral was held February 8, 1991.

We come to remember and honor the work of many, students
  and teachers and parents and friends, who put hands
and feet in the earth, who laid these walks and made these
  plantings of phlox and potentilla and hyacinth and grass;
Here in this long-discarded place they have laid walks to
  circle and intersect, paths asking our choice to remain
  here or pass on.
But we pause here for another purpose:
We dedicate this now dormant plot of ground and this water
  garden, this place in the process of becoming as we are in
  the process of becoming:
To friendships now dormant, to friendships enduring,
And to friendships yet to be made.

And as the water here ripples constantly, may these our
  friendships ripple out and renew themselves and others.

And as those who gathered the materials to construct this
  garden created order from disorder and beauty where
  there had been emptiness, so may we gather here again
  and again,

To repose here perhaps under the arbor or the gazebo
  to observe and consider how living things follow creation's
  process in planting and nurturing.

And here we may come to receive the planting of God's
  Spirit,
To recreate and reorder our lives, to nourish our friendships
  and then depart.

We dedicate this water garden and these plantings and these
  walkways and these places of repose and delight to the
  continuation of our friendships and to the honor of God.

The flag, Part II ... *cont. from page 173*

anthem absences had already taken place in the opinion columns of the local newspaper. This time as we visited a local school, a young man with a large flag on a long pole ran to and fro behind the Bruins bench where players and coaches could hear the loud rustle and snapping of nylon.

We were uncomfortable that season. But the discomfort came as a result of principle: our allegiance was not to the flag nor to the nation it represented but to God.

—*Jim Buller*

to minister in other arenas. The face of the faculty was changing. The veteran teachers were beginning to move on; youth and new energy would affect the nature of the Bethany community.

With the completion of the building program, Everett Thomas, a long-time presence in the school, both as teacher and then administrator, also left Bethany, now to provide leadership to the Mennonite Board of Congregational Ministries. During the first two years after his departure, the Bethany fundraising efforts were less successful. Operating losses hit a high of $128,007 in 1990 with a close second in 1991 of $98,283. Notes payable by the end of 1993 totaled $313,354, up from $133,641 in 1982.

The combined impact of these events—declining enrollment, mounting debt, and increasing faculty turnover—signaled that Bethany was entering a time of transition. The eighties, however, had provided Bethany with a firm foundation for the future, with principles to guide the school, by a well-defined administrative style reflecting the spirit of Anabaptism, shown by a sense of community enveloping both faculty and students. The structure too was well-wrought and durable, designed to promote the interweaving of Christian faith and the pursuit of academic excellence. The years ahead might demand modification of these, but the core values would remain.

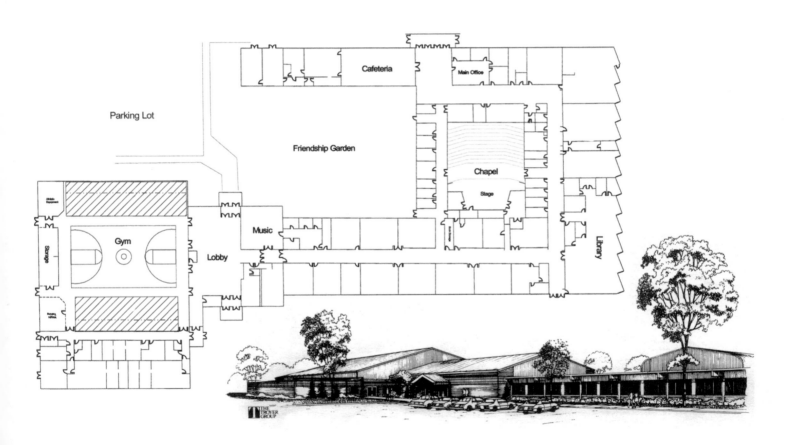

Parking Lot

Cafeteria

Main Office

Friendship Garden

Chapel

Stage

Gym

Storage

Music

Lobby

Library

THE TROYER GROUP

otes

. Bill Hooley, "Proposal for Balancing Program and Resources," (January 1981): 1-2. In his report, Hooley quotes two national publications, both of which projected lower secondary school enrollments in the 1980s. Indeed, the *Chronicle of Higher Education* report (January 7, 1980) projected that the number of high school graduates in Indiana would decline 26 percent between 1979 and 1995.

. Hooley, "Proposal," 38.

. Bill Hooley, interview by writers, August 3, 2001.

. Irene Gross, Roy Hartzler, Diane Schrock Hertzler, Allen Peachey, Patricia "Trish" Yoder, group interview by Sally Weaver Glick and writers, August 18, 2001.

. Bill Hooley, *Making a Good School Better,* "Enhancing Effectiveness and Accountability" (July 1987): 10-11.

. John Zook, *Making a Good School Better: A Summary Report of the First Year of Special Effort for Improvement at Bethany Christian High School*: 4-5.

. Zook, *Making A Good School Better,* Appendix A: 16.

. *Goshen News,* November 17, 1983.

. *Goshen News,* November 18, 1989.

2003-04 Board, seated: David Heusinkveld, Bob Steury, Eldon Heatwole, and Roger K. Miller. Standing: Ruth Miller Roth, Duane Stutzman, Jeanette Krabill, Randy Christophel, Fred Longenecker, Barb Slagel, and Marsha Hooley Miller.

Chapter 6

Building for the Future on the Past

1993-2004

by James R. Krabill

Above: 2003 Witmarsum, Vol. 49.
Left: Principal Allan Dueck.
Background: 2003 board-approved building plans.   Photos: BCS *Bulletin* (Fall 2003)

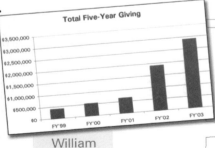

2002-03 Bethany Christian Middle School yearbook.

Jeff Bauman '03 and Eric Bixler '03.

2003 graduates Rachna Prakash, Rebecca Fath, and Kristine Bowman.
Commencement photos: 2003 *Witmarsum*

A 2001 survey of current Bethany high school students and recent alumni revealed that the national and global events making the biggest impression on students in the nineties were nearly all related in some way to tragedy, violence, or scandal. At the top of the list was the Columbine shooting incident, followed by the war in Kosovo, the Bush-Gore election dispute, Princess Di's tragic death, the Oklahoma City bombing, the Bill Clinton and O. J. Simpson trials, and the Monica Lewinsky scandal. This survey was conducted, it should be noted, before the September 11 World Trade Center attack and the subsequent "war on terrorism," or these events would have most certainly also rated high on student lists.

Yet despite—or perhaps because of—this rather dismal litany of world happenings, the children of the late nineties seemed to develop a keen sense of their generation's unique power and potential to make a difference in the world. According to Neil Howe and William Strauss in their book *Millennials Rising,* seven distinguishing traits best describe the "millennial generation"—those born in or after 1982. These children, say the authors, are special, sheltered, confident, team-oriented, achieving, pressured, and conventional. "Over the next decade," predicted Howe and Strauss in 2000, "the Millennial Generation will entirely recast the image of youth from downbeat and alienated to upbeat and engaged—with potentially seismic consequences for America."[1]

Peter Swartzentruber '03

... the children of the late nineties seemed to develop a keen sense of their generation's unique power and potential to make a difference in the world.

Above: 1993-94 choir. Photo: BCS files

Right: Board Chair Lovina Rutt presents a plaque to Bill Hooley. Photo: BCS files

'If John Steiner was the school's Abraham, William Hooley was its Moses.'

These events and circumstances then form the larger context in which Bethany found itself in the mid-to-late nineties as it prepared to leave one millennium and enter another. It was not particularly reassuring to realize that Bethany must make this journey without Bill Hooley, the school's faithful and trusted pastor-administrator, who had guided it with such great love and care through many troubled waters and for more years than most people could even remember.

Farewell to Bethany's "Moses"

"If John Steiner was the school's Abraham, William Hooley was its Moses," wrote Everett Thomas in his 1983 essay, "History of Bethany." For it was Hooley, says Thomas, who "reshaped the school's environment, objectives, faculty and the buildings themselves. He committed the school to being a servant of the church, and convinced the faculty and many students that BCHS must remain accountable to the [Indiana-Michigan] Conference."

Bill Hooley had the good fortune and blessing during his Bethany tenure to have received exceptionally strong support from three assistant administrators, each having uniquely complemented Hooley's academic leadership and his pastoral gifts. Two have already been discussed in previous chapters (Levi Miller and Everett Thomas); the first had worn the title of "principal" and the second "assistant principal." Then from 1989-98 Willie Kanagy served as "assistant principal." Kanagy brought an especially effective complement to Hooley. Well liked by both teachers and students, he was a man of the land, a farmer, teacher, and a person who provided consistent discipline with compassion to all students who came to his office. He gave the school strong supervision in its day-to-day functioning. By any measure, Kanagy was an outstanding administrator.

It was in the spring of 1994 that Hooley announced his resignation, effective at the end of the 1993-94 academic year. He had served for nearly a quarter of a century as Bethany's principal. "Looking back on 24 years of leadership at Bethany Christian High School and six additional years in other church schools, the strongest feeling that I have is deep gratitude," wrote Hooley in the school's spring 1994 *BCHS Bulletin*. "I have no regrets for having given 30 years of my professional life to church schools and I'd do it again!"

None of this, however, made it any easier to bid farewell to the school's "Moses." Hooley had been, in the words of Beth Yoder '95, a student writer for the May 1994 edition of the school's newspaper, "a constant fixture at BCHS." He had personally hired all but two of the 40-member faculty and staff serving Bethany at the time of his departure. He was, for much of the school's history, "the face" of the institution throughout the constituency, to the Goshen community, in Indiana-Michigan Mennonite Conference settings, and with the school's donors, supporters, friends, and alumni.

Mary Swartley served as interim principal, 1994-95. Photo: 1995 *Witmarsum*

The Bethany Board put in place a year-long search process for Hooley's replacement in late summer 1994, inviting nominations or applications up until November 1 of that year or "until the position is filled." Mary Swartley, completing her eighteenth year at Bethany as business teacher (also serving as half-time business manager the previous four years), was named interim principal for the 1994-95 academic year.

Swartley committed herself with great energy to the transitional task, stating from the outset her hope that "we may not miss a beat in carrying out the vision and mission of the school." In an inspiring editorial published in the fall 1994 *Bulletin,* Swartley spelled out Bethany's dual mission of providing "an excellent quality education" and encouraging and enabling students "in the development of Christian faith … I like to think of it as two distinctively different threads woven in a fabric," she wrote:

Global logo adopted
In 1992 a group of students was asked to write down in a few words what Bethany represented for them. After a period of brainstorming, the idea of global awareness developed. This grew to include global experience and appreciation, stewardship of global issues, and the development of a logo consisting of a globe held high by stick figures and encircled with the words: "church/home/school in partnership."

According to BCHS 1996 school records, over 60 percent of the school's alumni no longer lived in Northern Indiana, but in 49 states (none in Vermont) and 23 foreign countries spanning six continents.

—Adapted from BCHS Bulletin, *Vol. 41, No. 2 (Winter 1996)*

As threads in a woven fabric intersect at right angles to each other, so this dual mission of our school intersects at right angles … The mission of our school is the woof thread that weaves over and under the warp thread which represents the academic mission of our school … The warp threads prepare students for life in the twenty-first-century society, whereas the woof threads prepare students for life in God's kingdom. The warp threads help students acquire a positive self-identity, whereas the woof threads provide for students the view of themselves as Christians in a global community. Still further, the warp threads require that we model ourselves as an instructional institution that teaches English, history, math, science, arts, and skills. The woof threads require that we model ourselves after a community of Christian faith.

Hello, dolly! Director of Development Dennis Weaver '70 makes sure Cynthia Good Kaufmann gets to class on time.
Photo: 1995 *Witmarsum*

First day of school social. In front are Sosha Robinson and Tonya Swartzendruber '98. Photo: BCS files

1977 BCHS graduate Wes Bontreger returned to coach JV soccer from 1988-91 and also served on the Board, 1989-2003.
Photos: 1977 & 1992 *Witmarsums*

Warp and woof. Academic mission and religious mission. Excellent quality education and development of Christian faith. These are the threads woven into the fabric of Bethany's history and ongoing mission. This, of course, echoes the theme expressed in chapter one by writer Leonard Gross and two female students in his sociology class in 1964. Thirty years later these were among the notes sounded on the weekend of October 14-15, 1994, when more than 300 people gathered at Bethany to celebrate the school's fortieth anniversary.

Organized around the theme, "Keeping the Faith," festivities for the weekend included participation by alumni in chapel and classes on Friday and a dinner and program on Saturday evening. A special feature of the evening program was the performance by the school's concert choir of "Psalm 27"—a piece commissioned for the occasion and written by James Clemens, a 1983 Bethany alumnus. Using the first six verses of the psalm to bring together the past 40 years of the school's history, Clemens developed the themes of pain, doubt, hope, joy, and the celebration of God's everlasting faithfulness.

New leadership and new challenges

While there was much cause for celebration in the fall of 1994, there was also a growing awareness that change was in the wind, for several significant issues needing almost immediate attention began to emerge on a variety of fronts.

The first and most obvious challenge for the institution was that of making the transition to new administrative leadership in the wake of Hooley's recent departure. The question of whether Bethany should add a middle school to its operation had also found its way back on the table at this time and was gaining support in certain quarters. Some wondered whether and how such a move would fit into the school's long-term vision, goals, and objectives—which, others pointed out, were themselves outdated and in need of fresh evaluation and recasting.

Some teachers and Board members felt the time had come for another in-depth

Warp and woof. Academic mission and religious mission. Excellent quality education and development of Christian faith. These are the threads woven into the fabric of Bethany's history and ongoing mission.

While there was
much cause for celebration
in the fall of 1994,
there was also
a growing awareness
that change
was in the wind ...

Allan Dueck Photo: BCS files

Allan Dueck brought to the principal's office many of the qualities that the Board was looking for at this juncture in Bethany's history.

curriculum review. Others sensed the need for tightening up the supervisory functions and accountability structures for facilitating and strengthening faculty performance. Still others saw the urgent importance of upgrading Bethany's computer capabilities and program and of introducing advanced placement courses for college-bound students. Declining enrollment had also become a significant issue, with a student body of 208 during the 1993-94 academic year reaching a near record low, and then dropping even further the following year to 195—the first dip below the 200 mark since the late fifties.

And then there was the enormous challenge of the school's operating deficit, which had increased dramatically in the early nineties and escalated to a troubling $709,000 by the summer of 1995. All of these factors became important for the Bethany Board as it began to envision what kind of leadership would be necessary to carry the school beyond the Hooley era and into the next crucial chapter of its history. "There was one phrase that kept coming up over and over," said Roy Hartzler, Bethany science teacher (1976-97) and member of the search committee for a new principal. "We said what we really needed in a principal was 'a mover and a shaker.'"

Allan Dueck: Bethany's new principal

On the morning of March 3, 1995, the Bethany Board met with the faculty and announced its unanimous decision, after several months of interviews and deliberation, to invite Allan Dueck as Bethany's next principal. Dueck had furthermore accepted its invitation, the Board reported, and would begin his new assignment, effective that summer.

Allan Dueck brought to the principal's office many of the qualities that the Board was looking for at this juncture in Bethany's history. Educated in Canada and the United States, with specialties in English and theology and experience in directing drama, as well as coaching hockey and volleyball, Dueck also came to Bethany in 1995 with more than 20 years of teaching and administrative work in

Mission and Administration Subcommittee of the Middle School Planning Committee (1995-96): Allan Dueck (chair), Ruth Miller Roth, Lorie Vincent, and Jerry Garber. Photo: BCS files

Left: Fifty-two students, making up the newly formed middle school, occupy renovated space in the "barn" in August 1996. Photo: BCS files

Mennonite educational institutions at Goshen College, Hesston College, and most recently, at Mennonite Collegiate Institute in Gretna, Manitoba, where he had served for a decade as principal.

"Allan brings a strong commitment to Christian education within the Anabaptist Mennonite tradition," stated Board Chair Lovina Rutt in announcing Dueck's appointment in the spring 1995 *Bulletin,* "and he is a skilled and energetic administrator. We are confident that he will build on the substantial strengths of Bethany Christian High School and lead us into the twenty-first century with renewed vision and direction."

The middle school: new direction, new energy and growth

The search committee had been clear with Dueck from the outset that his new assignment might require his providing administrative leadership to not only one educational institution, but possibly two. No one could have guessed, however, that within a year, this second institution—the Bethany Christian Middle School—would

Ruth Miller Roth:
The middle school is born
"Looking back [to 1995], it's hard to know what exactly sparked the movement for a middle school at Bethany. At the time, I was a quiet homemaker, the mother of four young children, hardly an activist for educational reform. Yet when I heard about consultant Fudge's recommendation [that 'the time is not right'], something deep within me was moved to action.

I decided to put the consultant's recommendation to the test. I contacted all the area Mennonite churches, identified a contact person in each congregation and asked them to circulate a petition encouraging the Bethany board to establish a middle school for families in the church. Within two weeks, many signatures were collected from the participating churches."

Middle school orchestra directed by Brian Mast.
Photo: BCS files

be in full operation, staffed by three qualified sixth and seventh grade teachers in a newly renovated facility on the second floor of the "barn," the old industrial arts building, and ready to receive 52 students for the 1996-97 academic year.

The idea of a middle school was not new to the Bethany Board, which had given it serious consideration as early as 1980-81, then again in 1990-92, but on both occasions found insufficient support for the project. In 1994-95 faculty and Board committees explored for the third time the possibility by initiating new research and developed considerable enthusiasm for moving ahead. But plans were stalled once more when, on February 25, 1995, Don Fudge, an independent schools

Bethany Christian Middle School experienced considerable growth and vitality in its first five years after opening day in 1996, increasing its student body from 52 to 101 …

Middle school math teacher Ron Kolb-Wyckoff works with eighth graders Daniel Horst '01, Jeff Claassen '01, and Traci Yoder '01. Photo: BCS files

Above: Grade 6 students perform a musical, Livin' to Learn, Learnin' to Live, *written and directed by their teacher Eliza Jacoby. Right: BCHS facilities are shared with the new middle school.* Photos: BCS files

consultant hired by the Board, discouraged the project with the counsel that "there does not appear to be a compelling need to add these grades at the present time."

At this point a group of parents and faculty members requested an audience with the Board to urge reconsideration of the matter, based on their growing dissatisfaction with large public schools and their desire to have a school that could provide a safe learning environment, focused on Christian nurture and close teacher-student relationships. The Board listened carefully to the issues raised by the delegation at its next meeting on April 20, 1995, and eventually, with the assured strong support of both the administration and the Indiana-Michigan Conference, decided to move ahead with the proposal.

Allan Dueck, incoming principal, was assigned the task of organizing a committee to develop a plan for the school. Completing its work within five months, from October 1995 to February 1996, the committee turned over the next phase of responsibility to Bethany's administrative team who further fleshed out the details of important guidelines in key areas: Christian nurture, curriculum, teacher qualifications, facilities, co-curricular programming, budgeting, and so on.

By mid-March Bethany had 25 applications from students and on March 11 held an "information evening" with over 80 prospective students and their families in attendance. An additional "get-acquainted evening" was scheduled for May 23 and an orientation event in August, just one week before the school opened.

Bethany Christian Middle School experienced considerable growth and vitality in its first five years after opening day in 1996, increasing its student body from 52 to 101, doubling from one to two the class sections needed for each grade level, bursting from its facility into two supplemental modular units located adjacent to the "barn," and spilling over into the main high school building, occupying ever more space in commonly shared areas, such as the cafeteria, chapel, music room, and gymnasium. During this time, the Bethany Middle School established a solid reputation for the spiritual care provided by its teachers, for its annual musical and

Ray Gyori-Helmuth '80 taught in the high school (primarily Spanish) from 1993-98 before serving two years as assistant principal (1998-2000). Photos: 1980 & 1997 Witmarsums

Protesting the "School of the Americas"
On November 20, 1998, 13 Bethany students boarded a bus heading to Columbus, Georgia. There, they took part in a vigil with over 7,000 other people at the gates of Fort Benning. The students went hoping to draw attention to and protest the continued funding of the School of the Americas (SOA), a U. S.-based training facility for Latin American soldiers. The vigil marked the ninth anniversary of the killing of seven Jesuit priests, their housekeeper and her daughter by graduates of the SOA.

Several Bethany students joined over 2,000 activists in crossing into Fort Benning property. As a result they were bused to a local park and given orders to stay off the base for the remainder of the day, and then released.

—Adapted from the Reflector, Vol. 45, No. 5 (December 18, 1998)

Afghan pen pal responds
In January 2002 sixth grader Rachel Hollinger-Janzen received the first return letter from her pen pal in Peshawar, Pakistan. In mid-November 2001 students in J. D. Smucker's Grade 6 music class had sent letters to schools in Peshawar in an attempt to respond peacefully to Afghan refugees and help break down barriers of misunderstanding between people of different cultures and faiths.

"Our music teacher, Mr. Smucker, thought this would be a good way for us to learn about life in another country which we were bombing," said Rachel. "And our class thought that sounded like a great idea."

Rachel's mother, Lynda '73, a staff writer at Mennonite Mission Network, helped students locate the addresses of a boys' and girls' school in Peshawar interested in having pen pals. "You are now international diplomats," Smucker told his students, "but without the politics. Your goal is to be a peacemaker and build a relationship of trust and understanding."

—Adapted from BCS news release (2002)

Photo: 2002 BCMS yearbook

> ... the new administration set to work, putting into place a process designed to bring increased fiscal clarity and address the largest budgetary challenge in Bethany's history.

dramatic productions, its cutting-edge math program, its academic excellence reflected in repeatedly high ISTEP+ (Indiana Statewide Testing for Educational Progress) scores, and its creative cross-cultural learning events, field trips, and service projects throughout the Goshen community.

Looking back at the dramatic, fast-paced events of 1995-96, Ruth Miller Roth, one of the driving forces behind the parents' petition to the Board, said, "I give the Bethany Board and Principal Allan Dueck a great deal of credit for their vision, energy, and leadership in responding so positively and creatively to our challenge. It's still a mystery to me exactly what it was that made the *'no'* turn to *'yes'*—I like to think that it was just another example of God at work in the church."

Attention to the deficit, strategic planning, faculty-staff relations
Focusing such intense energy on launching the middle school did little to alleviate some of the other critical challenges Bethany was facing. Most urgent was the deficit, calling for immediate attention.

Beginning with a comprehensive review of the school's budgeting practices, salary policies, and accounting procedures, the new administration set to work, putting into place a process designed to bring increased fiscal clarity and address the largest budgetary challenge in Bethany's history. Two key initiatives early in this process were implementing the *Firm Foundations Campaign,* a 15-month fund drive focused on challenging a select group of high-level donors to assist in liquidating the school's accumulated operating deficit, and restructuring the *Partnership Plan,* a program through which congregations were encouraged to cover much or all of the tuition costs for young people choosing to attend Bethany Christian Schools—or BCS, as some now referred to it.

Other factors during this period—such as increased enrollment, a booming economy, and improved channels of communication with the constituency—no doubt also contributed to the successful launching of the middle school and the slow but steady turnaround of the high school's financial state.

Board Chair Wesley J. Bontreger '77 was able to state with considerable enthusiasm in his 2000-01 annual report that for five of the six preceding years, Bethany had ended the year with a cash surplus, that private gifts had experienced a steady increase, and that the schools' remaining debt had dropped to $396,000, just over half that of the 1995 figure.[2] Even more remarkable, given the financial restraints of the period, was the steady increase in teachers' salaries to a figure now 90 percent of that received by public school colleagues, up from 79 percent five years before.

In addition to the serious budget challenges facing the two schools, the new administration and faculty also embarked on a several-year process of long-range strategic planning for Bethany. One impetus for this initiative was the requirement of all non-public schools interested in maintaining state accreditation to participate in the state's school improvement planning process called Performance Based Accreditation (PBA).

During the 1997-98 year, the school invested considerable time and energy in the PBA process, with teachers, parents, board members, and administrators all engaged in conversations concerning Bethany's mission, curriculum, professional development, and school climate. Participants in the process were asked to identify both strengths and weaknesses in each of these areas and to develop specific action plans for improvement.

Growing out of the PBA evaluation, Bethany developed and implemented in 1998-99 a new process of curriculum review which emphasized rethinking all phases of the curriculum and ensuring appropriate sequencing of learning from one level to the next, from middle school through senior high. This resulted in the adoption of a five-year action plan that identified four school improvement goals, with strategies and a timetable for each to be monitored at regular intervals by administration and faculty.[3]

In addition to the PBA curriculum review, other initiatives were also put in place during this period to assist Bethany in various aspects of long-range planning:

In all, 12 long-time faculty members either retired or changed careers during the decade of the nineties ...

Above: Renee Glick '00 paints the face of a young patron at the 1997 Spring Fun Fest.
Below: Justin Zehr and Michael Honderich '04 plant flowers as a service day project.
Photos: BCS files

Jodi Kauffman '00: That stinkin' Fish Fry
"Fish Fry is in my opinion something that I didn't look forward to. You had to go out into the fish tent and work out there dipping fish and the only good thing is that you got cool T-shirts out of it. The bad thing was that the whole school smelled like fish for two weeks afterwards."

Wearing class T-shirts, Zac Boughner '99 boxes fish at the carry-out window while Lisa Bergey '99 restocks the pie table. Right: Joel Fath '00 readies tables for the next wave. Photos: BCS files

Strategic Goals, 1996-97; School Facilities Master Planning, 1997-98; *The Mennonite High School Project,* 1997-98; Capital Campaign Feasibility Study, 1998-99; and Strategic Operational Plan, 2001-02, with specific directives for how Bethany should work at issues related to seven spheres of its life: administrative and board leadership, faculty and staff, financial resources, facilities, marketing, and constituency relationships.[4]

Not all of the changes and new directions taking place at Bethany during this period were easy to accommodate for faculty and staff who had served the school under Bill Hooley's leadership. Allan Dueck's more formal, sometimes distant administrative style also required some adjustment on the part of those accustomed to Hooley's more engaging, pastoral approach. Some faculty chose this period of transition as a time to either retire or move on to other assignments. But, as they did, new teachers—usually younger—took their places, increasing the total number of faculty to 29 in 1999-2000, up ten from 19 in 1995-96. In all, 12 long-time faculty members either retired or changed careers during the decade of the nineties, six of those in the last four years of Hooley's tenure and Swartley's one-year interim (1994-95) and six in the first five years of Dueck's administration (1995-2000).

From old problems to new strength, achievement, and growth
Significant vitality and health were evident in at least six areas of Bethany's life during this period. These include the enrollment growth, academic achievement, technological improvements, sports explosion, blossoming of the arts, and faith development.

Enrollment growth. During the 1994-95 academic year, student numbers at Bethany dipped below the 200 mark, prompting the Board to do some projections of anticipated trends in the decade ahead.[5] Its prediction then was that high school enrollment would hold steady at 190 for several

'97 class officers: Wendy Yoder, Ben Hartman, ?ris Weaver, and Sarah Wenger, with English ?cher Devon Schrock in center.
?to: BCS files

1997 Academic Superbowl state champion teams (front): Coaches Beth and Malinda Berry, Rachel Koontz '98, and Tim Nafziger '99. Back: Coach Jack Hellenbrand, Ben Hartman '97, Hannah Stutzman '97, and Alison Dick '99.
Photo: BCS files

Anna Becker-Hoover '00, Sophie Charles '00, and "unidentified" clean litter from a one-mile stretch of C. R. 40, southeast of the school. Photo: BCS files

?ars, until gradually climbing back to a number over 200 in 2001-02. The middle ?hool, it projected, would start off in 1996 with around 40 students and grow to ?vice that number within five years. As it turns out, predictions proved low on both ?counts. The middle school opened in 1996 with 12 more students than anticipated ?d reached 101 during the 2000-01 year, 15 ahead of the number predicted. Already ? 1995-96, high school numbers had jumped back up to 216 and continued, for the ?ost part, on a steady incline throughout the remainder of the nineties. By 1999-2000 ?ethany had reached an all-time-high enrollment of 345—249 in the high school and ?6 in the middle school.

Of equal interest in the Board's 1995 projections were the stated goals of raising ?e percentage of local eligible Mennonite young people who would choose to ?tend Bethany as well as the number of "other than Mennonite" youths who might ?nroll. Numbers in the first category remained fairly constant at about 25-30 percent ?ver the next five years, but it was in the "other than Mennonite" (OTM) category ?at significant growth was to occur. Whereas only 27 OTM high school students

Above: While Marisa Yoder observes, Becky Wieand '96 demonstrates a classroom project. Left: Marisa Yoder receives the 1994 Elkhart County Conservation Award as "National Teacher of the Year." Photos: BCS files

Bethany figured at the top of the list [in area school SAT results for 2000 and 2001 academic years], scoring well above its nearest contenders in both 'verbal' and 'math' assessments.

Wilfred "Willie" Kanagy (1989-98) wore many hats during his nine-year tenure as assistant principal, including: grounds and facilities supervision, leading SALT groups, Key Club sponsor, administrative representative on the mascot research and name-change committees, and coaching girls' varsity basketball and softball.

Photo: 1990 *Witmarsum*

were enrolled at Bethany during the 1994-95 year, that number rose in the combined schools to over 90 in 1999-2000. Sixty OTM denominations or unaffiliated congregations had been represented in the student body in the prior decade (1987-95), but that number increased to 119 during the five years to follow (1995-2000). Not surprisingly, the ratio of Mennonite to "other than Mennonite" students experienced a significant shift during the decade of the nineties, moving from an 89-11 percent ratio in 1990-91 to a 75-25 ratio ten years later.

Academic achievement. On September 6, 2001, the *Elkhart Truth* ran a front-page feature article reporting on SAT score results from 11 area schools during the 2000 and 2001 academic years. Bethany figured at the top of the list for both of these years, scoring well above its nearest contenders in both "verbal" and "math" assessments. For 2001 Bethany's total "average score" for participating students was 1092 (541 for verbal, 551 for math)—a full 92 points above the state average and 72 points above the national average.[6] In that same year two students were named National Merit Finalists, a distinction achieved by less than 1 percent of students nationwide. It is worth noting that, for the decade 1991-2001, Bethany averaged just over two finalists per year, more than five times the national average.

Administration and faculty worked with great diligence in the last half of the nineties, not only to maintain but to improve Bethany's long-standing commitment to academic excellence. Of particular importance were the thorough music program evaluation (1995-96); the review of the small-group SALT and PEPPER programs (1996-97); the addition of upper-level electives for academically strong students (1996-97); the curricular initiatives for strengthening the senior year program (1997); the revision of Bible course requirements (1997-98); the entry of Bethany students into the Hoosier Academic Superbowl where winning state championships became an annual event (1987-2002); and the adoption of a new modified block schedule for the high school, designed with longer classes to facilitate more in-depth, uninterrupted study of certain subject matters (1999-2000).[7] In addition to these many significant initiatives, it should be noted that more than 25 new courses were added to the high school curriculum during the six-year period from 1995-2001.

Increased course offerings in science, with titles such as Eco-Topics, Environmental Science, and Biological World, attracted a growing number of students during these years, so that by the 2000-01 academic year, a full 86 percent of the student body was enrolled in at least one of the eight science courses available in the high school curriculum.

Teaching faculty and administration at Bethany have, over the years, set the tone for the school's emphasis on academic excellence. More than half the teachers in 2000-01 held master's degrees in their fields of expertise. And 80 percent of that year's 2001 graduating seniors were apparently interested in following suit by enrolling that fall in college programs.

Technological improvements. In the fall of 1996 two anonymous donors offered $40,000 to Bethany for use in computer education. Sixteen thousand dollars of that donation was designated for middle school computers and the remaining $24,000 was put to use in assisting classroom instruction.

Upgrading computer technology at Bethany was long overdue. Peter Hartman '98, a student reporter writing in the November 1995 issue of the *Reflector,* had expressed his desire to see the school emerge from "the stone age" by embracing this "incredible step in the BCHS educational system … Bethany is strong in many areas," wrote Hartman, "but the computer area is one of its weakest attributes."

In the same article Hartman reported on the School Board's recent decision to embark on a several-year plan to upgrade all office equipment, replace old student computers, create two separate computer labs, install Internet access, and develop courses in advanced computer application. This all sounded rather ambitious, almost outrageous, in 1995, but a quick glance at "Computer Resources" and

Teaching faculty and administration … set the tone for the school's emphasis on academic excellence.

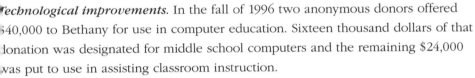

Above: BCS students benefit from ongoing technology upgrades. Photo: BCS files

Left: Andy Kehr builds a robot for an advanced computer course. Photo: 2003 *Witmarsum*

Cheryl Kaufman works with middle school students Michael Martin and Jennifer Manley.
Photo: BCS files

Athletic Director Allen Peachey (left) presents Dan Bodiker with a plaque in recognition of his 300th career win in varsity boys' soccer.
Photo: BCS files

Below left: 1965-66 basketball team members were honored a quarter of a century later. From left: Delvon Yoder '66, Coach Dan Bodiker, Dan King '67, Jay Hershberger '67, Allen Bontreger '66, Ken Thomas '66, Glen Yoder '67, Charles Steiner '67, and Larry Schrock '67. Not present: John Bontreger '67, Larry Miller '67, Sanford Schrock '67, and Craig Yoder '67. Photo: Chris Inebnit, 1992 Goshen News

From right: Jazz Band members Austin Scharf '02, Amy Leatherman '01, and Justin Heinz '03 provide basketball halftime entertainment. Photo: BCS files

"Technology Classes" on the Bethany Website in 2003 makes it clear that what was once but a dream had in a few short years become a reality:

- The two Bethany computer labs house 28 and 15 student workstations, respectively, with Pentium 350 MHz machines or faster.
- The library has 12 student workstations for word processing and Internet research.
- Students have access to 112 computers, all with high-speed Internet access.
- A class in keyboarding skills is required of all students.
- In the computer applications course, students learn to use Microsoft Office 2000 to make PowerPoint presentations, access databases, use Excel worksheets, and create Word documents, and they explore Website development, Photoshop, and robotics.

Sports explosion. In a high school survey conducted in 2001, Bethany students were asked to identify any and all activities in which they were involved. Options for selection included Foreign Language Club, drama, photography, yearbook-newspaper, chess, band, orchestra, choir, Academic Superbowl, intramural sports,

nd interscholastic athletics. Of the 167 students surveyed, 132 (79 percent) ndicated their involvement in "athletics," and 62 (37 percent) in "intramurals." The earest contender to either of these was "choir" at 46 (roughly 28 percent), making ports the hands-down winner of school-sponsored activities occupying students' me and energy outside of the classroom.

The intramural program during these years was a modest one, offering asketball, volleyball, and floor hockey for high school students, and indoor soccer nd volleyball for middle schoolers. But in the area of interscholastic athletics, Bethany saw a significant burst of energy and expansion.

Eight sports were offered in the high school athletic program throughout most f this period: baseball, basketball, cross country, golf, soccer, softball, tennis, and volleyball—many of which, though not all, existed in both "boys'" and "girls'" and in "varsity," "junior varsity," and sometimes "frosh" versions. Prior to 1997 Bethany teams had won only three sectional championships, one in boys' baseball (1987) and two in girls' volleyball (1976, 1980). But with the advent of Indiana's multi-class sport structure in 1997-98, winning sectional titles became virtually an annual Bethany event. Beginning with the remarkable victory of the 1997 girls' soccer team in their very first season of play, Bethany went on to win sectional championships in boys' basketball (1998, 2000, 2002—the first and last of which resulted in regional titles), girls' basketball (1998), girls' softball (1999), girls' soccer (2000, 2001), and girls' volleyball (2001).

… when he stepped aside as coach to become athletic director, 'Bod' had amassed over 900 combined wins …

Top and middle: The 1998 varsity boys' basketball team won the Class A regional championship, and the varsity girls were sectional champs. Photos: BCS files

Bottom: The 1997 girls' soccer team won a sectional championship in their first season. Photo: BCS files

Seniors Austin Kaufmann, Sarah Kingsley, Jeremy Friesen, Jen Mortrud, Dustin Miller, and Dawn Myers perform the song "Johnny Schmoker" for Spring Arts Day '94.
Photo: 1995 *Witmarsum*

Spring Arts Day, launched in 1991, continued to expand as an all-school competition in the fine arts, incorporating growing numbers of students …

Also cause for celebration during this period was the career of Dan Bodiker, spanning nearly two generations and almost four decades of coaching and teaching at Bethany. Between the fall of 1965, when he helped introduce interscholastic play to the school, and 1997, when he stepped aside as coach to become athletic director, "Bod" had amassed over 900 combined wins in boys' soccer, baseball, and various levels of boys' and girls' basketball.

Blossoming of the arts. The arts had for many years been an important feature of Bethany's life, but the nineties brought an even greater emphasis in this area. Spring Arts Day, launched in 1991, continued to expand as an all-school competition in the fine arts, incorporating growing numbers of students in "art and writing" (creative writing, drawing, painting, program cover design) and "performance" categories (drama, readings in poetry and prose, instrumental and vocal music).

A comprehensive evaluation of the BCS music program in the mid-nineties resulted in the launching of grade six choir, and middle school (seventh and eighth grade) choir, concert band, and orchestra. The program review also brought increased energy and set new directions for the high school's junior chorale (a requirement for ninth graders, an elective for tenth), Class Voice (a spring semester elective for tenth and eleventh graders), Jubilate Singers (an elective for all interested juniors and seniors), Cornerstone Singers (a select group of nine to 12 juniors and seniors), Chamber Orchestra, and Jazz Band.

Rescheduling high school orchestra practices and instrumental classes outside of regular class hours in time slots before and after school allowed for increased student

Middle school Agape Ringers handbell choir.
Photo: BCS files

J. D. Smucker directs Jubilate's 2002 Christmas concert.
Photo: 2003 *Witmarsum*

participation. The result was that the orchestra almost doubled in size during this time to an enrollment of 55 students in 2001-02.

The number of middle school students learning to play musical instruments also doubled in the last half of the nineties, with over 50 percent of the 2001 student body participating in either orchestra or a newer course offering, Beginning Instruments. During this period two middle school groups, Agape Ringers (a handbell choir), and Lightshine (a worship team), and one high school group, the String Chamber Ensemble, joined Bethany's music scene.

A particularly significant landmark event during these years was the 1997 staging of *Anne of Green Gables,* Bethany's first full-length musical, which incorporated the largest number of actors and instrumentalists in the school's 43-year history. Co-directed by Allan Dueck and J. D. Smucker, the production involved almost 70 students, one-third of the BCS student body, as cast, orchestra, or stage crew participants.

Other musicals or dramas produced during this period included:

A scene from the 1999 musical Fiddler on the Roof. Photo: BCS files

Year	Drama (BCHS)	Musical (BCHS)	Drama (BCMS)
2003-2004	The Chosen	You're a Good Man, Charlie Brown	Things My Mother Said
2002-2003	Play On	Cotton Patch Gospel	The Somewhat True Tale of Robin Hood
2001-2002	Do Not Go Gentle	Joseph and the Amazing Technicolor Dreamcoat	Stuart Little
2000-2001	The Foreigner	Amahl and the Night Visitors	Snow White
1999-2000	Twelve Angry Men	Fiddler on the Roof	Alice in Wonderland
1998-1999	January Thaw	Godspell	The Wizard of Oz
1997-1998	Quiet in the Land	The Sound of Music	James and the Giant Peach
1996-1997	The Orphans	Anne of Green Gables	
1995-1996	You Can't Take It With You		
1994-1995	Lost in Yonkers		
1993-1994	The Diary of Anne Frank		

A cornhusking scene from the 1998 drama Quiet in the Land. Photo: BCS files

Eileen Becker-Hoover Photo: BCS files

'Nurturing our young people' is, of course, an all-encompassing task and takes place at every moment and at every level of a school's existence.

Faith development. A 2002 promotional brochure designed for prospective BCS students and their parents presented the school by asking these questions: "Who is nurturing a *Christ-centered vision* in our young people? Who is building *community*, promoting *opportunities*, challenging them to *educational excellence,* and calling them to a life of *peace* and *service*?" The brochure then goes on to affirm: "These are the enduring values we strive to instill in each generation of students we serve at Bethany Christian Schools. *Discover the Difference!*"[8]

"Nurturing our young people" is, of course, an all-encompassing task and takes place at every moment and at every level of a school's existence. Nurture happened at Bethany during these years in the classroom, on class trips, in student-teacher relationships, during interterms, and in times of structured and unstructured small-group discussion. Nurture happened when Bethany athletes received state recognition for good sportsmanship, when sudden death on several occasions claimed the lives of parents or fellow classmates, and when

Beth Berry and Liz Hoover led an interterm group at Montreal's City Mission. Photo: BCS files

J. D. Smucker with members of his frosh SALT group. Photo: 2002 *Witmarsum*

Chapel is an integral part of the BCS program. Photos: BCS files

terrorists crashed into New York City's World Trade Center towers and the world, it seemed, also came crashing down.

Regular chapel experiences during this period offered a rich diet of spiritual reflection and cross-cultural challenge. A few titles illustrate the wide variety of topics treated:

"Science and Faith"
"My Faith Story" (Navajo minister)
"Mission in Africa"
"The School of the Americas"
"Responding to Injustice" (Filipino pastor)
"Dagestan Culture"
"Opposing Racism"
"The Holy Spirit in Our Lives"
"Choices" (substance abuse)
"True Love" (sexuality)
"Preparing Tables for our Enemies in Northern Ireland"

"New Age Movement"
"Songs of Justice"
"Celebration of Baptisms"
"Conflict Reconciliation"
"Cultivating Spiritual Life"
"Pathways to Peace"
"CPT Assists the Lakotas"
"Sports Be-Attitudes"
"Hearing God's Call to Mission" (India)

The Bible curriculum also underwent thorough review during these years, resulting in a more carefully sequenced, age-appropriate program for students from sixth through twelfth grades. Related to this initiative was a redesign and strengthening of the senior year program to help students in their final year "reflect on and consolidate the growth they've experienced in high school" and "prepare emotionally and spiritually for the upcoming transition to a new phase of their lives."[9] Included here were a reconfiguration of the senior year interterm and class trip experience, and the introduction of a new senior course, Christian Faith Journey, in which each student was required to reflect on his or her own personal faith pilgrimage, and then share a summary version of those reflections in a public setting—a group of invited friends, family members, classmates, fellow church members, or the entire student body in a Bethany chapel. For some students, and for some parents and teachers, this exercise became the highlight of their senior year.

International student accepts Christ
When Ulrike Voigt *(left)* came to Bethany from Germany in the fall of 1997 for a year of study, she knew very little about Christians, let alone Christ.

At Bethany she was exposed to Christian beliefs and practices through students and faculty, Bible class, and regular attendance at Waterford Mennonite Church with her host family, Delvon '66 and Shirley '65 Sawatzky Yoder.

At Christmas (1998) she wrote to principal Allan Dueck: "You [Bethany] had a great impact on my deciding to follow Christ now, and I'm very grateful."

—Adapted from BCS Bulletin, Vol. 44, No. 3 (Spring 1999) Photo: 1998 *Witmarsum*

Sarah Yoder '01:
"What else could Bethany do?"
"Bethany's atmosphere more than any other place has caused me to grow spiritually stronger. When I hear of parents who are disappointed that Bethany hasn't had more of a spiritual impact on their children's lives, I wonder: 'What else could Bethany do?'

For five years I've had teachers openly share and incorporate their faith into their classes. I've had chapels three times a week, discussion groups two times a week, and interterm, Spiritual Life Week, and Bible class every year. Bethany has provided me with so many opportunities to grow spiritually and of the ones that I have chosen to take advantage of, I have seen results.

Bethany cannot force anyone to grow spiritually, but has given me opportunities to develop my gifts and its teachers have been there to encourage me in my searching. I can't imagine spending my school years at a better place."
—BCS Bulletin, Vol. 46, No. 4 (Summer 2001)
Photo: 2001 *Witmarsum*

Persistence pays off
The opening of the Maple City Greenway's Winona Spur in spring 2001 was the culmination of a nearly 20 year effort by former Bethany teacher-administrator Everett Thomas (1972-89) to bring a bike trail from downtown Goshen to Bethany.

As more students became interested in biking to Bethany during the fuel crisis of the early 1980s, then-Assistant Principal Thomas became concerned that there was no environmentally friendly alternative to driving since the shoulder along State Road 15 was not paved. Inquiries into improving the roadside for bikers and pedestrians were not successful, and the railroad made a popular path along the tracks impassable.

Frustrated with the lack of concern for this issue, Thomas ran for Goshen City Council in 1991 and won, spurring the council to support the mayor to establish a master plan to connect all schools, parks, and public buildings in Goshen via a system of bike trails. However, building the spur to Bethany proved difficult since several affected landowners adamantly opposed the project. By 1997, many city officials had given up hope of having this spur built, but Thomas became more determined and met individually with residents over a several month period. Since he was also a property owner impacted by the proposed trail, Thomas was eventually able to convince his neighbors to support the trail.

Since the opening of the trail, pedestrian and bike traffic to Bethany has increased greatly. And for Thomas it is satisfying to ride the trail and see how many people are benefiting from his persistence.

—*Based on interview by J. Kevin Miller (above)*

Photos: 1985 *Witmarsum*; BCS files

Questions in Bethany's future

It is impossible to predict what will be the shape of Bethany's future. But repeatedly throughout the course of the research done for this final chapter, several key questions kept reappearing as important to consider in this regard.[10] At one point in the research, in spring 2002, BCS faculty and Board members were asked to take these questions and prioritize them in order of importance. They did this, not as a group exercise, but an individual one. And it is perhaps significant that the results produced no perceptible pattern of prioritizing, indicating that while there was some consensus about the importance of the questions themselves, there was little agreement about which should receive primary attention. Here, then, are the questions, simply presented from 1-12, with no attempt to place them in any particular order of ranking:

1. *Anabaptist-Mennonite focus.* What will be the impact of the school's changing demographics with a growing "other-than-Mennonite" student population? Will Bethany remain "Anabaptist"?

2. *Conference connections.* How important is it for BCS to stay connected to the Indiana-Michigan Mennonite Conference that helped give it birth? Is Bethany doing enough to cultivate that relationship? What is the level of Conference commitment to nurturing the connection?

3. *Staff-faculty-administration.* What kind of staff, faculty, and administrative leadership will shape Bethany's future? Will employment at Bethany be thought of primarily as a "job" or as a "ministry"? How important is it for staff and faculty to be both "professionals" and "people of faith" with significant involvement in local congregational life?

4. *Costs.* What will be the effect of the rising costs necessary to sustain the Bethany program? Will these costs eventually become prohibitive for all but a few?

5. *Larger community.* How will Bethany—as a largely white, middle-class school—relate with integrity to the multi-ethnic Goshen community in which it finds itself?

6. *Funding.* Bethany has struggled from the beginning with financial challenges. Will that pattern continue into the future? What will be the impact on the school of moving away from church-based ownership and funding to "big donor" or family financing?

7. *Balance.* How will BCS work to keep a healthy balance between various competing parts of its program: sports, arts, academics, faith development?

8. *Facility.* What kind of physical facility will be necessary to accommodate growing needs and assist the school in accomplishing its mission? Will the school be able to afford what is necessary? Can it thrive and survive without it?

9. *Spirituality.* In what ways will Bethany work to create an atmosphere of "spirituality"? What will be required in order to meet the spiritual needs of both faculty and students in this post-modern, pluralistic age?

10. *Educational trends in culture.* How will Bethany position itself in the wider cultural debate between advocates of private and public schooling, secular and faith-based education, formal and "non-formal" learning, classroom and Web-based instruction, "institutional" learning, and the home-schooling movement, etc.?

11. *Educational trends in denomination.* How does Bethany compare with and contrast to other sister institutions in the North American network of Mennonite schools with regard to trends and issues like enrollment patterns, tuition costs, church-

Bethany hosted the annual Mennonite Secondary Education Council Choir Festival in 2003. The mass choir is shown performing in the Goshen College Music Center. Photo: BCS files

What danger is there
in Bethany becoming
a cozy Christian community—
a 'holy huddle'—isolated
from the world around it?

Hannah Eash '02 Photo: BCS files

The first third-generation student, Joel Graber '99 stands between his grandmother, Eunice Troyer Miller '60 (Chupp) left, and his mother, Cathy Miller '77 (Graber) right.

Photo: BCS files

school relations, ratio of Mennonite to "other-than-Mennonite" students, racial-cultural composition, focus on Anabaptist-Mennonite education, etc.?

12. *Mission-service emphasis.* The BCS logo features "family, church, and school" against the backdrop of "the world." What danger is there in Bethany becoming a cozy Christian community—a "holy huddle"— isolated from the world around it? In what ways does Bethany work at equipping students to engage the surrounding culture, at training them for witness and service to the world? What specific role can and should Bethany play in helping the new Mennonite Church USA move toward becoming a "missional church"?

Asking questions of this nature and in this manner in no way suggests a faltering or failing on Bethany's part in realizing its historical calling. Quite to the contrary, it is precisely in the asking of such questions that Bethany and its supporting constituents can with integrity and renewed commitment take seriously the never-ending, ever-challenging task of "hearing the Teacher's voice" in the days and years ahead.

How faithfully has Bethany listened to "the Teacher's voice"?

Each decade in the last half of the twentieth century seems to have possessed its own unique personality. If popular music is any indicator of cultural trends, the fifties were best known for the tune, "Rock Around the Clock"; the sixties, "The Times, They Are A-Changin'"; the seventies, "Bridge Over Troubled Waters"; the eighties, "We Are the World"; and the nineties, "Candle in the Wind."[11] A few visual characterizations (see pages 208 and 209) provided by Neil Howe and William Strauss in their book *Millennials Rising* are another way to capture some of the cultural dynamics at work during this 50-year period.[12]

Constantly intersecting and interweaving with this larger American cultural tory was the Midwestern Mennonite story being played out in Northern Indiana and Southern Michigan. For, in the final analysis, the Bethany adventure described in these pages is much less about a *school* than about a *people*—a people emerging over the decades from rural, small-town isolationism into mainstream North American society, a people asking the hard question at every turn of the journey, 'How, in *this* time and place, do we remain faithful to our calling, our children, our church, and our God?"

One might wonder, given this perspective, what connection if any actually exists between the "early Bethany," so resistant to interscholastic sports activity, and the Bethany of the nineties, frequently splashed across the sports pages of local newspapers as champions in sectional and regional competitions. Similarly, one might ask what ongoing relationship still holds together the Bethany of the fifties, deeply immersed in discussions about dress codes and appropriate hairstyles, and

Class of 2006 members in the library: Nathan Kauffman, Darin Schwartzentruber, and Reanna Kuitse. Photo: BCS files

Post-September 11 sixth grade activities
Sixth graders were kept busy during the post-September period not only with their regular subject areas, but also with learning about Afghanistan, the people and their culture. They also explored the Arabic language, the Muslim religion, and the history behind the conflicts in the news of the day. Through guest speakers, learning the Lord's Prayer in Arabic, trying foods typical to that region, and discussions, sixth graders hoped to gain an understanding and compassion for the Afghan people.
—*Adapted from BCS "Keeping in Touch" monthly newsletter, Vol. 12, No. 3 (November 2001)*

Matt Lind '95: Sheltered from the world or suffering in it?
"Is [Bethany] a place to be sheltered? The answer is yes. Bethany lives up to its motto as a 'good place to grow.' As young plants here we find a safe, nurturing environment with fertile soil, relatively few herbivores, etc.

But the problem comes when we begin to think of Bethany as a place that gets us ready for isolated, secure lives. Bethany is a good place to grow, but only because a harvest is intended. This is fundamental to the school's Christian mission. Bethany is a safe place to prepare for life in a world of anguish. We are called to be light in the world, not to shut ourselves away.

Is Bethany a place to prepare for a life isolated from suffering, or a place that prepares us to suffer in the world with our Christ?"
—*Student editorial,* Reflector, *Vol. 41, No. 9 (May 26, 1995)* Photo: 1993 *Witmarsum*

There are good reasons to believe that Bethany Christian Schools are continuing to respond, imperfectly perhaps, yet faithfully, to the unique calling for which they were intended and designed.

today's school that chooses to feature sections in its 2000-01 yearbook on "Fashions," "Favorite Brand Names," and "Favorite In-Style Clothing Items"?

Such questions, though perhaps trivial and superficial to some, should be treated as the important and relevant questions that they are. For behind them is the ultimate question: How shall we be God's faithful people, "in, but not of" this world that God so dearly loves?

There are good reasons to believe that Bethany Christian Schools are continuing to respond, imperfectly perhaps, yet faithfully, to the unique calling for which they were intended and designed. One such illustration is the following report, filed only days after the tragic events of September 11, 2001, by Ryan Springer, seventh and eighth grade social studies teacher. Writes Springer:

When we first heard about the terrorist attacks, my grade 7 class was building cardboard ziggurats as a part of a unit on ancient Mesopotamia. The Mesopotamians believed that ziggurats, large pyramid-shaped structures with temples on top, connected heaven and earth—it is believed that the Tower of Babel in Genesis 11:1-9 was a ziggurat … When the Mesopotamians were building the Tower of Babel, they were attempting to reach God. Their tower represented security, closeness to God, and great achievement.

Ryan Springer with middle school social studies class.
Photo: 2001-02 BCMS yearbook

However, the only thing it achieved for them was confusion.

The attacks crushed my students' sense of security and safety. The political, economic, and military towers that our country has built were powerless against these attacks and created a false sense of security and protection. Students now realize that they are never truly safe and are confused about what is the right thing to do.

I hope my students learn from ancient Mesopotamians that no earthly or material entity can truly protect us, sustain us, or bring us closer to God. I hope they realize that ultimately our protection, comfort, and well-being come from God and our hope in Jesus Christ.

Furthermore, I hope to teach my students to build relationships of peace and love—true "towers" that work for the good of all people.

Justin Grossman '02 Photo: BCS files

In 1949 the Indiana-Michigan Mennonite Conference issued a statement titled "Why We Want a Christian High School." Heading the list of hopes and dreams for such a school at that time was the desire to place Christ at the center of the educational program. "We want our young people to study their history, science and literature in light of God's Word," the statement read. "We want to prepare them to make an effective, positive Christian witness to the world."

There are hopeful signs, 50 years hence, that Bethany, and the vision of its founders, is alive and well, and positioned to assist the church in facing the hard questions of what it means to be God's people in today's world. At the same time we know that the challenge set forth half a century ago is a never-ending one—one that requires of every generation, past, present, and future, the desire to hear more clearly and obey more faithfully the Teacher's voice.

Jennifer Klassen '04
Photo: BCS files

🙠 🙠 🙠 🙠

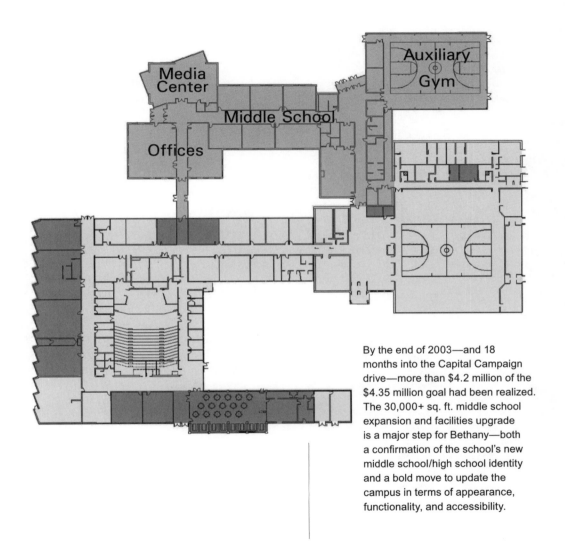

By the end of 2003—and 18 months into the Capital Campaign drive—more than $4.2 million of the $4.35 million goal had been realized. The 30,000+ sq. ft. middle school expansion and facilities upgrade is a major step for Bethany—both a confirmation of the school's new middle school/high school identity and a bold move to update the campus in terms of appearance, functionality, and accessibility.

Notes

1. Neil Howe and William Strauss, *Millennials Rising* (New York: Vintage Books, 2000). See especially 43-44.

2. In the 12-page "2000-2001 Annual Report," 3, included as an insert in *Bethany Christian Schools Bulletin,* Vol. 47, No. 1, Fall 2001.

3. For the full report, see the BCS administrative office files.

4. For more on any of these study documents, see the BCS administrative office files.

5. Statistics on the Board's 1995 growth projections have been taken from a document titled "Long-Range Planning (February 1995)," made available to writer by Allan Dueck.

6. The same article explores in some detail all the questions raised about the value of SAT tests and scores in truly monitoring aptitude in different cultural settings, etc. The scores are provided, nonetheless, as the best tool available until other instruments are put in place.

7. All of the study reports cited here can be consulted in full in the BCS administrative office files.

8. These themes of *Christ-centered, community, educational excellence, opportunities* and *peace and service* are developed more fully in the Spring 2001 issue of the *Bethany Christian Schools Bulletin,* Vol. 46, No. 3: 1-6.

9. For a full report of the Bible curriculum review, see the BCS administrative office files, made available to writer by Allan Dueck.

10. There were additional questions heard throughout the course of this research, but because of their less frequent occurrence, they do not figure in the list of 12 highlighted in the text of this chapter. Some of these included: "Why is the Mennonite Church willing to send its youth to National Youth Conventions for week-long celebrations, spending $1,000 for a week's activities, but many are unwilling to spend $6,000 for a full year of influence under Mennonite guidance?" "How would the Mennonite Church be different if its educational branches (high schools and colleges) were not in existence?" "How can Bethany keep a balance between the high academic students and those with learning disabilities?" "What relationship is there between Mennonite education and Mennonite lifestyle? Our schools are struggling for enrollment, but parishioners show up in the church parking lots to find many $25,000 vehicles parked there." "Does Bethany believe in 'mission'? How about our parishioners in general? We are, in many ways, what we get!" "Why did Conference discontinue the High-Aim Program, making it difficult for 'minority students' to attend Bethany?" "How decisions are made at Bethany is a crucial issue. There has been a shift in recent years to less consensus and a more unilateralist approach."

11. These are chapter titles in a book by Rick and Kathy Hick, *Boomers, Xers, and Other Strangers* (Wheaton, Illinois: Tyndale House Publishers, 1999).

12. Howe and Strauss, 17, 48, 202, 316, and 348.

Appendices

The tables in the appendices are
intended to provide specific data
of people, assignments, and
events. The tables have been
compiled from existing files and
records. In a few cases, the
records are not complete.
Omissions and errors are
possible. We apologize for that.
Should you notice an omission or
error, please e-mail the school at
info@bethanycs.net.

Bethany Operating Board members, with terms of service

A. Don Augsburger, 1965-67

Robert J. Baker, 1987-96

Lois Bare, 1983-85

Harold S. Bender, 1953-62

H. Ernest Bennett, 1953-59; 61-62

Melvin Birkey, 1960-62

Carol Birky, 1990-93

C. Franklin Bishop, 1962-65

Mary Bontrager, 1981-84

Wilbur Bontrager, 1985-86

Harold Bontreger, 1966-75

Wesley J. Bontreger, 1989-2003; chair, 1998-2001

Jim Boyts, 1968-69

Dean Brubaker, 1968-71

Lyn Buschert, 1999-2001

Loren Christophel, 1992-93

Randy Christophel, 2003-present

Willard Conrad, 1972-76

Bob Detweiler, 1970-73

Carrie Diener, 1972-75

Terry Diener, 2001-02

Stephen Dintaman, 1973-75

Bernie Eash, 1994-2000

Sanford Eash, 1962-66

Charles Gardner, 1953-54; 62-75; chair, 64-69

Del Glick, 1985-86

Dolores Graber, 1980-83

Virgil Graber, 1963-71

Dwight Grieser, 1978-84

Mary Grove, 1996-98

Harold Hartzler, 1989-99

Eldon Heatwole, 1997-present; chair, 2001-present

Sharon Heatwole, 1984-86

Dave Helmuth, 1980-83; 94-97

David Heusinkveld, 1998-present

James Hilty, 1970-71

Verle Hoffman, 1966-69

William Hooley, 1966-70

Martin Hoover, 1965-66

Glen Horner, 1972-75

Arlene Horst, 1996-2002

Amos O. Hostetler, 1953-66; chair, 53-61

Ernie Hostetler, 1986-95

Rachel Miller Jacobs, 1996-97

Deb Kauffman, 1990-96

Edith Kauffman, 1972-77

Gerald Kauffman, 1982-86; 90-91

J. Howard Kauffman, 1960-65

Sherm Kauffman, 1990-92

Nancy Kauffmann, 1991-92

Norman Kauffmann, 1981-90; chair, 85-90

John King, 1979-85

Keith Kingsley, 1991-93

Jeanette Krabill, 2000-present

Russell Krabill, 1953-54; 62-76; chair, 62-64

Alan Kreider, 1970-71

Anna Mae Lantz, 1983-86

Continued on page 220 …

Board members … *cont. from page 219*

Lee Leatherman, 1990-91

Cindy Lederman, 1997-2002

Russel Liechty, 1984-85

Fred Longenecker, 2002-present

Robert Mast, 1976-77

Herbert Maust, 1969-80; chair, 71-80

Ed Mendoza, 1981-86

Annas Miller, 1953-71; chair, 69-71

Carolyn Miller, 1981-84

David Ray Miller, 1970-73

Marsha Hooley Miller, 2001-present

Paul M. Miller, 1953-54 ex-officio

Robert J. Miller, 1977-80

Robert R. Miller, 1981-82

Roger K. Miller, 1999-present

Merrill Mishler, 1966-71

John Mosemann, 1976-79

Betty Mullet, 1984-86

Gerald Mumaw, 1979-80

Larry Neff, 1995-98

Franklin Newcomer, 1975-77

Nancy Nussbaum, 1996-99

Alice Roth, 1975-77

Arnold Roth, 1979-85

Ruth Miller Roth, 1999-present

Lovina Rutt, 1987-96; chair, 90-96

Vyron Schmidt, 1992-95

Dennis Schrock, 1976-79

Dale Shenk, 1990-93

Stanley C. Shenk, 1971-74

Barbara Slagel, 2003-present

Carl Smeltzer, 1981-86

Wayne Sommers, 1975-76

Leamon Sowell Jr., 1977-78

Elno Steiner, 1958-61

Bob Steury, 1995-present

Kathy Stiffney, 1991-97

Dan Stoltzfus, 1969-71

Phyllis Stoltzfus, 1974-76; 78-80

Rosalie Stoltzfus, 1978-81

Duane Stutzman, 1997-present

Ora Troyer, 1985-86; 90-91

Dennis Weaver, 1973-85; chair, 80-85

J. C. Wenger, 1954-56; 58-64

Gerald Wilson, 1977-80

David Yoder, 1968-70

Flossie Yoder, 1975-81

Glen Yoder, 1962-66

Leroy Yoder, 1985-86

Ora M. Yoder, 1953-56; 58-59; 61-70; chair, 61-62

Orris Yoder, 1973-74; 76-81

Paul Yoder, 2000-present

Richard Yoder, 1961-65

Roy Yoder, 1974-77

Winifred Yordy, 1993-99; chair, 96-98

Lester Zimmerman, 1966-68

Bethany administrators

C. J. Holaway, principal, 1954-62

John Steiner, superintendent, 1954-66

J. Marvin Nafziger, principal, 1962-65

Paul E. Yoder, superintendent, 1966-68

A. Don Augsburger, superintendent, 1968-70

Wade Bollinger, principal, 1970-73

William D. Hooley, superintendent, 1970-83; principal, 83-86, 87-94

Levi Miller, principal, 1973-76

Ed Herr, principal, 1976-78

Michael Lambright, principal, 1978-79

Everett Thomas, principal, 1979-82; assistant principal, 1983-86

Marlin Groff, principal, 1982-83

Mary Swartley, acting principal, 1986-87; interim principal, 1994-95

Gary Horst, principal, 1986-89

Willie Kanagy, assistant principal, 1989-98

Allan Dueck, principal, 1995-present

Ray Gyori-Helmuth, assistant principal, 1998-2000

Barry Johnson, assistant principal, 2000-present

Note: In 1983 Bethany switched administrative titles from superintendent/principal to principal/assistant principal.

Bethany Christian High School commencement record

Year	Date	Location	Speaker	# Seniors	Valedictorian	Salutatorian
1955	27-May	BC Auditorium*	Paul Mininger	26	Vivian Amstutz	Lora Eash
1956	25-May	GC Union**	J. Lawrence Burkholder	50	Mary Jean Yoder	Marion Yoder
1957	24-May	GC Union	J. C. Wenger	56	Rebecca Miller	Galen Eash
1958	23-May	GC Union	Harold S. Bender	62	Rosalyn Grieser	Richard Graber
1959	28-May	GC Union	Myron Augsburger	57	John Paul Wenger	Carolyn Schrock
1960	27-May	GC Union	Carl Kreider	82	Leah Beachy	Viola Christner
1961	26-May	GC Union	J. C. Wenger	78	Janet Moore	Margaret Mann
1962	25-May	GC Union	C. Franklin Bishop	65	Nancy Eash	Susanne King
1963	28-May	GC Union	Russell Krabill	75	Larry Mann	Leland Miller
1964	26-May	GC Union	C. Norman Kraus	76	Jeanette Slabach	Don Graber
1965	27-May	GC Union	B. Frank Byler	79	Lois Bixler, Fanny Mast	Marvin Miller
1966	27-May	GC Union	A. Don Augsburger	82	Leon Miller	Bob Troyer
1967	26-May	GC Union	Howard J. Zehr Sr.	84	Mary Ann Lehman	Diana Nafziger
1968	31-May	GC Union	Ray Pannabecker	84	Brian Martin, John Miller	
1969	30-May	GC Union	James W. DiRaddo	71	Becky Bair	Rodney Maust
1970	29-May	GC Union	David W. Augsburger	67	Judy Zimmerman	Evy Kreider, Deb Bontrager
1971	29-May	GC Union	Albert J. Meyer	76	Mary Jane Zimmerman	Joan Graber
1972	26-May	GC Union	A. Don Augsburger	63	Phil Shenk	Barb Nelson
1973	27-May	CMC***	John M. Drescher	73	J. Robert Gingrich	
					Student addresses	
1974	31-May	CMC	Don Jacobs	65	John Miller, Ellen Hoover	
1975	30-May	CMC	Calvin W. Redekop	71	Chris Hochstetler, Robin Helmuth	
1976	28-May	CMC	John Lapp	57	Christine Bowen, Bill Redekop	
1977	29-May	CMC	J. C. Wenger	66	Gretchen Metzler, Robert Kehr	
1978	28-May	CMC	Alice Metzler Roth	64	Audrey Roth, Greg Bontrager	
1979	27-May	CMC	June Alliman Yoder	75	Lorna E. Schwartzentruber, Thomas E. Charles	

Year	Date	Location	Speaker	# Seniors	Student addresses
1980	1-June	CMC	I. Wilmer Hollinger	70	Stephen Beachy, Cindy Hartzler
1981	31-May	CMC	J. C. Wenger	72	Brenda Chupp, Roger Kurtz
1982	30-May	CMC	James Lapp	66	Doug Bontrager, Joann McElmurry
1983	29-May	CMC	David Miller	61	Darla Schumm, Donald A. Wert
1984	27-May	CMC	Lee Roy Berry Jr.	47	Gregory L. Newswanger, Gwendolyn Joan Fike
1985	2-June	CMC	Laban Peachey	54	Margaret Jeschke, Randall Newswanger
1986	1-June	CMC	Diane Schrock Hertzler	44	Mark Guengerich, Heidi Kauffman
1987	31-May	CMC	Eileen Becker-Hoover	57	Doug Horst, Leisa Kauffmann
1988	29-May	CMC	Duane Beck	56	Chris Kauffman, Steve Longenecker
1989	4-June	CMC	Richard A. Kauffman	57	Jim Maust, Gretchen Nyce
1990	3-June	BCHS****	Shirley Showalter	55	Lori Mast, Eric Yordy
1991	2-June	BCHS	Nancy Kauffmann	52	Rachel Lapp, Samuel Miller
1992	31-May	BCHS	Lloyd Miller	66	Chad Smoker, Hannah Sommers
1993	30-May	BCHS	Dorothy Nickel Friesen	61	Danielle Miller, Benjamin Rutt
1994	5-June	BCHS	Devon Schrock	49	Austin Kaufmann, Jill Landis
1995	4-June	BCHS	Darla Schumm	50	Lisa Schmucker, Anthony Showalter
1996	2-June	BCHS	John D. Roth	46	Becky Wieand, Jason Miller
1997	1-June	BCHS	J. Lawrence Burkholder	45	Audrey Eash, Rafael Barahona
1998	31-May	BCHS	June Alliman Yoder	48	Matthew Krabill, Rebekah Yoder
1999	6-June	BCHS	Devon Schrock	57	Matthew Fisher, Stephanie Miller
2000	4-June	BCHS	Del Glick, Nina Lanctot	60	Chris Kingsley, Elisabeth Krabill
2001	3-June	BCHS	Shirley Showalter	53	Sarah Yoder, Seth Yoder
2002	9-June	BCHS	Victor Koop	51	Krista Bergey, Ted McFarlane
2003	1-June	BCHS	John D. Roth	54	R. D. Kuitse, Jenna Liechty

* Bethany Christian Auditorium
** Goshen College Union Auditorium
*** College Mennonite Church
**** Bethany Christian High School

Bethany Christian High School National Merit Finalist scholars

1979	Linda Metzler, Miriam Voran, Don Weaver		1991	Ryan Miller, Sam Miller, Paul Stauffer
1980	Deb Augsburger, Kathy Hochstetler		1992	Amy Kauffman, Nate Rempel
1981	Roger Kurtz		1993	Matthew Miller, Kerry Stump
1982	None		1994	None
1983	Peter Burkholder, Kelly Lerner, Jon Liechty, Elaine Moyer, Karl Steiner, Don Wert		1995	Jason Lehman, Kelly Short
			1996	None
1984	Scott Mark, Greg Newswanger		1997	Hannah Stutzman
1985	David Jeschke, Randy Newswanger		1998	Jennifer McFarlane
1986	Mark Guengerich		1999	Alison Dick, Matt Fisher, Tim Nafziger
1987	Jeremy Kropf, Jenny Smeltzer, David Wert		2000	Renee Glick, Andrew Histand, Aaron Lehman
1988	Steven Longenecker, David Schipani, Chris Stauffer, John Troyer		2001	Jeff Claassen, Jed Wulliman
			2002	Sarah Dick, Austin Scharf
1989	Jon Kauffman, James Maust, Gretchen Nyce		2003	Jon Meyer
1990	Cheryl Hochstetler, Lisa Stauffer, Mark Yoder			

Average: Last ten years (1994-2003)= 15 or 1.5 per year (over five times the national average)

Plays and musicals

1962	Handel's *Messiah*
1963	*Amahl* at school Christmas banquet
1965	*Our Town* – speech class *Gray Bread and Aria da Capo* – senior class Handel's *Messiah*
1966	*The Statues* – German class
1968	*Twelve Angry Jurors* – speech class
1970	*Amahl*
1972	*Amahl*
1974	*Amahl*
1975	*Ghost Dance*
1976	*Our Town*
1977	*The Crucible*
1978	*Martyrs Mirror*
1979	*Shut and Bar the Door* (one-act) *Amahl*
1980	*Pygmalion* *The Crucible* – junior class
1981	*Martyrs Mirror*
1982	*Twelfth Night*
1983	*For Heaven's Sake*
1984	*Arms and the Man*
1985	*Cheaper by the Dozen*
1986	*Bells on Their Toes*
1987	*The Carpenter*
1988	*Up the Down Staircase*
1989	*The Readymade Family* *The Little Tailor* – German club
1990	*The Miracle Worker*
1991	*Our Town*
1992	*The Curious Savage*
1993	*Nicholas Nickleby*
1994	*The Diary of Anne Frank*
1995	*Lost in Yonkers*
1996	*You Can't Take It With You*
1997	*Anne of Green Gables* (first full-length musical at BCHS) *The Orphans*
1998	*The Sound of Music* *Quiet in the Land* *James and the Giant Peach* (middle school)
1999	*January Thaw* *Godspell* *The Wizard of Oz* (middle school)
2000	*Twelve Angry Men* *Fiddler on the Roof* *Alice in Wonderland* (middle school)
2001	*The Foreigner* *Amahl* *Snow White* (middle school)
2002	*Do Not Go Gentle* *Joseph and the Amazing Technicolor Dreamcoat* *Stuart Little* (middle school)
2003	*The Chosen* *You're a Good Man, Charlie Brown* *Things My Mother Said* (middle school)

Senior athletes of the year

In 1997 Bethany began awarding the senior athlete award to anyone who played at least four varsity seasons as a junior-senior, earned a GPA of 3.0 or higher, and was active in church and community. An outstanding male athlete and an outstanding female athlete are chosen from these criteria (if there are no senior athletes for a gender, then no outstanding athlete for that gender is chosen).

1968	John S. Miller		1991	Phil Friesen and Heather Gusler
1969	Cal Frye		1992	Michael Bodiker and Audrey Schultz
1970	John Buller		1993	Ben Rutt and Danielle Miller
1971	Larry Gingrich		1994	Matt Weaver and Joanna Friesen
1972	Ron Gingerich		1995	Nate Lichti and Tara Swartzendruber
1973	Bob Gingrich		1996	Kevin Nice and Sheila Delagrange
1974			1997	Anders Weaver and Brooke Steury (Andrew Burkhalter, Eliot Friesen, Todd Sommers)
1975	Derald Bontrager			
1976			1998	Brad Schrock and Michelle Thomas (Dan Lanctot, Ryan Stiffney, Eric Yoder, Rachael Yoder)
1977	Wes Bontreger			
1978	Bryan Kehr and Barb Beachy		1999	Chris Nachtigall and Bess Steury (Amanda Friesen, Mike Malott, Stephanie Miller, Matt Plank, Erin Wentorf)
1979				
1980	Gary Bontrager and Lois Stoltzfus			
1981	Roger Kurtz and Karla Yoder		2000	Andrew Lanctot and Rachel Weaver (Jill Graber, Andrew Histand, Andrew Kauffman, Chris Kingsley, Aaron Lehman, Sam Nice, Brandi Schroeder, Rochelle Zehr)
1982	Doug Bontrager and Jessica Lapp			
1983	Loren Miller and Karen Miller			
1984	Greg Newswanger and Karen Yoder			
1985	Ric Troyer and Marta Brunner		2001	Tom Stahly and Sarah Yoder (Kate Showalter)
1986	Chad Sherman and Tina Lichti		2002	Jordan Buller and Sarah Thompson (Krista Bergey, Steve Ciesielski, Melanie Histand, Kayla Miller, Tara Plank, Emily Schulze)
1987	Myron Bontreger and Lynda Nyce			
1988	Scott Bodiker and Chris Kauffman			
1989	Nate Kingsley and Gretchen Nyce		2003	Brenna Steury (Hannah Kehr, Sarah Roth, Brittany Schroeder)
1990	Ryan Schrag and Lori Mast			

Post-season championship teams

Sectional

> Baseball – 1987
>
> Boys' basketball – 1998, 2000, 2002
>
> Girls' basketball – 1998
>
> Girls' soccer – 1997, 2000, 2001
>
> Softball – 1999
>
> Volleyball – 1976, 1980, 2001

Regional

> Boys' basketball – 1998, 2002

Faculty, staff, and special assignment personnel

Yr graduated		Assignment	Years of service
	James Acksel	volleyball coach	1984
	A. Don Augsburger	guidance, superintendent	1965-70
	Philip Barba	study hall supervisor	1967-68 (second sem.)
	Joanna Barkman	kitchen, library & office aide	1970-71, 87-93
	Tim Barwick	girls' BB, JV volleyball coach	2001-present
	Evelyn Bauer	art	1964-68
	Royal H. Bauer	librarian/media center dir./AV, English, speech, Bible	1955-88
2003	Jeffrey Bauman	chess coach	2003-present
	Naomi Baumgartner	middle school language arts	2003-04 (first sem.)
	Mark Beachy	custodian/maintenance	1984-89
	Shaun Beachy	custodian	1986-87
	Eileen Becker-Hoover	English	1979-82, 83-85, 90-pres.
	Winifred Beechy	home economics	1958-59
	Elizabeth Bender	algebra, English, German, Latin	1954-55, 58-59, 65-66
	Beth Berry	librarian, English	1988-present
	Laurie Bertsche	assistant girls' volleyball coach	1983-84
	Bonnie Birkey	admissions counselor	1998-99
	Mary Birkey	cashier, receptionist	1960-72
	Melvin Birkey	business manager	1959-69
	Jeanne Birky	receptionist	1974-75 (first sem.)
1988	Amy Birky (Birky Mounsithiraj)	receptionist	1998-2003
	Dan Bodiker	physical education, driver's ed, coach, athletic director	1964-present
	Wade Bollinger	English, principal	1970-73
1971	Becky Bontrager (Bontrager Horst)	English	1974-75
	Gladys Bontrager	cafeteria	1993-97

1955	Marion Bontrager	physical education, world history, athletic director	1961-62
1979	Rita Bontrager	library aide, cheerleading sponsor	1982-84
1978	Terry Bontrager	maintenance	summer 1978
1982	Cindy Bontrager (Hawkins)	JV volleyball coach	1985-88, 91
	Miriam Bontreger	assistant cook	1967-68
1987	Myron Bontreger	Spanish, Bible, soccer coach	1998-present
1977	Wesley J. Bontreger	JV soccer coach	1988-91
	Eva Borntreger	musical/drama costuming	2002-03
	Henry Braun	study hall supervisor	1967-68
	Anne Breckbill	English, volleyball coach	1985-90
	Sue Breiner	Bible	1975
	Timothy Brenneman	Bible	1966-69
	Jim Brubacher	custodian	1969-71
1966	Agnes Brubacher (Cross)	cook	1986-87
	Jennifer Bucher	physical education, assistant girls' BB/volleyball coach	1999-2002
	Neil Bucher	cross country coach	1996-2001
1971	Jim Buller	mathematics, guidance, coach	1979-present
	Lisa Burkey	science	1990-91
	Linda Butti	English, social studies	1974-76
	Archie Byler	bus driver	1958-59
	Gina Caligiuri	cheerleading coach	1997-98
	Karen Cender	cafeteria	2000-03
	Norm Cender	maintenance/custodian	2003-present
	Joe Christophel	industrial arts	1978-81
	Lucille Christophel	cafeteria assistant	1964-68
	Carl Chupp	custodian	1987-97
	Donna Chupp	office	1972-73
	Harvey Chupp	Bible, golf coach	1975, 90-92

Faculty, staff, and special assignment personnel ... *cont.*

1959	Loretta Chupp	receptionist	1975-92
	Eugene Clemens	history, physical education	1959-60
	James Clemens	library	1955-56, 57-59
	Randy Clouse	business manager	1995-present
	Elaine Clymer	home economics	1969-80
	Willard Conrad	English, German	1956-59
	Inez Culp	assistant cook	1956-57
	Lester Culp	science, agriculture	1954-87
	Brenda Daugherty	receptionist	2002-present
	Lee Dengler	sectional conductor	1995-97
	Susan Dengler	sectional conductor	1995-97
	James Derstine	Bible	1970-72
	Kenton Derstine	history	1983-84
1985	Cheryl Detweiler (Nester-Detweiler)	accountant	1992-95
	Diana Detwiler	business	1977-78
	Janelle Diller	English, social studies	1976-79
	Deb Drake (Witmer)	assistant volleyball coach	1979
	Allan Dueck	principal	1995-present
	Roger Dunn	physical education	1962-63
	Barbara Eash	admissions counselor	1995-98
	Ted Eash	grounds/maintenance	1998-present
	Joyce Eby	mathematics	1974-79
	Marsha Edwards	commerce	1972-77
	Sue Ehst	English, drama director	1997-present
	John Enz	orchestra	1969-70
	Robert Ewing	music	1954-59
	Stacey Farran	orchestra	1996-97
	Lois Fast	office	summer 1974

	Elaine Fidler	middle school drama director	2002-present
	Margaret Fisher	administrative assistant, structured study time tutor	1998-present
	Pauline Fisher	English	1961-62
	Aaron Fleming	cross country assistant coach	1999-2001
	Ron Friesen	biology, driver's ed	1963-67
	Rudolph Friesen	health	1967-68
	Walter Funk	mathematics	1965-66
	Lisa Gautsche	mathematics	1992-present
	Lori Gerber	JV softball coach	1999
1985	Mark Gerber	girls' JVBB coach	1991-93
	Nancy Gerber (Graber)	English, German	1965-68
	Dawn Gerber (Hankins)	JV volleyball coach	1988-89
	Lynn Geyer	cheerleading sponsor	1994-96
	Justin Gillette	custodian	2002
	Ray Gingerich	Bible, German	1968-69, 73-75
	Sam Gingerich	science	1971-73
	Susan Gingerich	development director	1997-present
	Aaron Gingrich	English, Spanish	1994-95
	Bruce David Glick	guidance	1977-78
	Craig Glick-Miller	girls' JV soccer coach	1997-98
1994	Chad Goertz	middle school mathematics	2002-present
	Mike Goertzen	science, coach	1997-present
	Cynthia Good Kaufmann	physical education, coach, admissions counselor	1993-2003
	Eric Good Kaufmann	art	1992-present
1977	Cathy Graber	cafeteria	1995-present
	Lewis Graber	custodian	1976-79
1978	Randy Graber	math, science, physical education, girls' BB coach	1997-99
	Richard Graber	mathematics	1965-68

Faculty, staff, and special assignment personnel ... *cont.*

	Viki Graber	assistant girls' BB coach	1987-88
	Wilma Graber	cook	1970-79
	Wanda Graber (Yoder)	cook	1977-78
	Beth Grieser	sixth grade	1999-present
	Marlin Groff	social studies, principal	1979-83
	Irene Gross	German	1970-96
	Leonard Gross	history, sociology	1959-64
	Gwen Gustafson-Zook	church history	2003-present
1980	Ray Gyori-Helmuth	Spanish, assistant principal	1993-2000
	Dawn Harms (Yoder)	music	1980-81
	Cindy Hartman	receptionist	1993-96
	Dean Hartman	mathematics, science	1959-68
	Donald Hartman	industrial arts	1967-68, 69-70
	Scott Hartman	middle school volleyball coach	2001
	Roy Hartzler	science, director of curriculum	1976-97
1982	Cindy Hawkins	volleyball coach	1985-87, 91, 95, 2003
1986	Beth Hawn	middle school science	2003-04 (first sem.)
	Bryan Heinz	coach	2000-present
	Jack Hellenbrand	German	1996-99
	Mary Helmick	secretary	1954-55
1977	Betty Helmuth (McFarren)	health, physical education, coach	1978-79, 82-85
	Ed Herr	mathematics, coach, principal, athletic director	1975-78
	Edith Herr	physical education	1954-55
	Ezra Hershberger	art	1955-64
	Floyd Hershberger	mathematics, science	1957-58
1961	Wilbur Hershberger	industrial arts, maintenance	1977-2000
	Dorothy Hershey (Hartzler)	home economics, English, typing	1954-56
	Nancy Hertzler	custodian	2001

aculty, staff, and special assignment personnel ... *cont.*

	Joy Hess	girls' tennis coach	1991-present
	Ruth Hilderbrand	study hall	1967-68
	James Hilty	business manager	1969-74
	Janell Hilty	girls' JVBB coach	1995-96
2002	Melanie Histand	coach	2002-03
	Arianne Hochstetler	head cook	1988-96
	Ritch Hochstetler	Bible	2003-04 (second sem.)
	Wendell Hochstetler	custodian	1965-67
	Bruce Holaway	business	1981-82
	C. J. Holaway	principal, Spanish, ass't to guidance counselor, superintendent	1954-62, 65-66
	Ruth Hollinger	drama director	1985-93
	Wilmer Hollinger	social studies, Bible	1965-86, 90-91
	Matt Honderich	chess coach	2003-present
	William D. Hooley	superintendent/principal	1970-94
	Florence Hoover	English	1969-72
	Saranna Hoover	cook	1987-94
	Elizabeth Hoover (Burton)	social studies	1986-97
1978	Carl Horner	algebra II	1983-84
	Barbara Horst	English	1982-83
	Carolyn Horst	physical education, history, girls' volleyball coach	1970-72
	Gary Horst	assistant principal	1986-89
	Ken Horst	science, mathematics	1973-76
	Oren Horst	science, mathematics, guidance	1968-71
	Darrel Hostetler	Bible, music	1967-75, 85-86
	Duane Hostetler	custodian	1989-96
	John Hostetler	business manager, commerce	1958-59
	Joyce Hostetler	interpreter	1990
	Jodi Huebert	computer, mathematics, economics	1996-present

Faculty, staff, and special assignment personnel ... *cont.*

1992	Tonya Hunsberger (Gaby)	girls' JV soccer coach	1996
	John Ingold	athletic director, driver's ed, biology, physical education	1959-60
	Eliza Jacoby (Stoltzfus)	sixth grade	1996-2001
	Scott Jantzi	English	1987-88
	Deb Johns	custodian	1997-2002
	Galen Johns	Bible, publicity/public relations	1968-70
1963	Steve Johns	publicity	1969-70
	Barry Johnson	assistant principal, coach	1995-present
	Chris Kahila	Bible	2003-04 (first sem.)
	Charleen Kanagy	supervised study time teacher	1989-93, 94-97
	Willie Kanagy	assistant principal	1989-98
	Byron Kauffman	music	1992-93
	Charles Kauffman	speech, Spanish	1967-68
	Katie Kauffman	cook	1961-63
	Sherry Kauffman	mathematics	1994-96
	Susan Kauffman	assistant cook	1958-59
1990	Tonya Kauffman (Miller)	girls' JVBB coach	1994-95
	Verda Kauffman	physical education	1960-61, 62-66
	Cheryl Kaufman Mast	seventh and eighth grade science	1998-present
1969	Rhoda Keener	language arts, learning disabilities	1986-94
1978	Bryan Kehr	middle school physical education, health, coach	1996-present
1956	Genie Kehr	cook	1977-88
	Julie Keim	drama director	1984-85
	Paul Keim	Bible	1979
	Pauline Kennel	piano	1954-55
1963	Arleta Kilmer	cook	1980-84
	Roy Koch	director of public relations/special gifts	1975-83
	Ron Kolb-Wyckoff	middle school mathematics, science	1996-2001

	Kathy Koop	German	2000-02
1975	Merrill Krabill	custodian	summer 1975
1975	Thomas Kreider	custodian	summer 1976
	David Kurtz	custodian	2002-present
	Michael Lambright	principal	1978-79
1991	Stephanie Lambright (Roth)	teacher's aide	1993-94
	Nina Lanctot	English, social studies	1977-79
	Emily Landis	assistant volleyball coach	1991
	Paul Landis	English, Bible	1972-73
	Paul Lauver	English, Bible	1958-59
	Ernest Lehman	algebra	1967-68
	Freeman Lehman	music	1959-67
	Jewel Lehman	physical education	1988-92
	Paula Lehman	art	1981-82
	Tim Lehman	seventh and eighth grade social studies, coach	2002-present
	Adele Leichty	middle school boys' soccer coach	2003-present
2000	Betsy Leinbach	middle school girls' volleyball coach	2002-present
	Roger Lengacher	custodian	1968-69
1984	Jay Little	cross country coach	1990-93
	Matt Litwiller	assistant BB coach	1993-94
	Wayne Litwiller	custodian	1967-68
	Jennifer Lucas-Germeyan	social studies	2001-present
1965	Marcia Mann (Troup)	mathematics	1968-70
	Tina Marsh	business	1988-89
	Samuel C. Martin	orchestra	1976-82
1968	Terry Martin	industrial arts	1975-77
	Miriam Martin (Friesen)	home economics	1960-68
	Brian Mast	instrumental music	1997-present

Faculty, staff, and special assignment personnel ... *cont.*

	Elsie Mast	home economics	1968-69
1981	John Mast	special services, girls' volleyball coach	1997-present
1980	Lois Mast	girls' volleyball, middle school girls' BB coach	1997-present
	Mafra Maust	cafeteria	2003-present
	Roseanne Maust	physical education	1954-56
1959	Wilmetta Maust	secretary	1977-94
	John J. McCarthy	music	1968-69
	Violet McColley	business education	1969-72
	Al McDowell	tennis coach	2002-present
1987	Edward McKenna	assistant custodian	1985-87
	René Mejia	custodian	1997
	Laura Metzler	secretary	1960-80
	Jacob Mierau	German	1964-65
	Beverly Jean Miller	cook	1978-80
	Catherine Miller	cook	1957-58
	Cliff Miller	Bible	1975
	Craig Miller	girls' JV soccer coach	1997-98
	Delmar Miller	English	1959-65
	Devon Miller	business	1959-61, 63-65
	Don C. Miller	mathematics	1980-94
	Fannie Miller	assistant cook	1970-71
	Gail Miller (Manickam)	orchestra	1981-82
	Grace Miller (Slaubaugh)	driver's ed, health, commerce	1956-57
1966	Henry Miller	custodian	1968-69
	J. Kevin Miller	communications coordinator	1994-present
1994	Jeff Miller	middle school soccer, JV baseball coach	1996-97
	Levi Miller	principal	1973-76
	Lloyd Miller	development director, campus pastor	1989-91

Faculty, staff, and special assignment personnel ... *cont.*

	Margaret Miller (Ingold)	home economics, girls' physical education	1959-60, 66-67
	Mark Miller	boys' JVBB coach	1993-95
1956	Marvin Miller	music	1963-64
	Mary Miller	head cook	1975-76
	Matt Miller	biological world	2003-04 (second sem.)
	Merv Miller	admissions counselor	2001-present
	Moses "Moe" Miller	custodian	1965-67
	Rachel Miller	head cook	1954-75
1979	Rachel Miller (Miller Jacobs)	English	1988-89
	Regina Miller	assistant softball coach	1990-92
	Sam Miller	custodian	1954-60
	Stephanie Miller	staff accountant	1995-present
	Sylvia Miller	cook	1964-67
1964	Verlin Miller	industrial arts	1984-85
	David Minter	study hall	1967-68
	Carol Morales	secretary	1990-95
	Marti Mosier (Kauffman)	cheerleading sponsor	1992-94
	Calvor Muchindu	International Visitors Exchange Program intern	1998-99
	Celia Mullet	teacher's aide	1997-99
	J. Marvin Nafziger	English, principal, guidance counselor	1954-58, 62-65
	Rhoda Nafziger (Schrag)	English, Bible	1963-65
	Beth Nebel (Stewart)	cheerleading sponsor	1979-80
	Boyd Nelson	publicity	1983-85
	Kristin Neufeld	science	1989-93
	Marilyn Nice	cafeteria	1992-present
	Mabel Nisley	art	1969-92
	Paul Nisly	English	1965-67
	Dave Nofsinger	art	1992-97

Faculty, staff, and special assignment personnel ... *cont.*

	Bettie Norman	orchestra director	1975-76
	Jennifer North (Bauman)	JV volleyball coach	1990
	Don Nussbaum	social studies	1982-83
	Tina Nussbaum Wagler	biology	1999-2000
	Dorothy Yoder (Yoder Nyce)	physical education	1961-62
1989	Gretchen Nyce	girls' JVBB coach	1993-94
	John Nyce	BB/volleyball coach	1961-62
	Patroba Ondiek	mathematics	1968-69
	Betty Otto	cashier	1956-59
	Galen Otto	commerce	1955-59
	Verna Oyer	cafeteria	2003-present
	Krysten Parson	health, physical education, coach	2002-present
	Allen Peachey	Spanish, athletic director	1970-83, 84-94, 95-96
	Mary Peachey	head cook	1996-2003
	Sara Penner	eighth grade mathematics	2002-03 (second sem.)
1990	Lauren Penner	summer help	1989
	Mark Plank	track/cross country coach	1985-88
	David Powell	mathematics	1964-65
	Betty Jo Ramser	cheerleading coach	1998-present
	Brent Randall	golf coach	1993-present
	Jon B. Reber	track/cross country coach	1988-89
	Brent Reinhardt	social studies, middle school and ninth grade baseball coach	1997-present
	Marla Reinhardt	middle school volleyball coach	1999
	Phyllis Rensberger (Kornhaus)	typing	1960-61
	Fancheon J. Resler	English	1966-67
1996	Sam Richardson	boys' JV soccer coach	1997
	Sandra Riegsecker	physical education, health	1966-68
1989	Denise Risser	administrative assistant	2000-present

aculty, staff, and special assignment personnel ... *cont.*

	Sheri Robinson	cheerleading coach	1996-98
	Arnold Roth	bus driver	1959-62
	Ruth Roth	library, English	1954-57
	Barb Roth (Horst)	English, coach	1982-83
	Vivian Schlabach	cook	1959-61
1955	Eudean Schlabach (Broni)	secretary	1959-60
	Mindy Schlegel	middle school volleyball coach	2003-present
	Dianne Schmidt	mathematics	1979-80
	Steve Schmidt	JV softball coach	2002
	Peter Schmitt	mathematics, physics	1955-59
	Keith Schrag	Spanish	1962-64
	Christine Schrock	cheerleading coach	1984-85
	Dan Schrock	guidance, coach	1963-64, 66-67, 73-77
	Devon Schrock	English	1977-99
	Tim Schrock	mathematics	1970-75
	Diane Schrock Hertzler	music	1975-87
	Dorothy Shank	English	1955-56
	Lydia Shank	French	1964-65
	Paul Shank	custodian	1979-82
	Susan K. Shank	music/orchestra	1973-75
	Bob Shantz	orchestra	1971-73
	Byron Shenk	physical education, health	1963-64
	Dale Shenk	Bible	1993-present
1968	Dan Shenk	golf coach, chess coach	1989, 1997-2003
1994	Jeff Shenk	frosh boys' BB co-coach	1996-97
	Karen Shenk	development assistant	2000-present
1968	Linda "Pert" Miller (Shetler)	physical education, health, girls' BB/volleyball coach	1972-79, 80-81
	Peter Shetler	technology/maintenance director	2000-present

Faculty, staff, and special assignment personnel ... *cont.*

	Melissa Shirk Jantz	seventh and eighth grade language arts	1996-present
	John Sholly	auto mechanics	1968-69
	Dawn Slabach	English	2000-01
	Neal Slabaugh	bus driver	1955-58
1965	Rosemary Slabaugh	physical education, girls' volleyball coach	1968-70
	Earl Slagell	custodian/maintenance	1971-84
	Joann Smith	social studies	1979-80
	Greg Smucker	orchestra	1983-86
	J. D. Smucker	choral music	1987-present
	Bruce Snyder	JV soccer coach	1984-87
	Debbie Snyder	cafeteria	2003-present
	Jean Snyder	English, music	1969-70
	Roxanna Sommers	family & consumer science	1989-99
	Ryan Springer	middle school social studies	2000-02
	Jackie Stahl-Wert	English	1975-76 (first sem.)
	Sharon Stauffer	orchestra	1982-83
	John Steiner	superintendent	1954-66
1961	Margaret Steiner	secretary	1972-73
1956	Marilyn Stephens	home economics	1975-78
	Rick Stiffney	sociology, boys' BB coach	1973-75
	Bryan Stoltzfus	driver's ed	1957-59
	Elsie Stoltzfus	cafeteria, cleaning	1969-70
	Grace Stoltzfus	receptionist/secretary	1973-74
	Ira Stoltzfus	custodian	1969-75
1966	Rosie Stoltzfus (Hartzler)	guidance	1984-85
	Donna Stuckey	receptionist/secretary	1973-74
	Keith Stuckey	mathematics	1976-80
	Arlene Stutzman	cook	1968-69

Faculty, staff, and special assignment personnel ... *cont.*

		Christine Stutzman	family & consumer science	1980-83, 99-present
		Dan Stutzman	bus driver	1956-58
1961		Duane Stutzman	middle school mathematics	2001-02
1960		Mary Stutzman	secretary	1980-86
		Mary Swartley	business, dir. of curriculum, business mgr., acting principal	1961-62, 78-95
		Larion Swartzendruber	shop	1970-75
		Clayton Swartzentruber	English	1957-58
		Bethany Swope	English, musical director	2001-present
		Everett Thomas	English, Bible, development director, assistant principal	1972-77, 79-89
		Richard Thomas	cross country coach	1994-95
		Nicole Tobey	middle school Spanish	2002
		Gordon Treesh	driver's ed	1967-71
		Effie Troyer	assistant cook	1984
		Jerome Troyer	custodian	1975-76
1966		Robert Troyer	physics	1969-70
		Velma Ulrich	cafeteria	1985-86 (first sem.)
		Mary Jo Unsicker (Martin)	JV softball coach	2000-01
1962		Alfonso Valtierra	Spanish, history	1967-70
		Marilyn Voran	home economics, girls' physical education	1956-59
		Pam Ward	sign language interpreter	1988-90
		Marcelo Warkentin	Spanish, JV soccer coach	2000-present
1970		Dennis Weaver	development director	1991-96
		Ivan Weaver	director of special & deferred giving	1983-85
		Shannon Wetzel-Gall	social studies, mathematics, JVBB coach	1999-2001
		Steve Wheatley	boys' tennis coach	2000-01
		Rachel Whitmer	English, German	1999-2000
		Dave Willig	softball coach	2001-02
		Richard Wineland	Bible	2003

Faculty, staff, and special assignment personnel … *cont.*

	Ruth Ann Wittrig	sixth grade	2000-present
	Rosemary Wyse (Reimer)	Spanish, English	1958-62, 65-66
	Betty L. Yoder	receptionist/administrative assistant	1995-98
	Carla J. Yoder	business	1985-87, 90-92
1973	Deloris Yoder (Hoover)	assistant cook	1976-77
1968	Don Yoder	custodian	1968-69
	Donna Yoder	commerce	1965-66
	Edith Yoder	cook	1966-67
1967	Edwin Charles Yoder	history	1984-85
	Faye Yoder (Mosemann)	music	1967-69
	Flossie Yoder	records	1967-68
	Fyrne Yoder	home economics	1955-56, 57-58, 59-60
	Gladys M. Yoder	English	1954-55
	J. Harold Yoder	tennis coach	1993-96
	Jill Yoder	middle school girls' BB/volleyball coach	1997-99
	Joy Yoder	cafeteria	1999-present
	June Alliman Yoder	drama director	1982-83
	Karen Yoder (Gyger)	coach	1978-80
	Larry Yoder	custodian	1967-69
	Lillian Yoder	business	1962-63
1978	Linda Yoder	cafeteria	1997-2000
	Marcia Yoder	cook	1985-87
	Marisa Yoder	science	1983-present
1957	Marvin D. Yoder	Bible	1976-91
	Ordo Yoder	custodian	1960-65
	Paul E. Yoder	superintendent	1966-68
	Pauline Yoder	typing	1967-68
	Renae Yoder	mathematics	1996-present

	Rhonda Yoder	business	1988-89
	Robert Yoder	bus driver	1958-59
1997	Rod Yoder	middle school soccer coach	1998
	Ruthie Yoder	cafeteria, assistant custodian	1987-present
	Sheila Stopher (Yoder)	sign language interpreter	1990-91
	Trish Yoder	physical education, health, girls' BB/volleyball coach	1981-88
	Vernon E. Yoder	Spanish, history	1964-67
1971	Warren Yoder	boys' BB coach	1979-80
	Albert Zehr	library	1962-65
	John David Zehr	church history	1965-66
	Kristen L. Zehr (Nussbaum)	earth science	1987-88
1983	Betsy Zook	girls' JVBB coach	1985-87
	Bonnie Zook	home economics	1983-89
	Herbert Zook	industrial arts	1960-67
	John Zook	guidance	1978-97

Bekki Fahrer '90 as Annie Sullivan, Michele Bontrager '91 as Helen Keller, and Director Ruth Hollinger in the 1990 production of The Miracle Worker. Photo: 1990 Bethany files

Class photos line both sides of the east-west hall and provide an interesting diversion for patrons waiting in line for the annual spring and fall fish fries.

Photo: Bourdon Studios

lass lists

Class of 1955

vian Amstutz (Headings)
arion Bontrager, **PR, F/S**
osa Cross (Borntrager)
ora Esch (Miranda)
on Farmwald
an Frey (Bouterse)
eland Haines
ewis Hochstedler
arol Hochstetler (Rhea)
arietta Hochstetler (Slabach)
owell Hoover
ark Hostetler
onald Martin
arol Miller (Zehr)
rancis Miller **VP**
oretta Miller (Kaufman) **TR**
ma Rangel (Ventura)
udean Schlabach (Broni) **F/S**
etty Slabach (Miller) **SE**
Villard N. Slabaugh
orman Stauffer
lwood Swartzendruber
orcas Troyer (Lara)
sther Weldy (Stichter)
sther Yoder (Kuhns)
ary Jean Yoder (Carlin)
. J. Holaway **SP**

Class of 1956

Mildred Bontrager (Wideman)
Charlene Borntrager Stutzman
Delta Byler (Basile)
Janet Cender (Zehr)
Harold Cross
Marion Ebersole (Kauffman)
Shelba Eby (Lenaburg)
Phyllis Eigsti (Troyer)
Clifford Frey
Dorthea Foster (Giddey)
Marie Gingerich (Miller)
Marlene Grabill (Eash)
Dennis Hartman
Lloyd Hartman
Eva Hershberger (Stutzman)
Winford Hershberger **PR**
Glen Hochstedler **VP**
Marilyn Hooley (Miller)
Carolyn Hostetler (Bauman)
Marilyn Hostetler (Stephens) **F/S**
Erma Kauffman (Swartzendruber)
Kenneth Kauffman
Mary Louise Kauffman (Meek)
Phyllis Kauffman (Kurtz)
Phyllis Keim (Beckler)
Doris Litwiller (Webber)
Morris Litwiller
Genevieve Metzler (Hershey)
Donald Miller
Genevive Miller (Kehr) **F/S**
Marvin Miller **F/S**
Truman Miller
John Mininger
Shirleen Oswald (Hochstedler)
Lurlene Rogers (Kedik)
Ruby Slabach (Hochstedler) **TR**
Loren Stauffer
Rosa May Stauffer (Hershberger)
Sylvia Steiner (Miller)
Melvin Stutzman

Ada Troyer (Beachy) (Hooley)
Arthur Troyer
Theresa Ventura (Hernandez)
Marian Weaver (Troyer)
Rhondal Wireman
Amzie Yoder
Charles Yoder
Joyce Yoder (Frantz)
Margaret Yoder
Marion Yoder
Mary Jean Yoder (Yoder) **SE**
J. M. Nafziger **SP**

Class of 1957

Norma Jean Baughman (Shenk)
Jean Bachman (Kauffman)
Jane Bartlett (Penland)
Evelyn Birkey (Yoder)
Rachel Bixler (Guedea)
Carolyn Burkholder (Bontrager)
Shirley Chupp (Glenn)
Shirley Crilow (Albrecht)
Galen Eash
Helen Good
Treva Gunden (Ritthaler)
Elinor Hallman (Good)
Lyle Hartman
Ralph Hartman
Richard Hershberger **TR**
Marybelle Kauffman (Beachy)
Mary Ellen Kaufman (Miller)
Joan Kuhns (Wood)
Birdena Lambright (Bollenbacher)
Warren Leichty
Joan Martin
A. J. Miller
Betty Miller (Yoder)
F. James Miller
Marlin Miller **PR**
Rebecca Miller (Fast)
Alvin Mullet
Paul Myers

Donald Newcomer
Barbara Plank (Slabach)
Marjorie Quiring (Troyer)
Leonard Ropp
Esther Rheinheimer (Hoover)
Verlin Riegsecker
Dale Schlabach
Janice Schrock (Prowant)
Mary Schrock (Yoder)
James Shank
Grace Sommers (Whitehead) **VP**
Janice Stahly (Yoder)
Sherry Stutzman (Weaver)
Verba Stutzman (Wilson) **SE**
Daniel Sutton
David Troyer
Janet Troyer (Weaver)
Esther Ventura (Garay)
Charlene Weaver (Farmwald)
Melba Weaver (Martin)
David Weldy
Daniel Wenger
Chris Yoder
Janet Yoder (Judy)
Leah Anne Yoder (Yoder)
Martha Yoder (Miller)
Marvin Yoder **F/S**
Patricia Yoder (Miller)
Robert Ewing **SP**
J. M. Nafziger **CS**

Class of 1958

Glen S. Bixler
Glenwyn Bollman (Cassel)
Ruby G. Bontrager (Bontrager)
Ruby S. Bontrager (Wilden)
Edwin Bontreger
Paul Borntrager
Jerry Burrows
Dewayne "Junior" Carpenter
Ferne Cender (Yoder)
Mary Ellen Dills (Miller)

Philip Dintaman
Roger Eby
Jeanette Eby (Hostetler)
Karen Erb (Schmucker)
Ruthann Gardner (Miller) **BM**
Marvin Gingerich
John Graber
Richard Graber
Rosalyn Grieser (Ledyard) **SE**
Gloria Guedea (Ventura)
Carolyn Hershberger (Miller)
Dorothy Hershberger (Hooley)
Rachel Holaway (Garot)
David Horst
Richard Hostetler
Virginia Hostetler (Wenger)
Sue Johnson (Brenizer)
James Kauffman
Lois Kauffman (Kaufman)
Marcile Kauffman (Miller)
Steven Kauffman
Pauline Kaufman (Borntrager)
Gerald Leinbach **TR**
Kathleen Martin (Ortiz)
David A. Miller
David Ray Miller **VP**
Fanny Miller (Yoder)
Joann Miller (Buerge)
Maurice Miller
Myrna Miller (Kauffman)
Ned Miller
Winifred Miller (Lehman)
Myrl Nofziger
Emerson Ropp
Mary Schrag (Kauffman)
Phillip Seitz
Mervin Slabach
Judy Slabaugh (Hochstedler)
Elson Sommers
Ann Stutzman
Elmer Stutzman
Carol Stutzman (Walls)
Georgia Thompson (Heard)
Floyd Troyer

Lavera Troyer (Hooley)
Louise Troyer (Beachy)
Larry Weldy **PR**
Larry Welty
Alice Yoder (Risser)
Edna Yoder (Brugger)
Rosa Yoder (Shetler)
Carolyn Yontz (Yoder)
Clayton Swartzentruber **SP**
Galen Otto **CS**

Class of 1959

Miriam Bauman (Slabach)
Loretta Birkey (Chupp) **F/S**
Howard Birky
Rosetta Bontreger (Miller)
Deloris Borntrager (Stalter)
Orvin Borntrager
Myrna Burkholder
Richard Carpenter
Richard Cender
Viola Gingerich (Miller)
Frances Hassencahl
Mary Ellen Hershberger (Miller)
Verl Hochstedler
Eva Hoover (Borntrager)
Sarah Hostetler (Halberda)
Rhea Kaufman (Biddle)
Mary Ruth Keim (Miller)
Alan Kreider
Marilyn Kortemeier (Welty)
Lois Lengacher (Delagrange)
Margaret Lengacher (Lengacher Potts)
Sharon Martin (Hill)
Wanda Mast (Frey)
Emery Miller
Larry Miller
Mary Kathryn Miller
Merlyn Miller
Steven Miller **PR**
John Mullet
Kenneth Mullett
Ruby Mullet (Farmwald)
Carol Mumaw (Miller)

Carolyn Myers (Chupp)
Keith Newcomer
Jane Osborne
Vera Pfile (Whitten)
Ivan Ramer
Ellsworth Risser
Carolyn Shrock (Hartman)
Marcile Smeltzer (Yoder)
Grace Snyder (Davidson)
Eleanor Sommers (Bieghler)
J. Stanley Steiner
Helen Steury (Nafziger) **TR**
Shelby Summer (Morrisey) **SE**
Grace Sutton
Ronald Swartzendruber **VP**
Shirley Tucker
Stanley Weaver
Janet Welty (Carpenter) **BM**
John Paul Wenger
Betty Yoder (Kauffman)
Betty Lou Yoder (Kendall)
Gloria Yoder (Eash)
Leon Yoder
Shirley Yoder (Lapp)
Verna Yoder (Trautman)
Wilmetta Yoder (Maust) **F/S**
Lester Culp **SP**
C. J. Holaway **CS**

Class of 1960

Eleanor Babcock (Buskirk)
Leah Beachy
Ernest Bennett
Ardys Book (Reinhardt)
Ervin Borntrager
Viola Christner
Richard Chupp
Ruby Cross (Bontrager)
Judy Crossgrove (Schwartz)
Martha Davidhizar (Timmons)
Ronald Davidhizar
Darrel Diener
Phyllis Dintaman (Stutzman) **SE**
Richard Eash

Lonnie Erb
Kenneth Farmwald
Royce Farmwald
LaVerne Good
Truman Good
Abraham Graber
Merlin Grieser
Richard Hallman
Leonard Hartman
Sharon Hershberger (Balyeat)
Rachel Holsomback (Yoder)
Leora Kauffman (Hodge)
Lila Kauffman (Miller)
Marcia Kauffman (Clark)
Shirley Kauffman (Steffen)
J. Evan Kreider **PR**
Robert Duane Kreider
Janice Lambright (Ropp)
Ann Lantz (Miller)
Larry Lehman
Karen Leinbach
Elenor Mann (Newton)
Ronald Martin
Waneta Mast (Haarer)
Dorcas Miller (Steider)
Dorene Miller (Kauffman)
Ervin Miller
Esther Miller
John Miller **TR**
Julia Miller (Miller)
Karon Miller (Weaver)
Lowell Miller
Martha Miller (Hartman)
Sharon Miller (Koelzer)
Shirley E. Miller (Miller)
Shirley J. Miller (Hamilton)
Dorothy Moore (Cramer)
Allen Morningstar
Lela Mullet (Rohrer)
Mary Mullett (Stutzman) **F/S**
Marilyn Quiring (Huffman)
Robert Ropp
Reita Seitz (Coblentz)
Norma Shaum (Peters)

Donald Stahly
Kenneth Stauffer
Guenn Stoltzfus (Martin)
Ron Stutzman
David Sudermann
Mary Swartzentruber (Stoll)
Donna Troyer (Sommers)
Dorothy Troyer
Eunice Troyer (Miller) (Chupp)
Walter Troyer
Larry Vardaman
Margaret Weaver
Arnold Willems
Veradine Wilson (Berkey)
Carol E. Yoder (Schaaf)
Carol J. Yoder (Munson)
David Yoder **BM**
Jon Yoder **VP**
Milo "Junior" Yoder
Roger Yoder
Ruth Arlene Yoder (Lengacher)
Sharon Yoder (Long)
Larry Yontz
Lester Culp **SP**

Class of 1961

Juanita Blough (Morningstar)
Elvie Bontrager
Robert Brenneman
Diana Burkey (Weldy)
Stanley Byler
Janice Carpenter (Miller)
Virginia Chupp
Ernest Crilow
Carolyn Dye (Marquand)
Marvin Eash **PR**
Phyllis Erb (King)
Gary Fulmer
Geneva Gingerich (Bender)
Edith Good (Kanagy)
Ben Graber
Gerald Gregory
Dwight Grieser **VP**
Carol Hartzler (Grieser)

Ernest Hartzler
Stanley Heer
Rachel Hernandez (Hensley)
Wilbur Hershberger **F/S**
Elsie Hochstedler (Hochstetler)
Amos Hostetler
James Hostetler
Charles Kauffman
Gerald Kauffman
Judy Kauffman (Kennel)
Verna Kaufman
David Lamar Knisley
Charles Kropf
Karen Lambright (Kotleba)
Karl Lambright
Jean Lehman (Moyer)
Letha Lehman
Rachel Leichty (Pittman) **TR**
Russell Leinbach **BM**
Margaret Mann (Steiner) **SE, F/S**
Valeria Mann (Dolph)
Bonita Martin (Kaufmann)
Carl Metzler
David L. Miller
David R. Miller
Evelyn Miller (Byler)
John Miller
Loren Miller
Betty Mullet (Hochstetler)
Phillip Mullet
Lamar Myers
Rollin Newcomer
Wayne Nissley
Paul Nunemaker
Sharon Nunemaker (Brooks)
Carlos Ovando
Irene Plank (Beachy)
Steve Richards
Carl Ropp
Don Schrock
Eugene Shrock
Marjorie Slabach
Shirley Slabaugh (Shoup)
Wayne "Arlee" Sommers

Wesley Steiner
Linda Stevens (Hugey)
Duane Stutzman **F/S**
Joyce Troyer (Troyer)
Phil Troyer
Lavon Welty
Mary Lois Wenger (Weaver)
Barbara Yoder (Nissley)
Esther Yoder (Kern)
Irma Yoder (Stutzman)
Lewis Yoder (Robinson)
Nancy Yoder (Nofziger)
Ruth Yoder (Neely)
Shirley Yoder (Yoder)
Warren Yoder
Freeman Lehman **SP**
Delmar Miller **CS**

Class of 1962

Margaret Baumgartner (Rippey) **TR**
Roger Beachy **PR**
Jonathan Billheimer **BM**
Phyllis Birkey (Fitchpatrick)
Perry Bontrager
Lois Book (Kipe)
Idella Borntrager (Otto)
Charlene Brown (Miller)
Marlene Brown (Coldren)
Robert Buzzard
Levon Christophel
Leroy Cross
Wayne Davidhizar
Carol Dintaman (Birky)
Andrea Eash (Yeager)
Nancy Eash (Myers)
Richard Friesen
Melba Good (Miller)
Josephine Guedea
Linda Hershberger (Wogoman)
Betty Holmes (Bollinger)
Gretchen Honderich (Yoder)
Vernon Hoover
J. Lloyd Kauffman
Susanne King

Simon Knepp Jr.
Arlene Koch (Holdeman)
Stanley Kulp
Sandra Leatherman (Kauffman)
Carol Lehman (Kampen)
Ann Lengacher (Reschly)
Ray Marks
David A. Miller
David R. Miller
Lynford Miller
Mary Ann Miller (Suter)
Willard Miller
Lowell Nunemaker
Ruby Ramer (Panyako)
Wayne Risser
Galen Schmucker
Judy Schrock (Stephenson)
Phyllis Showalter (Metzler)
Sharon Shriner (Stoll)
Betty Slabach
Cynthia Slabach (Stauffer)
Linda Slabaugh
Richard Slabaugh
Elaine Snyder (Yoder)
Dana Sommers
Janet Steiner
Eileen Stichter (Eash)
Fred Stoltzfus
Pauline Stutzman (Hochstetler)
Ruby Stoltzfus (Nofziger)
Burl Troyer **VP**
Nancy Troyer (Yoder)
Alfonso Valtierra **F/S**
Julia Weaver (Kennell)
Rodney Weaver
Gail Williams (Williams)
Elaine Yoder
Janis Yoder (Erb) **SE**
Rosemary Yoder (Detwiler)
Howard Zehr Jr.
Lester Culp **SP**
Herbert Zook **CS**

Class of 1963

Barbara Anderson (Graber) **TR**
David Bishop **PR**
David A. Bontrager
Mary Bontrager (Colwell)
Ola Bontrager (Cosby)
Earl Burkey
Joyce Byler (Slaubaugh)
Jerry Carpenter
James Chupp
John Chupp
Nancy Chupp (Garber)
Joyce Cross (Miller)
Rachel Cross (Brenneman)
Lavern Davidhizar
Sharon Delagrange (Mullett)
Clare Eby
Karen Esch (Patrick)
Karen Garber (Troyer)
Elizabeth Gingerich (Jones)
Judith Graber (Eash)
Lydia Graber (Kauffman)
Lynette Grieser (Slaubaugh)
Violet Hartman (Weldy)
Margaret Heer (Murphy)
Thelma Hershberger (Ramer) **SE**
John Histand
Wayne Hochstedler
Janet Hochstetler (Miller)
Keith Hoffman
Anita Hoke (Stoner)
William Hoover
Letha Hostetler (Bontrager)
Mary Etta Hostetler (Yoder)
Dolores Hughes
Brenda Jeffers
Joe Alan Johns
Steven Johns **F/S**
Dwight Landis
Jeraldine Lengacher (Bartels)
Larry Mann (Hesed) **VP**
Joseph Martin
Sherrill Martin (Vardaman)

Amanda Miller (Jacobs)
Daniel Miller
Leland Miller
Marcia Miller
Paul Miller
Ruth Miller
Sharon Miller (Ropp)
Sherrill Moore (Graber)
Jennie Morningstar (Kauffman)
Fanny Mullet
Carol Odell (Martin)
Jerry Richards
Arleta Schlabach (Kilmer) **F/S**
Mark Schrag
Frances Slabach (Bingaman)
Duane Snyder
Clair Stauffer
Glenn Stutzman
Sharon Stutzman (Chupp)
Ardis Summer (King)
Roger Tompkins
Mary Treviño (Nieto)
Janice Troyer (Hostetler)
Leona Troyer (Overholt)
Sally Troyer (Miller)
Verlin Troyer
Bonnie Weldy (Miesel)
Lee Weldy
Charles Yoder
Dennis Yoder
Leroy Yoder
Susie Yoder
Wealtha Yoder (Yoder Helland)
Leonard Gross **SP**
Dean Hartman **CS**

Class of 1964

Carol Bauman (Miller)
Elmer Beachy
Robert Beiler
David Berkey
Barbara Birkey
Sherlin Bollman
Shirley Bollman (Bricker)

Thomas Bontrager
Cecil Bontreger
Dale Burkey
Phyllis Burkey (Mast)
Paul Byler
John Christner
Janice Christophel (Langstaff)
Verlin Chupp
Max Cripe
Marilyn Davidhizar (Miller)
Aletha Doolin (Smithson)
Loren Eash
Ralph Erb
Carol Gingerich (Beachy)
Marjean Gingerich
Ronald Gingerich **VP**
Donald Graber **BM**
Dennis Hartman
Merlin Hartman
Carolyn Hershberger (Riegsecker)
Marolyn Hershberger (Yoder)
Rita Hooley (Troyer)
Ruby Hostetler (Brower) **SE**
Maxine Kauffman (Miller)
David Kaufman
Phillip Kilmer
Titus King **PR**
Yvonne Kraus (Forman)
Karen Kuhns (Chupp)
Wanda Lambright (Brotherton)
Philip Lehman
Janet Leichty (Brindle)
Maria Maniaci
Dana Martin
Manasseh Martin
Nancy Martin (Detweiler)
Marcia Middaugh (Schweitzer)
Inez Miller (Householter)
Karen Miller
Nancy Miller (Ketcham)
Verlin Miller **F/S**
Virginia Miller
John Mishler
Carolyn Mullet

Myrna Newcomer (Gerber)
Donald Nunemaker
Ronald Nunemaker
Mamie Ost (Markle)
Sandra Peebles (Peebles Linden)
Dorothy Schrock (Belile)
Marilyn Shrock (Stutzman)
Jeanette Slabach (Campbell) **TR**
Edith Slabaugh (Shanholt)
Darrel Sommers
Betty Stutzman (Miller)
Julia Treviño (Palos)
Rebecca Troyer (Christophel)
Marvin Troyer
Walter Troyer
Willis Troyer
Ronald Weaver
Cheryl Weldy (Martin)
Elisabeth Wenger
Kenneth Willems
Eileen Yoder (Miller)
Forrest Yoder
Lester Yoder
Paul Yoder
Rhoda Yoder (Troyer)
Miriam Martin **SP**

Class of 1965

Larry Austin
Marianne Bachman (Pletcher)
Veronica Beachy (Denlinger)
Ruth Ann Bender (Scott)
Lois Bixler (Martin)
Bessie Bontrager (Lehman)
Devon Bontrager
Esther E. Borntrager (Cross)
Esther J. Bontrager (Wenger)
Philip Bontrager
Robert Brundage
Clair Byler
Joe Christophel
Pauline Chupp (Diggens)
Richard Chupp
Sara Jean Chupp (Zook)

arvin Cross
aren Diener (Thompson) **SE**
homas Gardner **PR**
icki Gardner (Lichti) **TR**
arolyn Gingerich (Helmuth)
oise Gingerich
auline Gingerich (Liechty)
arol Hartman (Bontrager)
nita Hershberger (Myers)
leen Hoogenboom (Clemmer)
elmar Hooley **VP**
arie Hoover (Troyer)
oyce Hostetler
erda Hostetler (Bontrager)
oy Hunsberger (Beiler)
aymond Johnson
arrell Kauffman
nda Kauffman (Boyer)
Mary Kauffman (Hershberger)
Merlin Kauffman
onald Kaufman
oanne Kraus
aul Kreider
homas Lehman
dward Leichty
onna Lengacher (Ramer)
anet Lengacher (Lengacher Smith)
arrell Liechty
teve Liechty
Marcia Mann (Troup) **F/S**
da Martin
anny Mast (Lucius)
ldon Miller
oyce Miller (Borntrager)
Marvin Miller
herry Miller (Miller)
hirley Miller (Beach)
everly Moore (Stalter)
aVern Mullett
Dennis Myers
ue Neuhouser (Neuhouser Pownall)
Mary Jean Newcomer (Troyer)
ictor Ovando
teven Riegsecker

Marvin Schmucker
Dean Shetler **BM**
Joann Shrock (Mast)
Dorothy Slabach
Rosemary Slabaugh **F/S**
Carl Stauffer
Joan Stauffer (Chupp)
Gareth Stoltzfus
Ralph Stutzman
Rebecca Tyson
Andrea Valtierra (Britten)
John Valtierra
Daniel Ventura
Carl Weaver
Leona Weaver (Schmucker)
Barbara Welty (Eiler)
Anthony Yoder
Daryl Yoder
Phyllis Yoder (Gehman)
Waneta Yoder
Dianne Zehr (Schaefer)
Lester Culp **SP**
Herbert Zook **CS**

Class of 1966

Ken Anderson
Ruth Beachy (Wartell)
Gregory Beck
John Birkey
John Bishop
Allen Bontreger
Bethany Bontrager (Shetler)
Connie Bontrager (Parker) **SE**
Frieda Bontrager (Nisly)
Agnes Brubacher (Cross) **F/S**
Charles Cross
Roberta Davidhizar (Rexroth)
Virginia Davidhizar (Birky)
Cheryl Fogleman (Kersch)
Delores Gingerich (Kauffman)
Richard Gingerich
Carl Graber
Tom Graber
Curtis Grieser

Sharon Hartman (Swartzentruber)
Dolores "Dee" Helmuth (Birkey)
Mike Hershberger
Stanley Hershberger
Stanley Hoffman
Linda Hooley (Hochstetler)
Marsha Hooley (Hooley Miller)
Phyllis Hoover (Scanlon)
Lois Johns (Johns Kaufmann)
David Johnson
Pat Kauffman (Yoder)
Clara Keim
Carlyle Kuhns
Rosemary Kulp (Shirk)
David Leinbach
Jo Maniaci
Vera Metzler (Leinbach)
Barbara Miller
Elsie Miller (Horner)
Elwayne Miller
Gloria Miller (Hearten) **VP, FH**
Gordon Miller
Henry Miller **BM, F/S**
Leon Miller **TR**
Verna Miller
Victor Miller
Beverly Milne (Hershberger)
Ruth Mishler (Basinger)
Dallas Myers
Myra Nafziger (Oswald)
Dean Ramer
Micheline Rocourt (Rocourt Duskin)
Dennis Roth
Jeanne Shrock (Riegsecker)
Johanna Schulz (Daubenspeck)
Sharon Slabach (Bender)
Jerry Slabaugh
Dorothy Stauffer (Kropf)
Dennis Stichter
Rosemary Stoltzfus (Hartzler) **F/S**
Beverly Stutzman (Snyder)
Sharon Summer (Axline)
Kenneth Thomas
Gary Troyer

Jerry Troyer
Lena Troyer (Delagrange)
Robert Troyer **F/S**
Alice Trumbull (March)
D. Rex Tyson
Anna Marie VanVeen (Hooley)
Wilhelmina VanVeen (Dominiak)
Verda Weaver
Rex Wenger
Delvon Yoder **PR**
Dennis Yoder
Georgia Yoder (Davis)
Judy Yoder (Bontrager)
Malinda Yoder
Martha Yoder (Miller)
Rachel Yoder (Yoder Cook)
Raymond Yoder
Ruth Yoder (Dyal)
Joan Zehr (Link)
Dan Bodiker **SP**
Lester Culp **CS**

Class of 1967

Rosaleta Berkey (Miller)
Jay Bontrager
Thomas Bontrager
John Bontreger
Marvin Borntrager
Shirley Brenneman (Bontrager)
Philip Burkey
Dennis Byler
Jane Cripe (Schrock)
Jean Davidhizar (Griffin)
Nancy Davidhizar (Yoder) **TR**
Norma Davidhizar (Mast)
Craig Garber
Susan Gardner (Nelson) **FH**
Florence Gingerich (Ard)
James Gingerich **FH**
Kenneth Gingerich
Wayne Gingerich
Wanda Graber (Hagenbuch)
Margaret Groff **SE**
Lowell Haarer

Jay Hershberger
Sara Hershberger (Culp)
Jeffrey Hirschey
Cindy Hooley (Troyer)
Janalee Horst (Graber)
LeAnna Hostetler (Hochstetler)
Lila Hostetler (Fox)
Gay Hunsberger (Lehman)
Ray Hunsberger
Donna Johnson (Greenawalt)
Mary Ann Kauffman (Shultz)
Bonita Kaufman (Schultz)
Julie Kersting (Parcell)
Daniel King
Mary Ann Krabill (Hollinger)
Mary Ann Lehman (Wieand)
Ephraim Martin
Maxine Martin
LeRoy Mast
Betty Miller (Gruber)
Cynthia Miller (Mast)
Daniel Miller
Eugene Miller
Larry Miller **PR**
Ruth Ann Miller (Summers)
Sharon Myers (Birkey)
Diana Nafziger (Hershberger)
Benjamin Nelson **BM**
Judy Ramer (Martin)
Roger Rheinheimer
Esther Rocourt
Carol Schrock (Newhard)
Larry Schrock
Sanford Schrock
Verda Schrock (Fletcher)
Robert Slabach
Maria Smedzwick
Sherry Stahl (Mast)
Charles "Charlie" Steiner
Tim Stoltzfus
Robert Stutzman
Janet L. Swartzendruber (Reid)
Frank R. Treviño
Allen Troyer

Carol Troyer
JoAnn Troyer (Garber)
Kay Troyer (Schrock)
Dale Weaver
Esther Weaver (Yothers)
Fred Weldy
Rhonda Willems (Swartzendruber)
E. Charles Yoder **F/S**
Craig Yoder **VP**
Delores Yoder (Zehr)
Donovon Yoder
Glen Yoder
Gloria Yoder (Landes)
Jerry Yoder
Joan Yoder (Gingerich)
Retha Yoder (Baer)
David Zehr
Donna Zehr (Conrad)
Ellen Zehr (Zehr)
Dean Hartman **SP**
Wilmer Hollinger **CS**

Class of 1968

Jerry Albrecht
Susan Anderson (Weaver)
Phyllis Augsburger (Ressler)
John Bauman
Duane Beck
Kathleen Bennett (Stiffney)
Anne Birky (Birky Koehn)
Elroy Bontrager **BM**
Larry Bontrager
Mary Bontrager (Lakner)
Charles "Chuck" Bontreger
Deborah Brandenberger
Irene Burkey (Hargrove)
John Byler
Merle Christner
Sandra Christophel (Buss)
Donald Chupp
Dorothy Crilow (Schreck)
Mary Davidhizar (Lambright)
Audrey Gingerich (Miller)
Ronald Goetz

Robert "Bob" Graber **PR**
Linda Graber (Peterson)
Julia Hartman (Stech)
Paul Hartman
Barbara Helmuth (Albrecht)
Carol Helmuth (Honderich)
Martin Honderich **VP**
Glen Hostetler
Ronald Kauffman
Linda Kuhns (Unzicker) **SE**
Sandra Lambright (Yoder) **TR**
Weldon Lambright
Jan Leichty
Betsy Martin (Troyer)
L. Brian Martin
Terry Martin **F/S**
Carol Middaugh
Brenda Mierau (Yoder)
Carol Miller (Hostetler)
Cheryl Miller (Cotter)
Elroy Miller
Gary Miller
Gloria Miller (Miller Holub)
Gwendolyn Miller (Newcomer)
Jeanette Miller (Patches)
John S. Miller **FH**
Larry "L. G." Miller
Linda Miller (Shetler) **F/S**
Rachel Miller
Ralph Miller
Sheldon Miller
Jane Murray (Miller)
Gene Newcomer
Fern Nisley (Miller)
Dale Nunemaker
Ray Nussbaum
Janice Riegsecker (Yoder)
Susan Schertz (Moreno)
Stephen Shank
Dan Shenk **F/S**
Donna Shrock (Quiring)
James Shrock
Lowell Stoltzfus
Michelle Sullivan (Bontrager)

Keith Swartz
Daniel "Danny" Treviño
Barbara Troyer
June Troyer (Yoder)
Margaret "Peggy" Troyer (Garcia) **FH**
Verton Troyer
Brenda Tyson (Buller)
Owen Weaver
David Weldy
Donald Yoder **F/S**
Edna Yoder
Ernest Yoder
John W. Yoder
Leon Yoder
Richard Yoder
Rosalie Yoder (Monroe)
Sharon Yoder (Heatwole)
Wes Yoder
Daryl Zook
Wilmer Hollinger **SP**
Lester Culp **CS**

Class of 1969

Rebekah "Becky" Bair (Smucker)
Richard Baker
Norma Bauman (Bontrager)
Gary Beachy
James Beachy **VP**
Paul Beachy
Kathleen Beck (Martin)
Glen Blosser
David Blough
Elizabeth Bontrager (Schneider)
Tim Bontreger
Don Brenneman
Dale Brubaker
Darlene Cross (Plank)
Carolyn Davidhizar (Bitikofer)
Stephen Dintaman **FH**
Jay Friesen
Joan Garber (Gingerich) **FH**
Sharon Gingerich (Classen)
Shirley Gingerich (Nunemaker)
June Hershberger (Trcka)

ary Hershberger (Weldy)
oger Hooley
 Richard Hoover
elody Kilmer (Bechler)
mes "Jim" Krabill **PR**
uth Ann Lehman (Yoder)
arbara Leinbach (Lehman) **TR**
ennis Martin **BM**
odney Maust
onald Metzler
onnie Mierau (Bailey) **SE**
rian Miller
ugene Miller
va Miller (Burroway)
rieda Miller (Borntrager)
alen Miller
oy Miller (Gerber)
orris Miller
ynn Miller
ose Mishler (Miller)
onald Mullet
usan Nafziger (Bartel)
aul Nelson
enneth Schmitt
oger Schmucker
Harriet Schrock (Martin)
oseph Schrock
arl Schrock
hoda Shenk (Keener) **F/S**
aren Shrock (Miller)
uth Slabach
Marlin Slabaugh
herrill Slaubaugh (Brown)
orraine Sommers (Reinford)
David Stoltzfus
riscilla Stoltzfus (Trinkley)
Carmen Stutzman (Thompson)
Mavis Stutzman (Miller)
Miriam Sutter (Lapp)
Denver Troyer
aren Tyson
onald Tyson
Steven Valtierra
aren Weldy (Kaufman)

Bonita Yoder (Folkening)
Darrell Yoder
Jared Yoder
Marvin Yoder
Ronald Yoder
John Zimmerman
Wilmer Hollinger **SP**
Darrel Hostetler **CS**

Class of 1970

Steve Bauer
Andrea Bayer (Hudson)
Wayne Beall
Jane Birkey (Otto)
Albert Bontrager
Catherine Bontrager (Brubaker)
Debra Bontrager (Kauffman)
Gene Bontrager
Jason Bontreger
Lois "Tobi" Brenneman (Goldfus)
Stephen Chupp **VP, FH**
Sharon Cross (Bontrager)
JoEtta Culp
Mary Fisher (Mishler)
Calvin Frye
Roger Gingerich
Joseph Greaser
Marlene Hartman (Sutter)
Duane Hooley
Vic Hooley
John Hoover
Mardene Horst (Kelley)
Dale Hostetler
Lowell Hostetler
Rosalie Hostetler (Simon)
James Jacobs
Chuck Kaufman
Roger Kaufman
Jim King
John King
Evelyn Kreider (Martin)
Becky Lehman (Gascho)
Jim Leichty
Lois Martin

Patricia Martin (Bontrager)
Barbara Mast (Schlegel)
Jerry Maust **BM**
Ronda Maust (Chupp) **SE, FH**
Marie Metzler
Chuck Miller
Galen D. Miller
Galen J. Miller
Gary C. Miller
Geraldine Miller (Raabe)
Jane Miller (Leatherman)
Marilyn Miller (Riegsecker)
Philip Miller
Rosemary Miller
M. Reneé Minnich (Esch)
Carolyn Newcomer (Hochstetler)
Marilyn Nisley
Glenn Nunemaker
Tyron Pasley
David Schrock **PR**
Grace Shrock
Sigrid Simon
Randall Slabaugh
Robert Stuckey
Randy Stutzman **TR**
Carolyn Troyer (Hostetler)
Dorothy Troyer (Stutzman)
Denny Weaver **F/S**
Alvin Yoder
Golda Yoder (Wofford)
Jonathan Yoder
Russell Yoder
Judy Zimmerman (Herr)
Dan Bodiker **SP**
Al Valtierra **CS**

Class of 1971

Lola Albrecht (Gingerich)
Nancy Baker
Dave Beachy
Nedra Beck (Gnagey)
Larry Berkey
Carol Birkey (Miller)
Rebecca Bontrager (Horst) **F/S**

Mervin Bontrager
Linda Brubaker (Bergey)
Jim Buller **PR, F/S**
John Buller **BM**
Wilma Burkey (Kessens)
Shirlee Christophel
Greg Chupp
Ramona Chupp (King)
Pamela Dintaman
Paul Farmwald
Harry Funk
Gary Garber
Benjamin Gingerich
Merrill Gingerich
Larry Gingrich
Dennis Gongwer
Doris Graber (Mullet)
Joan Graber (Kauffman)
Coleen Harter (Steele)
Shirley Helmuth (Bachman)
Rebecca Hershberger (Horvath)
Phil Hoffman
Ken Holderman Jr.
Don Hooley
Steve Hooley **VP**
Dennis Hoover
Bev Hostetter (Wenger)
Caroll Hostetler (Beall)
Gloria Hunsberger (Schwartz)
Rodney Koch
Glendon Lambright
David Lehman
Charles Leinbach
Gary Martin
Patricia Mierau (Martin)
Ann Miller
Jenell Miller (Ulrich)
Norma Miller (Schrock)
Paul Miller
Retha Mishler (Filhart)
Karen Nisley (Givens)
Sandra Nunemaker (Garber)
Jan Schmitt (Orpin)
Cheryl Schrock (Dolson)

Kerry Schrock
Ruthy Schrock (Chupp)
Gaile Shaw (Shaw-Hill)
David Slabach
Barry Slabaugh
Fern Sommers (Delagrange)
Jane Stoltzfus (Stoltzfus Buller)
Jean Stoltzfus (Martin) **SE**
Shirley Stoltzfus (Aubert-Stoltzfus)
Salinda Stone (Robinett)
Ann Stutzman (Stevens)
Venesse Taylor (Yoder)
Jeannette Miller (Teall)
Pat Troyer (Weaver) **TR**
Judy Weaver (King)
Verl Weaver
Merritt Welty
J. Byard Yoder
Dennis Yoder
Lance Yoder
Nancy Yoder (Schaffer)
Ron Yoder
Warren Yoder **F/S**
Mary Jane Zimmerman
Brenda Zook
Lester Culp **SP**
Darrel Hostetler **CS**

Class of 1972

Steve Ball
David Bauman
Lavern Beachy
Max Beck
Elizabeth Bender (Barker)
Joan Bennett (Whicker)
Mildred Berry (Robinson)
Sheldon Blosser
Darlene Bontrager (Fanning)
Cliff Brubaker **BM**
Ernest Christner
Roger Christophel
Jeff Chupp
Judy Davidhizar
　　(Davidhizar Holmes) **SE**

Maribeth Diener (Friesen)
Howard Friesen
Ron Gingerich
Connie Graber
Richard Harder
Wanda Harter (Heckathorn)
Cecilia Hooley (Wyse)
Gail Kaufman (Brumbaugh)
Arlan King
Steven Kratzer
David Lehman **TR**
Sharon Leinbach
Murphy Lucas
Terry Marks
Rick Maust
Bryan Mierau **PR**
Carol Miller (Dulaney)
Charlotte Miller (Martin)
Dan Miller
Floyd Miller
Judy Miller (Cooper)
Kathryn Miller (Bontrager)
Lynn Miller
Miriam Miller
Rosa Miller (Chrzanowski)
Don Mishler
Glenda Myers (Ascencio)
Barbara Nelson (Nelson Gingerich)
Linda Nisley (Bontrager)
Beverly Ramos (Heller)
Diane Schrock (Hershberger)
Dina Sexton (Koch)
Philip Shenk
Paul Slagel
Elizabeth Snyder (Slagel)
Mike Stark
Karen Stichter
Mike Stutzman **VP**
Rose Stutzman (Baldridge) **FH**
Paul Sudermann **FH**
Sandi Troyer (Clark)
James Tyson
Jan Unoson
Gary Weaver

Frank Weldy
Mary Weldy (Clasen)
Derrise White
Jocelyn Yeater (Kauffman)
Norma Yoder (Buell)
Ron Yoder
Wilmer Hollinger **SP**
James Derstine **CS**

Class of 1973

Joy Bair (Martin)
Timothy Baker
Mary Ann Ball (Hooley)
Joyce Bontrager (Yoder)
Mark Bontreger
James Book
John Brenneman
Sarah Conrad (Yoder)
Larry Crilow
Charles Culp
Enos Davidhizar
June Davidhizar **FH**
Atsuko Endo
Cynthia Frey (Frey)
Gwendolyn Friesen (Hershberger)
Charles Garber
Gretchen Garber (Weaver)
Michael Getz
Joan Gingerich (Grossman)
Michael Gingerich
Susan Gingerich (Shetler)
J. Robert Gingrich
　　(Hooley-Gingrich) **PR**
Rosie Glick (Eash)
Dale Goetz
Deloris Graber (Hoover) **F/S**
Don Grieser
Donna Hershberger
　　(Ulbricht-Hershberger)
Wayne Hartzler
Betty Hershberger (Schmid)
Daryl Hershberger
Jeryl Hershberger
Lynda Hollinger (Hollinger-Janzen)

Keith Hooley
Carolyn Horst (Heydon)
Vaughn Hostetter
June Kauffman (Fowler)
Birdena Kaufman (Ringenberg)
Rose Koerner (Riehl)
Bonnie Kreider (Nussbaum)
Carolyn Martin (Hoover)
Treva Martin (Liechty)
Henry Martinez
Norman Mast
Stephen Maust
Gary Miller
James Mishler
Marcia Mumaw (Jantz)
Paul Newcomer
Marilyn Nisley (Frye)
Robert Nunemaker
Vitaris Ongoa
Sylvia Oswald (Beneze)
Sam Ovando
Tena Ramer (Stutzman)
Patti Schrock (Miller)
Dan Slabach
Cynthia Slabaugh (Dixon) **TR**
Jerry Slabaugh
Jeanette Slagel (Slabaugh)
Joan Steiner (Vogt) **SE**
Robert Steury **FH**
Danile Stoltzfus (Stoltzfus Martens)
Dick Stutzman
Mark Troyer
Randall Troyer
Kimberly Washburn (Williams)
Ellen Welty (Nussbaum)
Clint Yoder
Earl Yoder
Jonathan Yoder **VP**
Joyce Yoder (Bontrager)
Myron Yoder
Paul Yoder **BM**
Dan Bodiker **SP**
Al Peachey **CS**

Class of 1974

ebi Bontrager (Caprorotta)
eki Brenneman (Denman)
arlowe Buller
ennis Chupp
sa Comstock (Neff)
aul Conrad II
aren Coutts
loria Cross (Schrock)
yrna Drudge (DeAgostino)
hilip Frye
ene Gingerich
e Gingerich
ark Gingerich
haron Gingerich (Jakabosky)
onnie Gingrich (Brubaker) **BM**
achel Greaser (Good)
d Groff
onna Hartman (Caskey)
nita Helmuth (Showalter)
eronica (Roni) Henderson
hrisann Hensler (Longstreet)
isa Herr (Lederach)
hil Herr **VP**
ucinda Hochstetler (Neely)
athy Holderman (Allison)
llen Hoover (Stoesz) **TR**
Michael Hoover
uth Horst (Stoltzfus)
lden Hostetter
Anne Janz
enny Lee (Byrne)
ean Lehman (Patton)
iloria Leinbach
Naomi Marks (Otto)
Beverly Martin (Clindaniel)
udy Martin (Miller)
Alan Messersmith
Barb Metzler (Ramer)
Wendy Mierau (Wilson)
anet Miller (Kauffman)
ohn Miller **PR**
Kirby Miller

Randy Miller
Ruth Miller (Ortiz)
Garth Nauraine
Ken Nisley
Linda Nunemaker
Bonnie Regier (Donnelly)
Nancy Rupe (Cressy)
Donald Schrock
Sanford Slagel
Janice Snyder (Alexenko)
Rebecca Stichter (Brenneman)
Helen Stoltzfus (Bowman)
Ruth Sutter
Patricia Taylor
Anthony Troyer
Mervin Troyer
Maria Valtierra (Granado)
Lamortto Wofford
Beth Yoder (Jensen) **SE**
Bonnie Yoder (Gerber)
Dana Yoder
Roberta Yoder (Bontrager)
Carolyn Yutzy (Maust)
Rebecca Zook (Velasco)
Larion Swartzendruber **SP**
Lester Culp **CS**

Class of 1975

Merca Berry (Berry-Covert)
Derald Bontrager
J. Mark Bontrager
Rex Bontrager
Joanna Book (Robley)
David Brenneman
Steven Christner
Jee Yoon Chung
Ronald Chupp
Nancy Conrad
Mario Cordero
John Culp
John Davidhizar
Curt Farmwald
Rachel Friesen (Friesen Strombeck)
Gene Gamber

Jay Ganger
Pam Garber (Hooley)
James Gingerich (Nelson Gingerich)
Kevin Graber
James Harter
Elaine Helmuth (Jarvis)
Robin Helmuth
Sharon Hershberger (Zepeda) **SE**
Christina Hochstetler (Thurnau) **PR**
Karla Hochstetler (Brenneman)
Paul Hoffman
Eric Hooley **TR**
Brenda Hostetler (Hostetler Meyer)
Mary Hostetler (Glick)
James Kauffman
Don Kaufman
Stephen Kilmer
Marsha Koerner (Mast)
Merrill Krabill **VP, F/S**
Rosemary Kreider (Hess)
Thomas Kreider **F/S**
Marcile Lambright (Lindsey)
John Lowe
Michael Maust
Cynthia Miller
Don Miller
Gerald Miller
Judy Miller (Norris)
Steve Miller
Mark Mishler
Gloria Mumaw (Verbanac)
Sarah (Sally) Oyer
Linda Rheinheimer (Young)
Lyn Schlabach (Buschert)
Kathy Schrock (Hartzler)
Rachel Shank (Shenk)
Sharon Shumaker (Chupp)
Bill Skiles
Philip Slabach
Robin Slabaugh
Lester Snyder
Joe Springer
Carol Steiner (Scheerer)
Doug Steury

Miriam Stoltzfus (DeShield)
Dexter Stutzman
Gretchen Thomas
Reinhard Wolff
Mary Yoder (Garber)
Melody Yoder (Slabach)
Regina Yoder (Yoder)
Rita Yoder (Riggenbach) **BM**
Rick Yontz
Ronald Zimmerman
Cindy Zook (Stutzman)
Darrel Hostetler **SP**

Class of 1976

Wilmer Beachy
Denise Bontrager (Jensen)
Christine Bowen **VP**
Annette Boyts (Brant)
Annette Britton
Mary Brubacher
Myron Buller
Karen Burkey (Mishler)
Samuel Burkholder
Mark Chupp **FH**
Ruth Cocanower (Saunders)
Alan Davidhizar
Valerie Davis (Daw)
Bev Gingerich (Feyas)
Joanne Goetz (Sharick)
Joyce Graber (Cordero)
LaVon Gray
Mark Hartzler
Phil Herr
Pamela Holderman (French) **FH**
Lisa Hoover (Hnath)
Elaine Horner (Martin)
Janet Horst (Miller)
Anne Hostetler (Menahemy)
Bob Hostetler
Mike Hostetler
Jeff Kauffman
David King
Barbara Krobath
Duane Leatherman

Miriam Lehman
Charlotte Lindsay (Gregg)
Susan Mark (Landis) **SE**
Anita Martin (King)
Rachel Martin (Swartz) **BM**
Rebecca Martin (Picht)
Stan Martin
Steve Martin
Donna Maust (Graber)
Adrian (Ed) Mendoza
Peter Metzler
Dana Miller (Bontrager)
Karen Miller (Kubota)
Rebecca Miller (Holcomb)
Steven Miller
Donna Minter
LeAnn Mishler (Clark)
Bill Redekop
Eliza Salvador
Rodney Schmucker
Mike Schwartzentruber **PR**
Steve Shaum
Patricia Shumaker **TR**
Peggy Snyder (Goggins)
Carol Weaver (Pope)
Donna Weaver (Diener)
Leavett Wofford
Wilmer Hollinger **SP**
Irene Gross **CS**

Class of 1977

Manuel Aviles
Becci Bauman **TR**
Deborah Bender (Challenger)
Don Bontrager
Mable Bontrager (Mendoza)
Wesley Bontreger **F/S**
Bernardett Calbimonte
Ronda Christophel (Miller)
Kenneth Chupp
Teresa Chupp (Cripe)
Jerry Davidhizar
Ana Maria Espinoza
Daniel Ganger

Greg Garber
Kim Godshall
Anita Graber (Miller)
Cathy (Miller) Graber **F/S**
Suzanne Gross
Anna Hartman (Mast)
Betty Helmuth (McFarren) **FH, F/S**
Marcella Hershberger **BM**
Deb Hochstedler (Hershberger)
Kevin Hochstetler
Paul Hochstetler
Judy Hollinger (Bontrager)
Anita Hoover (Miller)
Randal Hoover
Robert Kehr **VP**
Jean Krabill (Miller) **PR**
Becky Kratz (Bening)
Franklin Kreider
Marlin Lambright
John Lantz
Diane Leatherman (Yoder)
Ed Lewis
Anita Martin (Yoder)
Janice Martin (Meyers)
Philip Martin
Grant Maust
Rebecca Maust (Schwartzendruber)
Gretchen Metzler
Michael Metzler
Philip Metzler
Anna "Ann" Miller (Beachy)
Daryl Miller
Jeff Miller
Keith Miller
Maureen Moore (Dreidger)
Mark Nafziger
Brian Nunemaker
Pam Ostrander (Grover)
Carmella Reyes
Louis Reyes
Kevin Roth
Dave Santiago
Rhonda Schmucker (Florian)
Daniel Schrock

David Schwartzentruber **FH**
Mike Slabaugh
Keith Snyder
Gloria Steiner (Hood) **SE**
Jay Swartzentruber
Mark Troyer
Judy Weaver
Richard Yoder
Mike Yutzy
Lester Culp **SP**
Diane Schrock **CS**

Class of 1978

Yolanda Aviles
Barbara Beachy (Yoder)
Lucyne Bonilla (Rodrigues)
Deloris Bontrager (Gibson) **SE**
Greg Bontrager
Patricia Bontrager (Shenk) **TR**
Terry Bontrager **F/S**
Jonathan Brenneman
Bill Bufton
Kathy Chupp
Nancy Chupp (Nunemaker)
Julie Dooley
Carolyn Dueck
Mary Eash (Winkelman)
Lorna Farmwald (Eames)
Rich Ganger
Randy Graber **F/S**
Stephanie Haines (Horner)
A. Chris Herr
Marla Hochstedler (Yoder)
Carl Horner **F/S**
R. Edward Horst **PR**
Barry Kauffman
Bryan Kehr **FH, F/S**
Linda Kilmer (Yoder) **F/S**
Deb Klopfenstein (Daw)
Sheila Koch (Graber) **VP, FH**
Pauline Krueger (Jackson)
Greg Kuhns
John Lapp
Mitch Mann

David Mark
Elnora Martin
Rachel Martin (Stutzman)
Fred Mast
Marcia Miller (Hamood)
Doug Minter
Timo Ovaska
Audrey Roth (Kraybill)
Pamm Roth
Kristine Schumm (Long) **BM**
Fernandez Shaw
James Slabaugh
Deborah Sowell (Blanchi-Sowell)
Terri Anne Stern (Troyer)
Charlotte Stichter
Densel Jay Stoll
Sonya Stutzman
Steve Stutzman
Angela Swartzendruber (Luedtke)
Mary Troyer (Hoefer)
Michael Troyer
Sharon Weirich (Plett)
Julie Wenger (Troyer)
Eric Wininger
Elaine Wise (Kennell)
Theresa Wofford
Anita Yoder (Yoder Kehr)
Diana Yoder
Joyce Yoder (Durfey)
Keith Yoder
Roger Yoder
Yvonne Young
Kathy Yutzy (Kappes)
Dan Bodiker **SP**
Linda Shetler **CS**

Class of 1979

Pamela Bechtel (Prough)
David Birky **PR**
Jacquelyn Boyer (Culp)
Diana Boyts (Young)
Jonetta Britton
Soo Yul Chae
Thomas Charles (Kopp Charles)

Mark Christner
Donald Diener
Donita Disbro
Leslie Fraser (Snyder)
Rob Ganger
Jon Gingrich
L. Pauline Glenn (Stutzman)
Rebecca Good (Sleeper)
Angela Graber (Ganger)
Galen Graber
Randall Graber
Valerie Gross
Lori Hershberger **SE**
Rita Hershberger (Bontrager) **F/S**
Brenda Hochstetler (Yutzy)
Conrad Hochstetler
Kenneth Hochstetler
Ken Hollinger
Connie Hoover (Mahaffa)
Loren Hostetter
Bill Kilburn
Julie Klopenstein (Brunstetter)
Cathy Kucinskas (Hampton)
Todd Lederman
Mary Lehman (Bettis) **BM**
Susan Loy (Sedam)
Elise Martin (Martin Coletto)
Michel Martin
Sherri Martin (Grindle)
Anita Maust (Snyder) **TR**
John Metzger
Linda Metzler
Kathy Meyer (Meyer Reimer)
Carl Miller
Clifford Miller
Denise Miller (Diamond)
Rachel Miller (Miller Jacobs) **F/S**
Rufus Miller
Rebecca Mishler (Korenstra)
Lorraine Morgan
Eric Mumaw
Connie Nunemaker (Haarer)
Lee Penner
Paul Reimer

Ronald Rheinheimer
Nele Schmidt
Donita Schwartzentruber (Rhodes)
Lorna Schwartzentruber **FH**
Karen Scott
Kimberly Shank (Snyder)
Randy Shaum
Teresa Shumaker (Swartley)
Marcia Slabach
George Smith
S. Michelle Smith
Dale Snyder **FH**
Cynthia Sommers (Huss)
Dallas Sommers
Edward (Gene) Stutzman
Kerm Stutzman
RoseAnn Stutzman (Mockler)
Miriam Voran (Faunce)
Debora Weaver
Donald Weaver
Rick Weaver
Ruth Weldy (Fitz-Gerald) **VP**
Loretta Yoder
Bob Zook
Al Peachey **SP**

Class of 1980

Deborah Augsburger
Stephen Beachy
Terri Blucker (Huber)
DiAnn Bontrager (Beachy)
Gary Bontrager
Roger Bontrager **VP**
Candace Bornman (Beck)
William Bowen
Bonnie Bufton (Blessing)
Nora Chavez (Morales)
Jonathan Eash
Christina Gingerich
Marla Graybill (Brenneman)
Steve Hanson
Cindy Hartzler (Hartzler-Miller)
Kay Hartzler (Reist) **FH**
Barbara Helmuth (Mast)

Ray Helmuth (Gyori-Helmuth) **F/S**
Charles Hochstetler
Grace Hochstetler (Sautter)
Kathryn Hochstetler (Hoover)
Lynette Hochstetler (Zimmerman)
Debra Homes (Krawiec)
Charity Hooley (Stutsman)
Roger Hoover
Wilbur Hostetler
Michael Howard
Eric Jeschke
Gail Kauffman (Maas)
James Kauffman
Dianne Kehr (Hogan)
Karen Krabill (Yoder) **BM**
Dawn Kuhns
Jennifer Lapp (Lerch)
Ronald Leatherman
Judith Martin
Rene Maust
Connie Miller (Prochno)
Cynthia Miller (Kauffman)
Karen Miller **SE**
Krista Miller (Murray) **PR**
Dunja Moeller
Wesley Parker
Outi Sarsa
Rodney Schmucker
James Shaffer
Bruce Slabaugh
Jeffrey Sluiter
Cathy Smeltzer (Erb)
Gregory Sommers
Timothy Stern
Lois Stoltzfus (Mast) **F/S**
Terri Stoltzfus (Swoveland)
Stephen Strasser
Kimberly Stutzman (Shearer)
Richele Thomas (Hofsommer)
Cynthia Troyer (Lederman) **TR**
Rik Troyer
Carol Weirich (Piekunka)
Pauline Wickey
William Wiggins

Rachel Wise (Martin)
Chris Yoder
Colleen Yoder (White)
Curtis Yoder
Dwight Yoder
Kevin Yoder **FH**
Lori Yoder (Stutzman)
Renette Yoder (Borton)
Marcus Zimmerman
Marvin Yoder **SP**
Lester Culp **CS**

Class of 1981

Dawn Birky (Steiner)
John Bixler
John Blosser
Donna Bontrager (Miller)
Ginny Bontrager (Miller) **TR**
Roger Bontrager
Roz Brenneman (Desch)
Jay Bufton
Brenda Chupp (Hershberger)
Mark Eash
Linda Eckert (Casper)
Christine Ettling
Tracy Farmwald
Angela Fetz
Debra Fisher (Sweetser)
Todd Friesen
Robin Garner (Clark)
Michael Gingrich
Susie Glick (Richardson)
Victor Carlos Gonzales
Starla Graber **VP**
Carla Gunden
Jeff Hartzler
Kent Hershberger **PR, FH**
Phil Hertzler
Carmella Hochstedler (Walters)
Rachel Hochstetler (VanderWerf)
Brenda Hooley (Nebel)
John Hooley
John (Eric) Hostetter
Grace Hunsberger (Roth)

Tyrone Hunt
Carla Inbody (Bailey)
Belva Keene (Elliott)
Kendra King (Shickel)
Jeryl Kolb
Cheryl Kropf (Miller)
John Roger Kurtz
Craig Martin
Janell Martin (Atkinson)
John Mast **F/S**
Brent Miller
Jane Miller **SE, FH**
M. Eric Miller
Marty Miller
Randall Miller
Sharla Miller (Cox)
Vi Miller (Delagrange)
Anita Musselman (Eisenbeis)
Zondra Nussbaum (Resh)
Sandy Peachey (Slabaugh)
Nathaniel Regier
Julia Reimer
Douglas Rheinheimer
Peggy Schrock (Stickler)
Scott Slabaugh
Gregory Smucker
Susan Stauffer (Schnupp)
Paul Steury
Brenda Stoltzfus (Toews)
Ray Stutzman
Roger Swartzendruber
Joyce Tyson (Dreier)
Steve Voran
Tamara Walters (Snodgrass)
Arlen Welty
Jeff Wenger
Ron Whiteford
Charlotte Yoder
Karen Yoder (Wyse)
Karla Yoder (Minter)
Lori Zook (Stanley)
Dan Bodiker **SP**
Linda Shetler **CS**

Class of 1982

Judy Augsburger
Marcus Beachy
Anne Bender (Plyler) **FH**
Gay Birky
Marleen Birky
Cheryl Bontrager (Fickus)
Cynthia Bontrager (Hawkins) **F/S**
Delton Bontrager
Douglas Bontrager
Todd Borntreger
Terry Brandeberry
Bruce Buller
Ed Crowder
Tony Dávila
Linda Dintaman (Martin) **TR**
Lorne Dueck
Laurel Elias (Crawford)
Benjamin Espinoza
Elizabeth Espinoza
Lily Espinoza
Sheila Felder (Johnson)
Mary Gingerich (Reitz)
George Graber
Susan Graber (Detweiler)
Stacy Haines (Krahn) **SE**
Jeannie Hochstedler (Gascho)
Linda Hochstetler
Kirk Hoover
Carmen Hopkins Jr.
Michael Houser
Samuel Hower
Tony King
Lisa Kratz
Jessica Lapp (Herzler) **PR**
Lee Leatherman
Bradley Lehman
Joseph Lehman **VP**
Maria Lehman (Hostetter)
Suzan Lehman (Hutchinson)
Kelly Lerner
Roma Martin (Miller)
Tracie Mast (Spurlock)

Joann McElmurry (Elder)
Dawn Metzler
Carey Miller
Cheryl Miller (Beachey)
Jenny Miller (Hooley)
Ann Minter (Fetters)
Karen Mishler (Heed)
Donna Parcell (Leatherman)
Beulah Perkins (Sparkman)
Reuben Reyes
Lisa Roth (Walter)
Mona Schertz (Seaver)
Ron Schmucker
Dwight Schumm
Corinne Slabaugh (Burckhart)
Sherwyn Smeltzer
Conrad Smucker **FH**
Thad Stern
Diane Steury (Maust)
Gordon Stichter
Lyn Stutzman
Brenda Troyer (Hendryx)
Diane Yoder
Renee Yoder (Miller)
John Zook **SP**
Mary Swartley **CS**

Class of 1983

Robert Beachy **PR**
Eric Bechtel
Tina Birky
Cae Borntreger
Peter Burkholder
Brent Chupp
Nancy Chupp (Krabill)
Jim Clemens
Rhonda Clemens (Talbott)
Mark Crisantez
Wendy Eash
Lynda Gingrich (Troyer)
Anthony Godshall
Roland Helmuth
Melissa Hershberger (Jones)
Courtney Hess

Pam Hochstedler (Landis)
Janet Hooley (Kercher)
Shawn Horton
Bruce Hostetler
Ardith Hostetter (Kauffman) **TR**
Krista King (Powell)
Dan Liechty (Koop Liechty)
Jon Liechty
Paul Mark
Chris Matsuda (Bast)
Crystal Maust (Graber)
Janell Maust
Elaine Meyer (Lee)
Karyn Mierau (Flaming) **FH**
Angie Miller (Shetler)
Beth Ann Miller (Beitzel)
Bryan Miller
Darby Miller
Karen Miller (Miller Rush) **SE**
Ken Miller
Loren Miller
Lynelle Miller (Clark)
Sharon Miller (Smith)
Elissa Miranda (Ohlwiler)
Jill Newcomer (Erb)
Marcia Powell (Schrag)
Durrell Ramer
Cheryl Roth (Kauffman)
Darla Schumm (Harris)
Suzanne Shenk (Painter)
Annette Slagel
Deb Smucker
Lisa Steffen
Karl Steiner
Malinda Stoltzfus (Sanna)
Jeff Strasser
Tony Torrejon
Rebecca Troyer (Fontaine)
Eric Unzicker
Don Wert **FH**
Colleen Yoder (Nafziger)
Kyle Yoder
Lyndon Yoder
Lynette Yoder (Singleton)

tsey Zook **VP, F/S**
rc Zook
lmer Hollinger **SP**
rlin Groff **CS**

Class of 1984

becca Bare
nise Bontrager (Williams)
chelle Bontrager (Ismert)
se Ann Bontrager (Schrameyer)
binzine Bryant **VP**
ta Burkholder (Greger)
 Eugene Cross
yrta Cruz (Lowe)
thony DePew
mothy Eash
rlin Elias
wendolyn "Wendy" Fike (Good) **FH**
muel Hooley
lie James (Bishopp)
enda Janz (Hoover)
ruce Janz **PR**
eidi Kauffmann
hn Kolb
bert Kurtz
homas Lantz **FH**
 Michael Lapp
awn Leatherman
hannes Lichti
mes Little **F/S**
cott Mark
harles Martin **TR**
athy Mast (Slabaugh)
aren McElmurry (Pfaler)
rian Metzler
leen Miller (Myers)
imberly Miller (Judy)
andall Miller
harman Miller (Reimer)
ickie Miller (Scaletta)
regory Newswanger
hristine Reimer
ike Schleining
isa Shank (Fannin) **SE**

Jerrol Shaum
Tammy Stern (Miller)
Sheri Walters
Ronald Welty
Karen Yoder (Kym)
Karmen Yoder
Michael Yoder
Rebecca Yoder (Stichter)
Tenley Yoder (Starks)
Dan Bodiker **SP**
Roy Hartzler **CS**

Class of 1985

Jonathan Bornman **VP**
Lisa Brandeberry (Avedician)
Karl Brugger
Marta Brunner **PR**
Darrin Cross
Cheryl Detweiler
    (Nester-Detweiler) **F/S**
David Eash
Douglas Fisher
J. Darrell Gascho
John Gerber
Mark Gerber **F/S**
Darrell Gingerich
E. David Godshall
Larry Guengerich
Jennifer Herr (Drescher)
Randal Hertzler
Rene Horst
David Jeschke
Margaret Jeschke
Kevin Kauffman
Douglas Kaufman **FH**
Harold Kosteck
Jeanne Liechty
Vonda Litwiller
Brian Loucks
Romelia Luna
Kimberly Martin (Main)
Linda Martin (Martin Burkholder)
Julio Martinez
Eric Mast

Brent Metzler
Anita Miller (Yoder)
Cedric Miller
Darren Miller
Jerald Miller
Kevin Miller
Lorraine "Lori" Miller (Nester)
Robbie Miller
Eric Miranda
Keith Mullett
Randall Newswanger
Kimberly Riegsecker (Lehman)
Troy Risser
Robert Douglas Schleining
Susan Schmidt (Funk)
Timothy Schmucker
Lonna Stoltzfus
Leslie Stutzman
Eric "Ric" Troyer
Laurel Voran **TR**
Carmen Weaver (Smucker) **FH**
Andre Yoder
Barbara Yoder (Yoder Stutzman) **SE**
Matthew Zook
Jim Buller **SP**
Trish Yoder **CS**

Class of 1986

Elizabeth Bare (Hawn) **F/S**
Joseph Bare
Sandra Blosser
Shanda Blosser (Weaver)
Carl Bontrager
Stacy Bontrager
Valerie Bontrager
David Bornman
Steven Collins
Crystal Cross (Troyer)
Lisa Dintaman (Skinner) **TR**
Chad Friesen
Cynthia Friesen
Lloyd Gingerich
Mark Guengerich
Arlene Hostetler (Schrock)

Mark Houser
Heidi Kauffman (Kurtz)
Ronald Krabill **VP**
Michelle Lehman
Christina Lichti (Bornman) **FH**
Caterina Martinez
Audrey Mast (Oostland) **SE**
Joy Maust
Bruce Miller
Jodi Miller (Coblentz) **PR**
Starla Miller (Borror)
Tonia Mullet (Immel)
Wanda Mullet (Donohau)
Lisa Nunemaker (Weaver)
James Powell
Camela Reimer (Reeves)
Connie Sark (Eash)
Royce Schrag
Pamela Shank (Knight)
Maria Shenk **BM**
Chad Sherman
Jeffrey Smith
Kent Smith
Gregory Stauffer **FH**
Benjamin Stutzman
Lyle Stutzman
Jeffrey Swartzendruber
Allan Yoder
Lester Culp **SP**
Wilmer Hollinger **CS**

Class of 1987

Todd Bontrager
Trenton Bontrager
Myron Bontreger **F/S**
Pat Burkholder
Craig Chupp
Gary Chupp
Judith Clemens
    (Clemens Smucker) **VP**
Daniel Diener
Gail Eash (Schrock)
Marlis Farmwald (Chupp) **FH**
Douglas Friesen

Tiffany Friesen
Charlotte Gascho (Hunsberger)
Diane Gingerich (Miller) **SE**
J. Alvin Godshall
Eric Helmuth
Pedro Hernandez
Dawn Hochstetler (Weaver) **TR**
Julie Hochstetler (Van Oss)
Lois Hochstetler
Oren Douglas Horst **FH**
Lori Kauffman (Nordman)
Leisa Kauffmann
Brian Kilmer
Arthur Jeremy Kropf
Marla Lantz (Cole)
Philip Lapp **PR**
Alejandra (Alex) Luna (Montelonge)
Kimberly Mast (Bollinger)
Sheila McElmurry
Edward McKenna **F/S**
Coretta Miller (Haines)
Robin Miller (Jacobs)
Steven Miller
W. Todd Miller
Yolanda Miller (Pawlyshyn)
Janet Moyer
Robert Newcomer
Kendall Newswanger
Lynda Nyce
Kristina Peachey
Randall Riegsecker
Scott Schmucker
Thomas Shenk
Jenny Smeltzer
Lisa Stauffer
Kent Steiner
Curtis Stoltzfus
Rebekah Stutzman
Teresa Troyer (Zook)
Jan Vardaman
Regina Weaver
David Wert (Hockman-Wert)
Tyler Wyndham
Alev Yoder

Debra Yoder (Nelson)
Justine Yoder (Nettrour)
Dan Bodiker **SP**

Class of 1988

Leo Akins
Mike Babin
Ly-Ly Beane (Rose)
Tammy Beck (Markham)
Amy Birky (Birky Mounsithiraj) **VP, F/S**
Scott Bodiker **PR**
Dawn Bontrager (Schwartz)
Lynn Borntreger (Brubaker)
Stephanie Brown (Hudson)
Sharon Brugger (Norton) **TR**
Alan Chism
Mark Claassen
Ken Cross
Denise Diener (Diener-Perez)
Joylin Elias (Ykimoff)
Carl Friesen
Colleen Gerber (Guengerich)
Joe Gerber
Kirstin Golden
Jay Guengerich
Lisa Helmuth (Liras)
John Hershberger
Karis Hirschler (Corbett)
Carrie Hochstetler
Kenton Hostetler
Lisa Kaiser (Klingshirn)
Chris Kauffman (Weaver) **FH**
Karl Kauffman **FH**
Tony Kauffman
Steve Longenecker
April Miller
Carla Miller (Thompson)
Devon Miller
Kerwin Miller
Liana Miller (Gott)
Tim Miller
Jane Moore (Wilson)
John Moyer
Shane Mullett

Tony Norris
Eric Risser
Olivia Sanchez (Rittenhouse)
Rafael Santos
David Schipani **SE**
Terry Seiler
Brett Sherman
Chris Stauffer
Dawn Summerton
Matthew Thompson
John Troyer
Rosie Vazquez (Puente)
Vonnie Weirich (Berkey)
Angie Wenger (Nord)
Greg Yoder
Rick Yoder
Yolanda Yoder (Brunsma)
Jim Buller **SP**
Trish Yoder **CS**

Class of 1989

Paul Alvey
Frances Barkman (Webb)
Eric Beck **PR**
Austin Birkey
Marc Blosser
Mark Bontrager
Wendy Bontrager (Nunemaker)
Joseph Braun
Brenda Briseno (Haraguchi)
Suzanne Brugger (Brugger Kanode)
Peter Carpenter
Todd Christophel
Matthew Fisher
Bradley Friesen
Michael Gingerich
Rachel Hahn (Hoover)
Jennifer Helmuth (Shenk) **FH**
Jonathan Helmuth
Sara Hershberger (Mast)
Eric Horst **FH**
Cara Jones
Patricia Jones (Depew)
Nathan Kingsley

Susan Lambright
Rebecca Lichti (Randolph)
Jered Liechty
Kay Mast (Bigler)
James Maust **TR**
Curtis Miller
Lance Miller **VP**
Susan Miller (Beasy)
James "Jamie" Mullet
Brent Nunemaker
Gretchen Nyce **F/S**
Franklin Kent Oyer
Tamara Riegsecker (Miller)
Deanna Risser
Denise Risser **F/S**
Maria "Lola" Romero (Campos)
Cynthia Sark (Miller)
Kristina Schlabach
Stacy Schmucker (Stoltzfus) **SE**
Janell Steider (Harris)
Kristine Steiner
David Stoll
Timothy Strouse
Calvin Swartzendruber
Jason Swihart
Michael Thomas
Jill Troyer (Miller)
Heather Wengerd
Jerod Hank Willems
Erika Yoder (Meyer)
Holly Yoder
Monica Yoder (Roth)
Nicole Zehr
Rebecca Zook (McDowell)
Roy Hartzler **SP**
Marisa Yoder **CS**

Class of 1990

Ryan Beck
Joseph Berry **TR**
Melinda Birky (Brown)
Carla Chupp (Johnson)
Ana Colon (Davis)
T. Ed Detwiler

eila Eash (Beachy)
becca "Bekki" Fahrer
therine Friesen
sannah Gerber (Gerber-Lepley)
cilia Godshall
n Hahn
dre Hirschler
eryl Hochstetler (Hochstetler Shirk)
onda Hochstetler (Martin)
isten Hoober
rmen Horst
lene Hostetler (VonGunten)
evin Kauffman
onya Kauffman (Miller) **PR, F/S**
oy Kauffman
Heather Kropf
na Martin (Weaver)
ochelle Martin **FH**
ockelle Martin (Saupe)
ri Mast (Miller)
avid Miller
ffrey Miller
el Miller
arla Miller (Shepard)
aron Mortrud
avid Muntukwonka
hristi Newcomer (Schrock)
mes Noffsinger Jr.
auren Penner **F/S**
eather Pipkin
di Risser
esley Rutt (Rutt Dyck) **SE**
yler Sawatzky
larisa Schipani (Klopfenstein)
yan Schrag **FH**
ennifer Slaubaugh (Baldwin)
latthew Smith
inia Marisa Smucker
isa Stauffer (Stauffer Wengerd)
my Stoll (Gardner)
lissa Stutzman (Gongwer)
ebra Swartzendruber (Gascho)
aniel Thut
ffrey Vardaman

Douglas Yoder
Mark Yoder
Robby Yoder
Eric Yordy **VP**
Tonja Zook (Nicholas)
Dan Bodiker **SP**
Elizabeth Hoover **CS**

Class of 1991

Tony Beiler
Alison Birkey (Sties) **FH**
Stephanie Black (Chlebek)
Tricia Blosser
Michele Bontrager
   (Bontrager Showalter)
Kristin Borntrager
Margaret Broni (Miller) **TR**
Kira Cunningham
Kristine Detweiler
David Diener (Moyer-Diener)
Darryl Eichorn
Bryan Falcón
Philip Friesen (Zook Friesen)
Kevin Gascho
Mark Gingerich
Heather Gusler (Gingrich)
Cindy Harshberger (Ross)
David Helrich
Dawn Hoover
Rebecca Howland (Robinson)
Eric Kauffman
Jay Kauffman
Philip Kaufman
Stephanie Lambright (Roth) **F/S**
Rachel Lapp **SE**
Luke Lefever
Eric Martin
Brandon Miller
Karl Erich Miller
Ryan Miller
Samuel Miller
Sarah Miller (Miller)
Toya Miller
Grant Newcomer **VP**

Kevin Newcomer
Travis Nunemaker
Kenya Ray
Ramphis Rodriguez
Outi Saari
Larissa Schmidt
Jennifer Shell
Carrie Snoke (Kovac)
Paul Stauffer
Ami Steiner (Damer)
Rosetta Stoltzfus (Landis)
Deidre Summerton (Summerton-Bias)
Timothy Swartzendruber **PR**
Rebecca "Becky" Thut (Thut Witmer)
Bradley Weirich **FH**
Rebecca Wenger
Brent Yoder
Brian Yoder
Jim Buller **SP**
Jewel Lehman **CS**

Class of 1992

Nina Bailey (Bailey-Dick)
Dallas Barkman
Andy Beck
Malinda Berry
Michael Bodiker
Jasmine Cataldo
Craig Christophel
Jennifer Christopel (Christophel Lichti)
Daniel Chuen
Walter Cortes
Darrin Eichorn
Steven Gingerich
Julie Golden (Feathers)
Steven Hahn
Joel Hartzler **TR**
Shelly Heatwole (Kirkendall)
Maria Hershberger **SE**
Lenora Hirschler
Tonya Hunsberger (Gaby) **F/S**
Amy Kauffman
Jeremy Kauffman
Mark Kauffman

Tina Kauffman (Laws)
Michelle Kaufman (Strite)
Britt Kaufmann **PR**
Aaron Kingsley (Sawatzky-Kingsley)
Leon Ma
Luis "Alex" Martinez (Francisco)
Craig Mast
Jeremy Mast
Beth Miller
Brent A. Miller
Brent L. Miller
Elsie Miller
Ross Miller
Krystie Morales (Bond)
Katrina Mullet (Siegrist)
Kent Myers
Stacy Nunemaker
Jason Oswald
Nathan Rempel (Mateer-Rempel)
Karmen Riegsecker (Clark)
J. Stephen Sauder
Lorraine "Lanie" Schmucker (Cole)
Audrey Schultz (Bollinger)
Jon Shenk
Tiffany Slabaugh (Swihart)
April Slaubaugh
Chad Smoker **VP**
Hannah Sommers
Ryan Stauffer
Daniel Stoltzfus
David Swartzentruber
Mai Takeuchi (Shimiz)
Jeff Unzicker
Andres Valtierra
Justin Weaver
Jeremy Weishaupt
Isaac Wengerd
Karl Yoder
Laura Yoder (Moshier)
Marla Yoder (Jones)
Mary Yoder (Chamberlin)
Mike Yordy
Trista Zook (Nunemaker)

Marisa Yoder **SP**
John Zook **CS**

Class of 1993

Jason Birky
Matthew Bollman
Jeffrey Bontrager **VP**
Amy Bontreger (Stutzman)
Nathan Boughner
Renee Brooks (Stuckman)
Emily Burkhalter
    (Burkhalter-Blosser) **TR**
Alana Dennis (Stuckman)
Audra Detwiler (Hoover)
Anthony Gerber
Laura Gilbert (Moon)
Lisa Gingerich (Keim)
Tina Gingerich (Showalter)
Heather Graber (Potsander)
Nicole Greenawalt (Berkey)
Lisa Guengerich
Keri Hiatt
Tim Hochstetler
Ronda Hoffman (Weldy)
Joshua Kanagy (Phillips-Kanagy)
Monica Kaufman
Steven Kaufman
Bradley LaFollette
Seung-Eel Lee
Linda Luna (Luna-Zalazar)
Chad Martin
Derek Martin
Joel Martin
Shane Martin
Amber Maust
Danielle Miller
Karena Miller (Hixon)
Kevin Miller
Lisa Miller (Miller) **FH**
Matthew Miller
Megan Miller
Michael Miller
Rachel Miller
Mark Moyer

Jessica Mumaw (Mast)
Gretchen Newcomer (Miller)
Maria Nice (Chupp)
Carla Nunemaker (Richer)
Eric Risser
Benjamin Rutt
Virgil Sauder
Heather Saupe
Catherine Schmidt
Matthew Schmidt **PR, FH**
Andrea Slegel (Slegel-Pressler)
Kris Sommers (Shenk)
Jason Steiner
Kerry Stump
Elizabeth Swartzendruber
    (Swartzendruber-Goertzen
Philip Swartzendruber
Ryan Troyer **SE**
Margaret Turco
Stephanie Vasbinder
Jessica Whicker
David Wieand
Rachel Yoder (LaPorta)
Roxanna Summers **SP**
Dan Bodiker **CS**

Class of 1994

Stacy Beiler (Weaver)
Aaron Bennett
Anne Berry
Kristian Bontreger
Victoria Bontreger (Blosser)
Ami Butler
Willow Cataldo
Jonathan Christophel **VP**
Carleigh Cleveland **PR**
Jennifer Eiler
Jeremy Friesen
Joanna Friesen (Friesen Parks) **TR**
James Garber
Chadrick Goertz **F/S**
Ryan Hochstetler
Jennifer Hostetler (Chizum)
Bradley Hunsberger

Glen Kauffmann
Julian Kauffmann
Austin Kaufmann
Sarah Kingsley (Kingsley Metzler)
Rodney Kiogima
Jill Landis **FH**
Tamara Lehman
Carrie Martin
Brian Maust
Joe Menadue
Dustin Miller **FH**
Eric Miller
Jeffrey Miller **F/S**
Lana Miller
Marijohn Mininger (Mosemann)
Kyro Morales
Jennifer Mortrud (Bennett)
Dawn Myers (Warkentin) **SE**
Jessica Oswald
Randall Pflederer
Megan Ramer
Kristina Riegsecker
Tamara Sawatzky
Nadia Shank
Jeff Shenk **F/S**
Kathryn Sommers
Phillippe Stoltzfus (Weaver-Stoltzfus)
Heather Stutzman
Daniel Weaver
Matthew Weaver
Jason Witmer
Eric Yoder
Jim Buller **SP**
Cynthia Good Kaufmann **CS**

Class of 1995

Heather Birky
Ryan Bontrager
Susan Christophel
Iris Cortes
Jonathan Eash
Jason Garber
Freman Fritz Hartman
A. Jon Hartzler

Jonathan Hartzler
Rachel Hershberger
Elizabeth Kanagy (Miller)
Rachel Kauffman
Kenneth Keesling
Rebecca Kiogima
Lisa Koop
Julie Landis (Smith-Landis)
Jason Lehman
Jewel Lehman (Yoder)
Nathan Lichti (Christophel Lichti)
Mateo Lind
Natasha Loop (Hartman)
Brook Martin
Debra Miller (Hickman)
Jeffrey Miller
Nakeisha Miller
Steven Miller **TR, FH**
Michelle Norman
Monica Reinford (Stutzman)
Crystal Rogers (Hoover)
Sandra Rolon (Miller)
Jason Rupp
Lisa Schmucker (Showalter)
Wesley Schrock
Ryan Schumm **VP**
Kelly Short (Muhonen)
S. Anthony Showalter
Erika Smoker
Kristin Stiffney (Grantham) **PR**
James Strouse
Tara Swartzendruber
    (Swartzendruber Landis) **SE**
Matthew Thomas
Amy Thut
Kurt Vasbinder
Amanda Yoder (Yoder)
Andrea Yoder
Beth Yoder
Charity Yoder **FH**
Joshua Yoder
Terah Yoder (Goerzen)
Todd Yoder

n Zook **SP**
risa Yoder **CS**

noel Alves
neson Bell
ron Berkey
ristopher Black
na Blough
tricia Borntrager (Chico)
dre Brito
lin Burkholder
rtis Burkholder
an Camacho
salina Cortes
eila Delagrange
erri Delagrange (Gyrion)
chole Fanning
elissa Fisher (Fisher Fast) **PR**
elody Gerber (Wilson)
adley Gerbrandt
an Gingerich
son Golden
nne Horst
ynthia Lambright **SE**
hn Leigh
harles Love
aren Martin (Martin Schiedel)
eidi Miller
son Miller **FH**
nnie Mininger
athy Morales (Fisher) **TR, FH**
mes Neff
evin Nice
rooke Nunemaker (Martin)
amuel Richardson **F/S**
amaris Rodriguez (Diaz)
imothy Schmidt
yle Schrock
shua Sohar
nathan Stoll
mily Ulrich
sther Valdez
usan Wenger

Derek Wentorf
Leanne Whicker
Rebecca Wieand (Bateman)
Anne Yoder (Potoczky)
Rachel Yoder (Moscript)
Tonya Yoder (Rupp) **VP**
Roxanna Sommers **SP**
Dave Nofsinger **CS**

Class of 1997

Nate Arbuckle
Rafael Barahona
Anthony Bontrager
Jessica Bontreger
Andrew Burkhalter
Michael Cross
Tony Detwiler
Audrey Eash
Brent Falcón
C. J. Friesen
Eliot Friesen
Michael Frischkorn
Mary Garboden
Maria Gnagey (Woelk)
Aaron Graber
Ben Hartman **PR**
Jason Heatwole **TR**
Sarah Kanagy
Joe Keesling
Carmen Kingsley
Jay Lapp
Cory Livengood
Traci Maust (Vermilion)
Ana Mejia
Lori Miller
Matthew Miller
Erica Mishler (Amsinger)
Cordelia Nance
Tina Nunemaker
Todd Sommers
Greg Stahly **VP**
Michael Stellingwerf
Brooke Steury (Clemmer)
Hannah Stutzman

Sally Suarez
Katie Turco
Joaquin Valtierra
Anders Weaver **VP**
Chris Weaver
Sarah Wenger
Teresa Witmer **FH**
Matthew Wyse
Kent Yoder
Rodney Yoder **FH, F/S**
Wendy Yoder (Nice) **SE**
Cynthia Good Kaufmann **SP**
Dale Shenk **CS**

Class of 1998

Sandrina Berkau
Heidi Birky
Lena Buckwalter
Nick Clark
Matthew Eash
Angela Garber
Marcos Garber
Gretchen Gusler (Sommers)
Preston Hall
Chris Harris
Pete Hartman
Tony Hartman
Brad Hoffman
Kent Holsopple
Kim Kaufman
Rachel Koontz
Matthew Krabill
Alyssa Kreider
Daniel Lanctot
Kevin Lehman
Mary Leigh
Carlene Mast
Daniel Mast
Jennifer McFarlane
   (McFarlane Harris) **PR**
Kyle Miller
Melinda Miller **FH**
Josh Nice
April Nofziger

Rachel Paulovich
Sara Penner
Derrick Ramer
Eric Reinford
Brad Schrock **VP**
Brian Short
Nate Sohar
Laura Sommers
Ryan Stiffney **FH**
Tonya Swartzendruber **SE**
Michelle Thomas
   (Thomas Brenneman)
Rachel Wenger-Keller (Brice)
Kara Westerbeek
Alyssa Wyse (Ray)
Anita Yoder (Miller)
Eric Yoder
Justin Yoder
Rachael Yoder
Rebekah Yoder **TR**
Troy Yoder
Jim Buller **SP**
Marisa Yoder **CS**

Class of 1999

Christopher Atkins
Lisa Bergey
Megan Berkey (Gingerich)
Lee Bolt
Zacary Boughner
Kristin Buller **LG**
Conrad Burkholder
Daniel Charles
Heather Clark
Alison Dick
Matthew Fisher
Brittan Frey
Amanda Friesen **LG**
Adam Gascho
Benjamin Gerig **FH**
Anthony "A. J." Graber
Joel Graber
Brenda Harley
Sharyn Harley

Brian Hite
Reid Kaufmann **LG**
Cecilia Lambright (Lambright Nuzum)
Sallie Landis
Sara Lederach
Hannah Livengood
Michael Malott
Jennifer Mast
June Miller
Stephanie Miller **FH**
Andrea Milne
Brian Mullet
Greg Myers
Christopher Nachtigall
Tim Nafziger
Karisa Oswald
Melissa Oyer
Robin Paulus (Van Gundy)
Matthew Plank
David Richardson
Erin Rosenogle
Rachel Schultz
Nathan Shenk
Erin Smoker
David Snider
Jay Stahly
Joel Stair
Bess Steury
Heidi Stoltzfus
Rachel Stump
Ryan Swartzendruber
Kellie Thomas
Jeffrey Weaver
Erin Wentorf
Emily Yoder
Julie Yoder (Dick)
Landon Yoder
Troy Yoder **LG**
Jodi Huebert **SP**
Dan Bodiker **CS**

Class of 2000

Anna Baer
Anna Becker-Hoover

Mary Beechy
Lisa Bently
Erin Bontrager
Derek Bontreger
Elizabeth Brett
Jason Bryant
David Byler
Sophie Charles **LG**
Christopher Clark
Jordan Cross
Kenton Delagrange
Adam Derstine
Lindsy Diener
Daniel Eash **FH**
Joel Fath
Gloria Figueroa Vargas
Bradley Gingerich **LG**
Jennifer Gingerich
Renee Glick **LG**
Jill Graber
Alisa Hartzler
Carrie Hartzler
Anna Hershberger
Andrew Histand **LG**
Johannah Isaacs
Andrew Kauffman
Jason Kauffman
Jodi Kauffman
Amber Kaufman (Butler)
Christopher Kingsley
Elisabeth Krabill
Laura Kraybill
Andrew Lanctot
Carrie Landis
Aaron Lehman
Jessica Lehman **LG**
Elizabeth Leinbach **F/S**
Anne Liechty
Emma Loewen
David Martin
Jason Maxwell
Eric Meyer
Bess Miller
Gretchen Miller (Kingsley)

Janice Miller **FH**
Jesse Miller
Sarah Miller
Joshua Newtson
Samuel Nice
Forrest Ramser
Eric Saner
Brandi Schroeder
Rachel Weaver
Elizabeth Weidner (Abrahams)
Christopher Westerbeek
Aaron Wieand
Kevin Witmer
Rochelle Zehr
Eileen Becker-Hoover **SP**
Dale Shenk **CS**

Class of 2001

Jessica Berkey **FH**
Elizabeth Bolt
Joel Bontrager
Jeremy Braun
Kristin Bycroft
Andrea Chupp
Jeffrey Claassen
Stephanie Cox
Jonathan Fridley
Benjamin Friesen
Lavon "Tony" Ganger
Richard Gasa
Andrew Gingerich
Nick Gingerich
Jennifer Gingrich
Kevin Gnagey
Matthew Gongwer **LG**
Daniel Horst **FH**
Lane Kaufmann
Joel Koeneman
Amy Leatherman
Bethany Lehman **LG**
Jeremy Leinbach
Joshua Miller
Sarah Miller
Mariko Miyama

Mike Nachtigall **LG**
Anna Newburn
José Ortiz
Jonathan Paulovich
Sandhya Prakash
Justin Ramer
Laura Rheinheimer
José Rivera
Medardo Rosario
Jayme Sample
Michael J. Sharp **LG**
Joanna Shenk
Kathryn Showalter **LG**
Andrea Skyrm
Anthony Slabaugh
Melissa Sobraski
Thomas Stahly
Rebecca Steury
Gretchen Stoltzfus
Kyle Thomas
Crystal Wentorf
Jed Wulliman
Adrienne Yoder
Rebekah Yoder
Sarah Yoder
Seth Yoder
Traci Yoder
Sue Ehst **SP**
Mike Goertzen **CS**

Class of 2002

Zachery Albrecht
Joshua Anderson
Krista Bergey
Heidi Buller
Jordan Buller **LG**
Phoebe Christophel
Stephen Ciesielski **LG**
Traci Davidhizar
Sarah Dick
Hannah Eash
Lora Fernatt
Matthew Getz
Katrina Gingerich

Justin Grossman
Melanie Histand **FH, F/S**
Kevin Hochstetler
Benjamin Hoffman
Kyle Huffman
Andrew Kaminskis
Heather Kaufman
Gregory Koop
Kyle Leeper
Nick Loewen
Katrina Maust
Theodore McFarlane
Kayla Miller
Lance Miller
Vanessa Mishler
Matthew Morgan
Abigail Nafziger
Timothy Nice
Kristen Oswald (Hochstetler)
Sonia Oswald **LG**
Ryan Peachey
Tara Plank
Kyle Reinford
Erin Richard
Daniel Rodgers
Austin Scharf **FH**
Emily Schulze
Rebecca Selman
Rebecca Shantz
Elisabeth Short
Brett Snider
Scott Stahly
Michael Stroud
Jacob Stucky
Sarah Thompson
Alisha Walz
Laurel Yoder **LG**
Natalie Yoder
John Mast **SP**
Ranae Yoder **CS**

Class of 2003

Brianne Austin
Gabriel Baker

Bryce Barwick
Bethany Bauman
Jeffrey Bauman **F/S**
Eric Bixler
Amanda Boehlke
Kristine Bowman
Jesse Butler
Nolin Chatterjee
Joy Ciesielski
Heidi Claassen
Jared Clemens
Daniel Cowells
Russell Coy
Eric Diener
Natasha Diener
Rebecca Fath **LG**
Bradley Ganger
Uryna Gerber
Jonathan Gingrich
Julia Gingrich
David Glick
Aaron Gnagey **LG**
Joyce Graber
Dori Hartzler
Justin Heinz **FH**
Jared Herschberger
Veronica (Nicki) Hoffman
Julia Hollenberg
Hannah Kehr
Roelf "R. D." Kuitse **LG**
Jenna Liechty **FH**
Matthew Loucks
Elizabeth Martin
Mary Jo Martin
Stephanie Martin
Nathan Mast
Elizabeth Nachtigall
Megan Pletcher
Rachna Prakash
Seth Ramser
Sarah Roth **LG**
Maegan Schmidt
Brittany Schroeder
Mandy Schwartzentruber

Laura Sharp
Abigail Sohar
Brenna Steury
Robert Steury
Gary Surface
Simon Peter Swartzentruber
Victoria Vallejos
Timothy Yoder
Eric Kaufmann **SP**
Jodi Huebert **CS**

Index